Mastering RMI

Developing Enterprise Applications in Java™ and EJB™

Rickard Öberg

Wiley Computer Publishing

John Wiley & Sons, Inc.

NEW YORK · CHICHESTER · WEINHEIM · BRISBANE · SINGAPORE · TORONTO

This book is gratefully dedicated to my Maria.

Publisher: Robert Ipsen
Editor: Robert M. Elliott
Assistant Editor: Emilie Herman
Managing Editor: John Atkins
Associate New Media Editor: Brian Snapp
Text Design & Composition: MacAllister Publishing Services

Published by John Wiley & Sons, Inc.

Published simultaneously in Canada.

Library of Congress Cataloging-in-Publication Data:

ISBN: 0-471-38940-4

Printed in the United States of America.

10 9 8 7 6 5 4 3 2 1

CONTENTS

INTRODUCTION

Mastering RMI is a tutorial on Remote Method Invocation. This book will show you the concepts involved in designing and building RMI applications, including the most common design patterns. It will teach you how to take advantage of all the advanced features of RMI and give you many examples of how to build RMI systems. And it will show how RMI relates to other technologies that build on RMI. After reading this book, you will know how to best use RMI in your own work. More importantly, you will not only know what to do, you will also know why you should do it that way. (Knowing why you do things in a certain way is crucial to understanding any subject, RMI included.)

Distributed computing in general and RMI in particular are quite complex. They involve many things that make it much harder than regular Java programming. While this book aims to make it no more complicated than is necessary, you should be aware of the inherent complexities involved. We will take it from the beginning, so you do not need to know anything other than Java in order to read the book. Prior knowledge of networking and its principles is recommended but not required.

Although RMI is useful on its own, it is much more powerful when complemented by other technologies. This book uses quite a few such technologies, and you will probably want to download and read the specifications for these as you proceed through the book. References to these specifications are provided last in this book in the section titled "Further reading." The book's accompanying Web site will also contain links to these specifications and technologies.

Organization of the Book

The book is organized into four parts.

Part 1 begins by introducing you to the client/server architecture. We will define the words client and server and look at the concept of n-tier systems. After that, we will see what it takes to create a remote method invocation mechanism in general and what problems it's meant to solve. Next we will look at a couple of examples of current client/server architectures and how each of them has solved the problems we defined. The second chapter is a crash course in the RMI architecture. We will go through the entire design of RMI, and see how it implements the tasks that must be taken care of. We will cover the internals of an RMI implementation, such as threading, serialization, and dynamic classloading, so that you have a clear picture of what happens inside RMI when you use it. These two chapters will give you a solid ground on which to proceed with the applied chapters. Very experienced readers may want to skim Chapter 1. However, I recommend that all readers at least review the Tip and Warning sections in Chapter 2, as they contain quite a few interesting tips and tricks.

Part 2 takes you through the process of creating basic RMI applications. We begin in Chapter 3 by creating a simple HelloWorld example that shows the minimal required steps. We look at how to structure the application so that it is easy to package and deploy. We also follow an RMI call from the client to the server and back again. This will give you a clear picture of the flow of an RMI call, which is an important key to understanding RMI in general. Chapter 4 takes the HelloWorld example from Chapter 2 and enhances it by changing the client to an applet, using dynamic classloading with a Web server, and using the *Java Naming and Directory Interface* (JNDI) to hide the naming service behind a standardized naming API. Experienced readers may skip Chapter 3 and go directly to Chapter 4, but readers who are new to RMI should read both chapters.

Part 3 deals with the more advanced features of RMI. We will use the basic HelloWorld example from the previous part of the book and let each chapter show how the particular feature can be used to enhance the example. The features described are custom connection management (a.k.a. custom socket factories) and activation. Custom socket factories allow you to have control over how network connections are handled between clients and servers. Activation will let you activate your server on demand and also provides remote object stubs that can survive server failures. Custom connection management is a good way to secure your servers, and activation is a very useful technique if you are programming Jini, so these chapters should prove interesting if you plan to use these features.

Part 4 investigates two technologies that have been built on top of RMI: *Jini* and *Enterprise JavaBeans* (EJB). Jini was initially marketed as a technology for building networked devices that could collaborate in a flexible and fault-tolerant way. As it turns out, the scope in which Jini can be applied is much more far reaching than that. All networked services that want to collaborate with other services and do so in a fault tolerant way (i.e., more or less all networked services) can make use of Jini. We will see just what kind of magic Jini provides that makes it so useful, and we also enhance our HelloWorld example to illustrate how Jini improves the situation. The last chapter deals with EJB. The purpose of EJB is to provide a model for creating portable Java components that help you deal with complex business logic for such functions as transactions, databases, and security. It also helps you tie such components together into applications in a flexible way so as to make the components as reusable and loosely coupled as possible. We will look at what an EJB server provides for you and what you need to do to develop EJB components. Last, we create a simple EJB component to illustrate the steps involved.

Illustrations in the Text

All illustrations, except screenshots, use the *Unified Modeling Language* (UML). UML is the standard methodology for creating software diagrams. If you are not familiar with UML, I recommend that you read the book *The Unified Modeling Language User Guide*, by Grady Booch, et al. (Addison-Wesley 1999), which shows how to use UML effectively. UML is a very important tool in any serious developer's toolbox, and is highly recommended as a way to convey your ideas and designs to other developers. The diagrams in this book have been created with the UML tool Together/J from TogetherSoft.

Examples Used

I decided to use the classic HelloWorld example as a base for many of the examples in this book. This allow us to focus on the things that are required to use RMI, and not bother so much with the details of the application used as an example. While this is probably not a very exciting example, it does give you bare bones code that you can use as a base for your own applications.

That said, I have also chosen to include two full sample applications. One is a mobile agent system that highlights quite extensively how to use the dynamic classloading feature of RMI. The other is a chat system that shows many important design patterns that are useful when designing real RMI applications. These two should give you a more complete picture of how larger RMI applications are designed and implemented.

We finish the book by presenting one Jini example and one EJB example. Here we go back to the HelloWorld type of sample code, but this should be enough to show you what interesting things the two technologies can do.

Conventions Used

The following conventions are used in this book: All new concepts and terms are shown in *italics* on first usage. All class names, method names, or similar, is shown using a `mono-spaced` font.

The Companion CD-ROM

On the accompanying CD-ROM, you will find all the source code from the examples in this book. They are complete with build structures and make files. I have chosen to use the excellent Ant make tool, which is an Apache project. You can find more information about this tool at `http://jakarta.apache.org`.

The EJB example can be run using the JBoss application server, which is included on the CD. JBoss is free for all uses, so you can safely build applications on JBoss without worrying about license issues. One of the most important goals with EJB is to allow the components to be portable between different EJB servers, and hence the example does not contain anything that would tie it to the JBoss server. For more information about JBoss, see its homepage at www.jboss.org.

For the Jini example, you will have to download and install the Jini 1.1 (or better) toolkit from the Jini homepage at www.sun.com/jini/.

The examples have been developed and tested on Sun's Java Development Kit v1.3. You will have to download and install it (or a later version of the JDK) before you can compile and run the examples. For more information regarding the examples, please see the documentation on the CD-ROM.

The Companion Web Site

Of course the book has an accompanying Web site, which I will use to notify you of updates to the book, including:

- Error corrections from the text
- Links to RMI resources
- Any updates to the source code examples

I would recommend that you check the Web site before reading on, as there may be important changes there that have been made since the book was published. The Web site is at: www.wiley.com/compbooks/oberg.

Feedback

I would love to hear about your own RMI projects, and any experiences you have had working with RMI, Jini, or EJB. You are welcome to e-mail me with examples, case studies, horror stories, or tips that you have found helpful in your experiences. With your consent, I will put some of these on the Web site for others to share. You can reach me at rickard@dreambean.com.

ACKNOWLEDGMENTS

While there is only my name on this book, this book would not have happened if not for the help and inspiration of a number of people. To begin with, I want to thank Ted Neward for giving me the idea to write the book in the first place. I would also like to extend my warmest kudos to the reviewers Rob Castaneda, Niclas Hedhman, Karl-Fredrik Blixt, and Marc Fleury. You guys were just excellent, and have had a significant, positive impact on both the content and quality of this book.

On a more personal level, there is of course my love Maria, who helped me at all times and was always at my side, even when things got tough. (And believe me, writing a book is no easy ride). I must also thank both my own family and Maria's for their support during the past year!

Next there is all the inspirational folks who have helped me grasp all of this: the all-knowing RMI team at Sun, including Ann Wollrath, Peter Jones, and Adrian Colley; the insightful members of the RMI-USERS mailing list, including Stu Halloway, Brian Maso, Jeff Kesselman, and Erez Katz; the incredibly talented people in the jBoss development team, including Dan O'Connor, Aaron Mulder, and Oleg Nitz. And a bunch of other people—you know who you are!

Finally, there are of course the wonderful people at John Wiley & Sons. You guys have been a dream to work with! In particular I would like to thank Bob Elliott, Emilie Herman, and Dawn Kamper for their excellent attitudes and work.

Basic Principles and Architecture

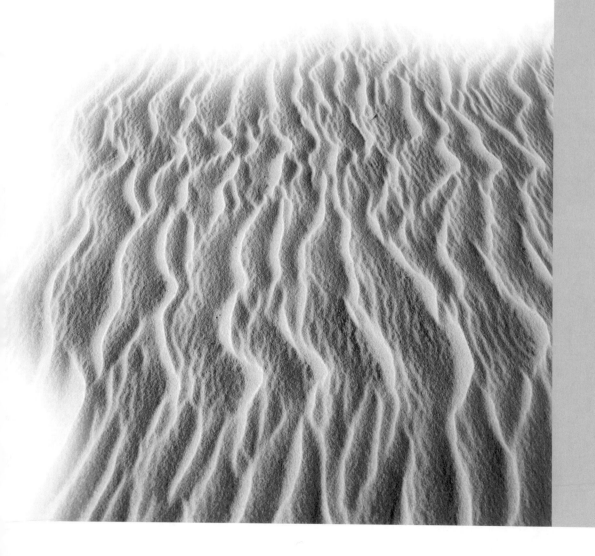

The first part of this book explains the basic concepts and principles of client/server architectures. Once you have an understanding of the different components needed in such architectures, you will be introduced to Remote Method Invocation (RMI) architecture. The different parts of RMI are then explained. This gives you a good understanding of the design and reference implementation of RMI, which makes it substantially easier for you to start developing applications.

You might ask why a whole chapter in a book about RMI is dedicated to basic client/server concepts. I have been working with the RMI technology for quite some time, and I often see that many problems arise because developers don't understand the underlying principles. Learning everything about the "how-to" is useful to a certain point, but after that you need to understand why it works the way it does. And this is what is discussed in Chapter 1. Once you have looked at what problems should be solved in order to create an RMI, you will see that each part of RMI is targeted at solving one of these basic architectural problems.

Chapter 1 begins by investigating the principles of all client/server architectures and the reasons for using such architectures. Key concepts shared by most client/server systems are identified, and a brief look at the history of client/server architectures is also provided. Once you have gained an understanding of the basics presented in this chapter, the specifics of RMI will be much easier to understand.

Chapter 2 explains in detail what RMI is, its design, and the implementation of RMI that is provided with the standard Java Development Kit (JDK), the Java Remote Method Protocol (JRMP). The general design of RMI/JRMP is explored as well as some of the basic parts of RMI required to implement a remote object. As you read this chapter, I will also show you how different parts of RMI relate back to the general concepts presented in the first chapter.

CHAPTER 1

Client/Server Architectures

In this first chapter, we look at the characteristics of client/server architectures: what the components are, what the common concepts are, and why one would want to have them. Finally, we examine some of the most popular examples of client/server architectures.

We begin by looking at the basic definition of what a client/server architecture is. It is very likely that you already have some understanding of what client/server architecture is all about; however, let's start by reviewing the basic definition to ensure that you have a well-defined base to work with.

We then take a look at the most common concepts that are involved in creating a distributed architecture, such as RMI. I have identified what I feel are the core parts of just about every distributed architecture, and when we get to the specifics of RMI, you will see how different parts of the RMI design relate to those basic building blocks.

In the last part of this introductory chapter, I show you a couple of different client/server architectures and give you a brief overview of how they have implemented the concepts that have been described in this chapter. This will make it much easier to see how RMI fits in and how it differs from other architectures.

(If you're tempted to skip directly to Chapter 2, first take a brief look at the sections under "Basics of Networked Computing," as I will be referring to those concepts when I describe the RMI architecture.)

Client/Server Basics

Let's begin by looking at what a client/server architecture is and define the notions of client and server. Most people have an intuitive idea of what they are, but with the introduction of the Internet, the words client and server are often used in different contexts. Their meaning therefore slightly differs depending on usage.

Once you have a clear picture of what a client/server architecture really is, we take a brief look at the reasons you might want to use one and whether or not there are alternatives.

The Definition of Client and Server

If you look at the main characteristics of clients and servers, you can use the following definition, which works in most cases:

- A server is a software program that provides one or more services that can be used by zero or more clients.

- A client is something that uses at least one service provided by at least one server.

These definitions are illustrated in Figure 1.1.

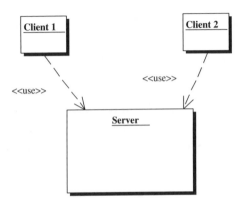

Figure 1.1 Client and server.

And that is really all there is to it. As you can see, this definition is quite broad, and thus can be used in many different situations. One of the most important things to notice is that this definition allows a server to be a client of another server. In practice, this is a very common occurrence. For example, a Web server that provides documents accessed by client browsers through the HyperText Transfer Protocol (HTTP) may use a logging server to store a list of all accesses. It may also use a disk server, which provides the physical storage of the documents to be transferred.

In the preceding definition, there is nothing that says that a client/server architecture is based on network communication between different physical machines. However, because this book is dedicated to the RMI architecture, let's assume this additional characteristic. Although the server and client may be executing on the same physical machine, the most common case in a networked environment is that they are not.

Why Use a Client/Server Architecture?

Client/server architectures are becoming more popular every day. More and more applications that have traditionally been desktop applications, such as office suites, are adopting the notions of clients and servers. Some of the motivations for using a client/server architecture are:

- **Resource sharing.** The most common reason for using a client/server architecture is that a resource located on one machine needs to be shared between several clients, where there is often a one-to-one mapping between a client and a physical user. A popular example of this is the World Wide Web (WWW), where documents need to be accessed from a particular Web server by several surfers, often simultaneously.

- **Accessing remote resources.** This item is related to the preceding item, but is somewhat different. In some cases, a particular resource can only be available on a specific physical machine, which means that the only way to access it is to use a client/server architecture that allows this resource to be accessed. For example, the popular messaging system ICQ creates a server on each user's machine, which can receive messages for the user located at that machine. This server, which is actually the ICQ client, in turn uses the centrally located ICQ server in order to send messages to other users.

So in this case, both the ICQ program located on the user's machine and the ICQ master server are both servers and clients! This architecture is shown in Figure 1.2.

- **Delegating responsibilities.** Some tasks that are common to many clients may be put on a server that all clients can access. By doing this, these common tasks are centralized, which makes them easier to maintain and control.

- **Performance distribution (bandwidth, CPU, memory).** Sometimes a particular task can be very expensive to perform. If every computer had enough hardware to perform this particular task, it might become a rather expensive solution. Instead it is usually a better idea to invest in one high-performance server and keep the client hardware to a minimum, thus reducing overall cost. Adding clients in such a scenario also becomes much cheaper.

- **Security.** Some applications might require data that is of a sensitive nature. In these cases, keeping the data on every computer that is able to access it is a bad idea. Someone wanting access to the data could easily steal the computer and simply examine the computer's storage to get to it. By placing the data in a highly secured server, you are able to have very strong security restrictions on its usage. Users wanting to access the data would have to verify their identity in some way, and it would also be possible to let different users access different kinds of data.

As you can see, the rule of thumb is that if you need to use a network in order to implement an application, you need to use a client/server architecture.

The use of client/server architectures, and their design and implementation, is continually changing. One of the first client/server architectures was the mainframe computer—a megalithic server with vast computing resources accessed by client terminals with little or no computational power. Today, of course, the designs and implementations are significantly more complex.

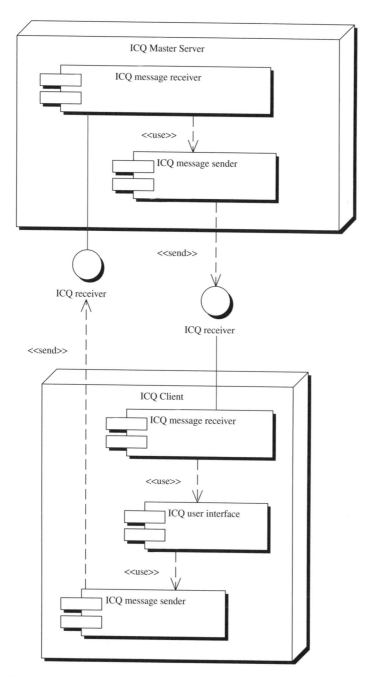

Figure 1.2 The ICQ architecture.

It is amusing to listen to the discussions of whether client/server as a programming paradigm is dead or not. Some claimed that the introduction of the personal computer would make the client/server paradigm obsolete. However, as you probably all know, the Internet changed all that. And now client/server architecture is huge, with new distributed standards and products emerging at a very rapid pace.

As long as there are networks there will be client/server architectures. They will no doubt be very different from the ones used in the beginning of the networking paradigm, but the basic ideas—and problems—will essentially still be the same.

N-tier Systems

Client/server architecture can be described as a two-tier system. One tier is the client, and the other tier is the server. Each of these tiers has well-defined responsibilities, and the interfaces between them are very strict. You can also extend these tiers to any depth, which are called *n-tiers*. Why would you want to do this? A very common reason is to narrow the scope of responsibilities for a particular tier, and by doing so, maximize the reuse of the software design.

Let's look at a typical example. Assume you have a SQL server, which is highly optimized for storing organized data. The client to this server could be the computer used by the end user, but allowing the end user to access the SQL server may not be a good idea. Two reasons for not allowing end user access to the SQL server are security concerns and the possibility of excessive server resource consumption (letting each client have its own database connection does not work well if there are many clients). Also if you need to upgrade the behavioral model of the database system, you need to upgrade all the clients simultaneously. Therefore, you can introduce a middle tier, which handles all the behavioral models of the database system. The client at the end user only contains the visuals, showing the end user the visual perception of the data. If you then make the client completely generic (in the sense that it is not tied to a particular application), such as a Web browser, Portable Document Format (PDF) viewer, or Virtual Reality Markup Language (VRML) navigator, the middle tier is the only part that is unique to the system. Maintenance becomes easier and upgrading only takes place at a single point.

Observe that the middle tier in the preceding example is the client to the SQL server and the server to the view client. The client/server architecture was extended to a three-tier system. It could have been extended to any depth, but the important thing to remember is that each tier introduces a new set of interfaces, which must be maintained at all times.

Basics of Networked Computing

Now that you have a rough idea of what a client/server architecture is, the next step is to investigate how it is typically implemented and what you need to understand in order to successfully design such a system.

We cover this information in a bottom-up fashion by beginning with the lowest level—the network communications—and work our way up through object marshalling, distributed proxies, and naming. Once these concepts have been covered, you should have a pretty good idea of what kinds of services RMI provides in order to be a good client/server architecture.

Network Communications

Whenever you are dealing with client/server architectures in a distributed computing context, one of the core technologies that is used is the network communications layer. For a client to be able to talk to a server that is located on some other physical machine, it needs to be able to send data to it and get a response somehow.

Connectionless Protocols

There are basically two different modes of communication in network programming: connectionless and connection-oriented. Connectionless protocols send one packet of data at a time, and the sender and receiver does not have to agree on anything beforehand. There is usually no guarantee for the sender that the packet actually reaches the receiver. It may get lost on the way for a number of reasons, and the only way for the sender to notice is if the receiver has to acknowledge the packets. In the world of Internet and Java programming, Universal Datagram Protocol

(UDP) is used for connectionless communication. UDP is a standardized protocol that is widely used. It is a protocol that is built on top of the IP protocol, which is the base data transmission protocol used on the Internet.

Figure 1.3 shows how the UDP protocol works. Somewhere a receiver listens for incoming packets on a particular *port*. A port is basically just a number that identifies a particular listener. If there was no notion of a port, there could only be one listener per machine, which is a bit limited. Typically, you want to have quite a few listeners on a networked machine, each implementing some specific application protocol. The port number that the listener uses is related to the application type that it implements. This way, a sender that implements the client-side of an application can send the data to the known port number and know that the listener understands the content and structure of the sent data.

For example, the popular computer game Quake communicates in multiplayer mode by using UDP, and the server listens for data on port 27015. Because it uses UDP, it means that it is not the end of the world if some of the sent data is lost. Either the data is resent, or data may come in at a later point in time, which replaces the data that was lost. UDP is also popular in applications where packets are seldom sent and where the overhead of setting up a connection would be greater than the actual data that is sent. The popular instant messaging application ICQ is such an example, where each message is sent as a UDP packet to the server. It, however, has to have some protocol of its own on top of UDP to make sure that any sent message actually reaches the server. Lost messages are not acceptable in the ICQ application.

Figure 1.3 The UDP protocol.

Connection-Oriented Protocols

Connection oriented protocols have a couple of phases that have to be completed in order for a sender to communicate with a receiver. First, the sender connects with the receiver. After a connection has been established, it is viewed as a stream of data through which the sender and receiver may communicate. The sender can send whatever data it wants to this stream, and thanks to the connection abstraction, the sender is guaranteed that the data will reach the receiver. If the transfer fails, then the sending operation fails, and the connection is closed. But if the send operation is successful, you can be certain that the data made it through.

In most protocols, the receiver is also allowed to be a sender, in which case, the connection is bidirectional. When the communication is done, either party may close the connection. Any attempts at writing data to the connection after that point will fail. The standardized connection-oriented protocol that is used in common Internet and Java network programming is called Transport Control Protocol (TCP/IP), which, like UDP, works on top of the IP protocol (hence the name).

Most network programming libraries, including those available on the Java platform, abstract the usage of the TCP/IP protocol by using *sockets*. A socket contains the necessary operations to establish a connection with a remote machine, communicate with it (preferably using streams), and terminate the connection. These commands, however, are not performed by the socket itself, but instead the socket delegates the commands to the TCP/IP implementation, which does the actual work. By using sockets, network programmers have a simple way of dealing with the network. All the complicated details of TCP/IP, such as resending lost packets, are taken care of at the protocol level, which the programmer does not have to bother with. All you need to care about at the application level is that you can connect to another machine and send and receive data while connected to it.

Marshalling

Once you are able to connect to other networked computers, you want to be able to send data that is useful for the particular applications that you want to create. The data is very specific to each application, but some common notions are used. For simple applications, such as sending e-mail through the Simple Mail Transfer Protocol (SMTP) protocol, you usually just send strings of commands and data from the client to the server. This is the simplest case, and it is very convenient if the application does not have many requirements on the available commands and data.

However, if the application is more complex and especially if it is object-oriented, on one hand, you run into the problem of having applications that deal with structures of data or objects, and on the other hand, having a stream-oriented network connection that send bytes or blocks of bytes. How do you deal with this difference? You need some way to push your objects through the connection pipe in a format that the connection can handle.

The solution is what is commonly called *marshalling*. Marshalling is a process that converts a complex object into a byte stream, and then converts it back to an object using the reverse process, *unmarshalling*. The Java platform implements this through the *serialization* specification and accompanying Application Programming Interface (API).

The basic idea is shown in Figure 1.4. On the left is a live object, in the middle is a connection, and on the right is the object that was re-created from the data transferred through the connection. Note that although a network connection is used in these discussions, any binary storage or medium, such as a plain file, e-mail attachment, or a Java byte array could be used.

Let's take a simple example of an object and see how it can be marshalled. The class is constructed as shown in Figure 1.5. It has a simple String attribute and a reference to another object of the same class. Let's see how this can be converted into a stream of bytes, so that you can

Figure 1.4 Object to byte to object conversion.

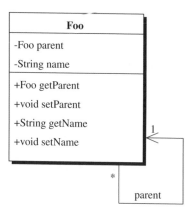

Figure 1.5 Marshalling example class.

transfer it over a network connection or perhaps store it on a disk, which also requires the object to be transformed into a stream of bytes.

The actual scenario that is used is shown in Figure 1.6. It contains two instances of the preceding Foo class, and one of the objects references the other through the parent association. This object graph needs to be transformed into a stream of bytes. I will not use any actual implementation of marshalling, such as serialization, but rather a pseudotype process that hopefully is easy enough to follow.

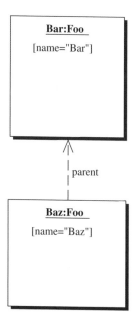

Figure 1.6 Marshalling example scenario.

Let's begin by stating that it is the Baz object that is to be marshalled. Some meta information is stored first, specifically the class of the object and a unique identification number. The class name is used to instantiate the correct class during the unmarshalling process, and the latter is used if some other object to be marshalled needs to reference this object, in which case, it simply marshalls the identification number. The name of the object, Baz, is then stored by converting the string into a series of bytes.

An interesting problem arises: You now need to store the parent attribute that points to another Foo object, namely Bar. How should this be done? Well, because the Bar object has not yet been marshalled, in which case, you would simply store the unique identification number that it had been assigned, you need to do marshalling of the Bar object. This is done in the same way as with the Baz object. The class name and identification number is stored first, then the name of the object, and lastly a token that represents "null." This last part is necessary because the unmarshalling process expects a reference to another Foo object, but because there is none, you must use some data that the unmarshalling process can understand as being a null reference.

After you have completed marshalling the two objects, you have a stream of bytes that contains the following:

```
<class: Foo><id: 1><String: Baz><class: Foo><id: 2><String: Bar><null>
```

Once you have a stream of bytes, there is no problem sending it through a socket to another networked computer. The application that receives this stream of bytes at the other end simply applies the reverse process, unmarshalling, to convert the stream back to an object graph.

The marshalling process that has been described is a simplified version of marshalling, and the one used in Java programming, which is called serialization, is much more advanced. However, the basic concept is the same, and it is vital that you understand this process if you are to do any serious work with client/server architectures, especially object-oriented ones as is the case in RMI.

Proxies

Now that you can connect networked computers, send data between them, and also convert objects into streams to simplify sending this data, what is left? Well, you could start working with only this basic knowledge, but you would soon realize that it is a rather awkward way of writing distributed applications. The application code, in general, looks something like the following code. You can assume that issuing a command involves sending some data to the server, that is, the name and parameters of the command, and then receiving a response as a result of some computation based on the input.

```
// Connect to the server host
Socket s = new Socket("myserver.mydomain.com", 1234);
// Get the out stream
OutputStream out = s.getOutputStream();
// Attach a stream that takes care of the serialization of objects
ObjectOutputStream oo = new ObjectOutputStream(out);
// Write an object that is to be used by the server
oo.writeObject(someObject);
// Get the in stream
InputStream in = s.getInputStream();
// Attach a stream that takes care of the deserialization of objects
ObjectInputStream oi = new ObjectInputStream(in);
// Read the response from the server
Foo bar = (Foo)oi.readObject();
// Close the streams - the underlying streams will be closed implicitly
oo.close();
oi.close();
// Close the connection
s.close();
```

The server executes similar code, but in reverse, that is, it reads something, does some computation, and then writes the result.

As you can see, this is quite a lot of code (and note that the preceding code does not include any exception handling, which should be added for completeness). What is important is that the only part that is directly relevant to your application is the fact that you are sending someObject, and receiving a Foo object. The rest is generic code that is used for all communication. This means that much of the code could possibly be reused for all applications.

One of the properties of the preceding code is that you are exposed to many details of the transferring of objects to and from the server. Preferably, you would only want to say, "Hey, send this to the server at this location, and give me the response." Also, all of this should preferably be done by talking to an object that has the operations that are relevant to your specific application. For example, wouldn't it be great if the preceding operation could be done by simply using the following code line:

```
Foo bar = server.doSomething(someObject);
```

This would be much easier to code, and you would not be directly exposed to the fact that the call involves quite a lot of network communication. It is all hidden away behind a nice little Java object.

This actually can be implemented by using *proxies*. A proxy is an object that implements a given interface, but does not directly execute some code to compute a result, rather it delegates to some other object that performs the actual computation. This concept is shown in Figure 1.7.

There is one interface in the figure, `MyServer`, which is implemented by both `MyServerProxy` and `MyServerImpl`. However, only `MyServer-Impl` actually performs any computation when `doSomething` is called. `MyServerProxy` only sends the call to the delegate and returns the result—nothing more. However, it is only this simple if the two objects `MyServerProxy` and `MyServerImpl` are in the same physical Java Virtual Machine (JVM). What happens if they are not? This scenario is shown in Figure 1.8.

The proxy has to do something similar to the pseudocode shown in Figure 1.7, or it could delegate to some other library or something similar that performs the network communication on its behalf, which is how RMI works. The proxies, or *stubs* as they are called in RMI lingo, do not handle the network communication themselves, but rather use a subsystem to perform this work. This relationship is explained in detail in Chapter 2.

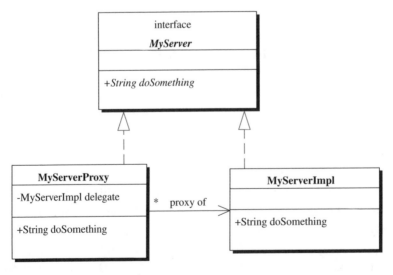

Figure 1.7 Proxy example.

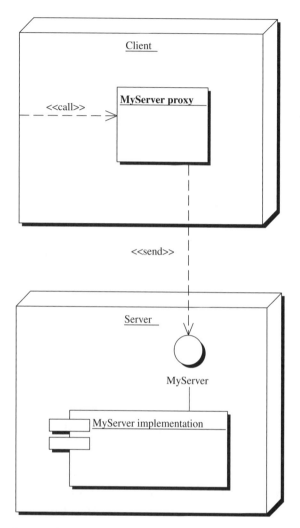

Figure 1.8 Proxy example scenario.

One very important aspect is how the proxy that references the object that resides within the real server is constructed. Obviously, it cannot have a real Java reference because a Java reference only works if the objects are located within the same physical JVM, so another scheme has to be used. Exactly how to implement this differs between different client/server systems, but the general idea is to assign the server object some unique identification key, which the proxy holds, in addition to the name of the host where the object lives. This information is then used whenever the server object is called. The contents of such a remote reference in the case of RMI is discussed in Chapter 2.

To summarize, proxies provide you with a Java object model of remotely accessible objects, and they hide all the details of network communication. If you did not have this abstraction, a significant amount of your application would have to deal with these issues, which is both time-consuming and rather difficult to get right.

This proxy pattern is one of the most useful patterns in distributed application programming. The use of proxies in this way is probably the most common, but there is nothing to stop you from putting yet another proxy on top of the current one on the client or placing a proxy in-between the client proxy and the server implementation. It may, for example, perform some tasks that should be handled regardless of the interface and object implementation. Examples of such tasks are automatic error handling, security management (such as data encryption and client authentication), and so on. The idea that proxies can be chained in this way is a very powerful idea and should be used as much as possible in order to reduce the complexity of an application.

Naming

Now that you understand network communications, how to send objects using marshalling, and how to abstract all of the details by using proxies, what is left? Well, there is still the issue of how the client acquires the proxy.

One way for the client to acquire the proxy is to create it directly on the client. However, this requires a lot of knowledge on the client's behalf. It needs to know how to construct the internal remote reference that contains the unique object identifier and host name, how the proxy deals with network communication, and how to initialize the proxy with the remote reference. These are things that you preferably do not want to deal with in the client, especially if the server object's identifier is not known, perhaps because it was assigned a random one when the server started.

What do you do in this case? Often, you can introduce a layer of indirection that abstracts all of these things. What you really want to do is say, "I know that my server is called Foo. Give me something that allows me to talk to it." This concept of retrieving something by using a name, or a set of known properties about it, is called *naming*. The primary goal of naming is to simplify the task of acquiring an object by using its name. This can be implemented in lots of ways.

One popular naming implementation is the Domain Name Service (DNS), which is frequently used for translating an easily remembered computer name into the IP address of the named computer. For example, you could ask a DNS server for the IP address of a computer named "www.mydomain.com," and it will look in its translation tables for it, or perhaps ask another DNS server if it does not have the answer in its own tables.

Using this approach, the client only has to care about the name of the server object and where it can get the real proxy in exchange for this name. In the case of RMI, the most commonly used implementation of naming is the RMI registry, which is provided with the Java Development Kit (JDK) distribution. This service has `bind` and `lookup` operations that allow you to store proxies to the server objects using a name as an association and later to look up these proxies using these names.

But you might wonder: isn't this just a way to put the problem off, as you now have to get the proxy to the naming service, which is more or less the same problem as discussed previously. The naming service itself can be seen as a remotely accessible object whose proxy has a set of operations that delegate to this server object. The only reason it is easier now is because the naming service generally has a given object identifier through which you can access it, and an API is also generally available, which can be used to easily construct a proxy to a naming service. This makes it different from the other objects. This is shown in Figure 1.9.

One useful way to take advantage of the naming concept is to chain names. This means that if you look up a name in a naming service, the result may not be the proxy but yet another name to be looked up using another naming service. If you follow the chain of names, eventually you reach the object. Preferably, the naming service should perform this chain following on its own, so that the client only needs to look up a name by querying the first naming service.

All of the information provided thus far, which has been greatly simplified, constitutes everything you need to know about client/server architectures to be able to understand the RMI architecture. The RMI architecture is a fairly advanced architecture, but all of its parts map

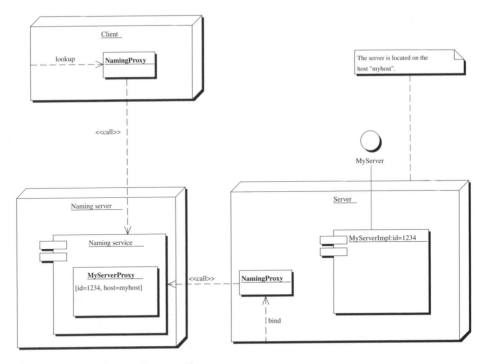

Figure 1.9   Naming usage scenario.

quite well to the fundamental concepts that have been discussed in this chapter. Chapter 2 describes in detail how all of these basic concepts have been designed and implemented in the case of RMI.

Other Types of Client/Server Systems

Before we delve too deeply into the mysterious and fascinating world of RMI, let's take a look at a couple of other client/server architectures. These have much in common with RMI, namely they all use the previously mentioned concepts but in different ways, and all pave the way for RMI as the latest step in the evolution of client/server architectures.

The preceding comment is perhaps only half-true, as you might argue that RMI is not as powerful as, for example, Common Object Request Broker Architecture (CORBA). Although this is true, in my opinion, one of the great strengths of RMI is its focus on the Java programming model and its seamless integration with the Java syntax. This results in a very simple distributed programming environment. It focuses clearly on the problem of remote object communication. Everything else that programmers may want to have in a distributed application, such as transactions, security, and persistence management, are specified in other standards that are part of the set of enterprise APIs defined by Sun through the Java Community Process. It is hard to hear the whole orchestra if you only listen to the violin. In order to understand how to create full-featured distributed applications, I suggest that you also take a look at the other specifications defined by Sun and its partners. Later chapters in this book deal with two of the most important RMI-based technologies: Enterprise JavaBeans and Jini.

The World Wide Web

One of the best, and most popular, examples of client/server architectures is probably the Web and its associated standards HTTP and HyperText Markup Language (HTML). There are lots of books available on HTML and HTTP, so I will not detail their characteristics, but it is important for you to see how HTTP and HTML map to the basic concepts that have been defined in this chapter.

The HTTP Protocol

Basically, the Web is a way to access documents that are located on servers around the world. This is accomplished by using HTTP. HTTP is an example of a simple text-based protocol. Because of the simplicity of the protocol, it is easy to implement using almost any programming language. The HTTP protocol was initially created by Tim Berners-Lee, a researcher at the CERN institute in Switzerland, for the purpose of easily accessing documents that were located on CERN's intranet.

Using a greatly simplified description, the HTTP protocol works in this way: The client sends a string to the server that contains information about what document to retrieve. An example of such a string is as follows:

```
GET HTTP/1.0 /index.html
```

The server interprets this string so that the GET command is performed on the file "/index.html." Basically, this means that the server should return the contents of the index.html file. The "HTTP/1.0" string is a hint to the server as to which version of the protocol is used. If a command is issued and the server does not understand this command because it had been written for an earlier version of the protocol, the server may return an error response.

```
Every document that may be accessed is given a unique name called a Uni-
form Resource Locator (URL). These names look something like this:
http://www.somedomain.com:81/somedirectory/somefile.html.
```

The first part of the URL, http://, indicates that this name points to something to be accessed by using the HTTP protocol. Other possible protocols include File Transfer Protocol (FTP) (in which case the prefix would be ftp://), gopher, Wide Area Information System (WAIS), and so on.

The second part is the name of the computer that hosts the Web server and the TCP/IP port that this server uses to listen for incoming requests. If the port is omitted, then the value of 80 is assumed, which is the default port in the case of HTTP. Each protocol has a default port.

The third part is the name of the file relative to some directory on the server, which only the Web server knows about.

When the preceding URL is given to a Web browser, it breaks it up into its components and issues a GET command, as shown earlier, for the *somedirectory/somefile.html* document by contacting the Web server on the host www.*somedomain*.com, which is using port 81 for communication.

The URL maps, more or less, to the naming concept. The client need only know the name of the document in order to retrieve it.

The HTML Format

The HTML format, which is used to encode most of the documents that may be accessed, is the Web's equivalent of the marshalling format. A complex document is flattened out to a simple text document, which can easily be sent to the client, who can unmarshal it by using a Web browser to view the page. The browser can be compared to a proxy, which the real client, in this case the physical user, may use to easily access and view the documents. The following is a simple example of what HTML looks like:

```
<HTML>
<HEAD>
  <TITLE>A document</TITLE>
</HEAD>
<BODY BGCOLOR="yellow">
<H1>Some title</H1>
Text that is <STRONG>important</STRONG>!</P>
</BODY>
</HTML>
```

As you can see, HTML contains both meta information about the document, such as its title, as well as information that is directly related to its presentation, such as the background color and a hint that some text should be visualized using an emphasized font (represented by the <STRONG> tag). This is only a simple example. The complete HTML language is rather complex, and it is constantly evolving, but the basic idea is very similar to that of marshalling formats.

Remote Procedure Call

The next level of client/server architectures calls software libraries that are located on a networked computer. Typically, a library is just a set of functions that can be executed, so no objects and state is involved beyond the simple variables that the library may contain. In a sense, you can think of libraries as being only one object with a bunch of methods that can be called.

The technique of calling functions over the network is commonly called Remote Procedure Calls (RPCs). This was, and still is to some extent, a very common way of calling libraries that were programmed using a programming language that is not object-oriented, such as C or Pascal. The basic idea of RPC is shown in Figure 1.10.

The main difference between simple RPC and RMI is that there may only be one "instance" of MyLibrary, as it is not an object but rather just a set of functions that can be invoked remotely. Because of this the remote reference to an RPC library usually only contains the name of the library, the name of the machine that is hosting the library, and the port to which it is listening.

The proxies used to communicate with RPC libraries are often generated by first defining the interface of the library using an Interface Definition Language (IDL), and then using some implementation specific

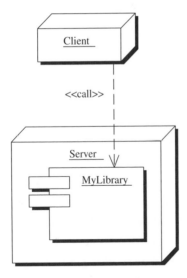

Figure 1.10   RPC.

tool to generate the proxies or stubs as they are also commonly called. These stubs control how the communication between the client and the server is handled and takes care of the marshalling and unmarshalling of parameters and result values.

Ironically, despite the fact that RMI is based on an object-oriented language, many RMI applications treat it as a simple procedural language and only use one remote object on the server-side, usually called "The Server," with which to communicate, essentially making the architecture RPC-ish. This simplifies the design of the application in some cases, but may also often be too much of a restriction as the full power of the Java language and RMI is not being utilized.

CORBA

The next step towards creating a distributed object architecture is to start dealing with real objects. There are quite a few such architectures available, but one of the most important ones, especially from our point of view, is CORBA.

What Is CORBA?

CORBA is a unified standard for distributed object systems. The Object Management Group (OMG) first created the CORBA standard in 1989. OMG is an industry consortium that works to define these standard specifications, which the different products offered by the vendors implement.

CORBA contains several specifications that deal with the different aspects of a distributed system. These include, for example, the Internet Inter-Orb Protocol (IIOP) network protocol specification, which defines how clients and servers communicate; the COSNaming specification, which defines how naming is done; and the OMG IDL, which defines a way to describe object interfaces in order to be able to generate proxies that can talk to them. The entire CORBA standard contains many more such specifications, each covering some piece of a distributed system that needs to be defined.

One of the most important features of CORBA is that it is platform and language independent. This means that a CORBA client can be written in one programming language that runs on one platform and be able to talk to a CORBA server that is written in a completely different language and runs on some other platform. For example, a C++ client running on a Windows computer is able to talk to a Java server on a system running the Solaris operating system. This makes CORBA a very convenient way to integrate different systems, especially to do what is often called "legacy system integration," that is, when you have an old system that needs to be integrated with a newer one.

How Does CORBA Work?

CORBA has many similarities with RMI, so understanding how CORBA works is a good way to get some idea about how RMI works. A CORBA client first acquires a proxy to a CORBA object by using the COSNaming service and approximately implements the features described in the Naming section. The object may reside on the same computer or some other computer in a network. This proxy has been generated by running a tool that takes a description of the object, written in OMG IDL, as input. The created proxy is specific to the particular language and platform that the client uses.

When a method in the proxy is called, the proxy communicates with the local Object Request Broker (ORB), which is responsible for forwarding the call to the object. In case the object is not managed by the local ORB, the call is sent over the network to the computer that hosts it. On the receiving host, there is another ORB, which accepts the method invocation request. The communication between the two ORBs uses the IIOP, which is a protocol that is specifically designed to allow the platform and language independence that is one of the most fundamental features of CORBA.

Once the receiving host has accepted the request, it looks up a proxy that can accept this request and passes it on to the object. This proxy, which resides on the server-side, is called a *skeleton*. Early versions of RMI also used server-side skeletons, but since the reflection API was introduced in JDK1.2, this has been changed so that the RMI runtime can now call the object directly without the need for such a skeleton. The entire CORBA scenario is outlined in Figure 1.11.

This figure does not show how or from where the client acquires the stub, which it can use to call the object. As I said earlier, the client uses the COSNaming service to accomplish this. Similar to what was explained in the Naming section, the COSNaming service can be used to look up a stub when provided with a name that the stub has been associated with. This association is typically set up by the server upon startup of the system.

Why Use CORBA?

CORBA is very similar to RMI in that it is an object-oriented way to call objects over the net. If you are able to call your Java objects from clients that are potentially not written in Java or if your objects themselves are not in Java, then it makes sense to use CORBA. CORBA also has many helper services to assist you in making larger systems, and the vendor support for CORBA is fairly sizable.

With the recent introduction of RMI over IIOP (RMI/IIOP), there is now a marriage between the two worlds, which gives you, as a developer, the best of both worlds: platform and language independence through the IIOP protocol as well as the easy to use programming interface RMI. RMI/IIOP allows you to make remotely accessible objects that can be accessed by CORBA clients, but which are substantially easier for you to create by using the RMI interface instead of CORBA during develop-

Client/Server Architectures 27

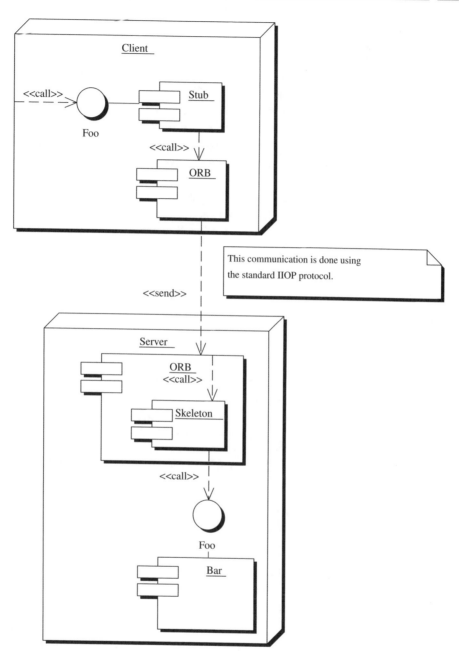

Figure 1.11 A CORBA scenario.

ment. RMI/IIOP is also the technology used to bring interoperability into the Enterprise JavaBeans API, which makes it even more useful to know about.

RMI/IIOP Limitations

Beware however; although RMI/IIOP makes it easier to use CORBA, it is significantly less flexible than the RMI/JRMP combination used in Java. In fact, so many features of RMI have been removed that I believe the name should be changed to "RMI"/IIOP. So, if you have a situation where you know that both the clients and the server are going to be in Java and you do not foresee any change to this in the future, I would recommend that you use the standard RMI/JRMP implementation.

Features that are not available in RMI/IIOP include distributed garbage collection, dynamic classloading (or at least very few vendors implement it), and custom socket transports. It is also more difficult to write RMI/IIOP clients.

Summary

This chapter began by stating some basic definitions, such as that of client and server. The important notions of n-tier systems were then defined. When working with client/server systems, it is always important to note which layers in the architecture perform what tasks, and the n-tier paradigm gives you a good understanding of this.

Subsequently, some of the key concepts involved in client/server architecture were discussed:

- **Network communications.** Network communication is all about how two systems on potentially different computers in a network communicate with each other.

- **Marshalling.** Marshalling is used to transform objects into byte streams, which can easily be sent over the network, and then transformed back into in-memory objects.

- **Proxies.** By using proxies you hid many of the details of network communication and marshalling, and instead were able to use a simple Java object to communicate with a remote object.

- **Naming.** Naming helps you locate proxies, which can be used to talk to remote objects.

The last part of the chapter showed some examples of client/server architectures and how they relate to the basic concepts that were defined. Some of them are very different from RMI, whereas others (such as CORBA) are very similar.

Next, we take an in-depth look at RMI and see how it is mapped to what has been discussed so far. That discussion will conclude our introductory coverage, and we will then take a look at how to actually start coding RMI objects.

Essentials of Remote Method Invocation

N ow that you have a reasonably good idea of what distributed architectures are all about, it is time to introduce the star of this story: Remote Method Invocation (RMI). This chapter describes RMI in detail as well as the Java Remote Method Protocol (JRMP) implementation that is provided with the Java Development Kit (JDK). You learn what RMI is, how it relates to Java programming in general, some of the practical details involved, and what lies under the hood of the JRMP runtime engine.

After completing this chapter, you should understand how RMI works and why it works the way it does. RMI is not hard once you understand the reasoning behind its design and implementation. If you manage to get through this chapter and understand everything, I promise you that the more applied chapters to come will be a breeze, a stroll in the park, a piece of cake.

What Is RMI?

Let's start off with the question: What is RMI? Well, RMI is a specification for how Java objects can be accessed remotely—that is, from Java Virtual Machines (JVMs) other than the one that hosts the particular object. These may reside on the same physical machine as the hosting JVM, or they may be located on other machines that are connected to the hosting machine (the server) through some network. The specification includes rules for how these objects should be coded, how they can be located and called remotely, and how method parameters and computation results are passed between JVMs. In short, it contains definitions of how all the concepts that were discussed in Chapter 1 should work.

What RMI Is Not

Before getting too far into the specifics of RMI, there is one misconception that should be straightened out right away. It is easy to think that the APIs and implementation that come with the JDK is RMI. It is not. What you get are the interfaces that are defined in the RMI specification, which are contained in `java.rmi` and its subpackages, as well as the default implementation of RMI, which is called JRMP. Well, actually JRMP is the name of the wire protocol that is used by the implementation that comes with the JDK, but lacking a better name, this is what it is usually called. Sometimes you see the name combined with RMI, which results in RMI/JRMP.

So, when discussing RMI, it is important to remember what the general characteristics are as defined by the RMI specification and what the specific issues are that only apply to the JRMP implementation of RMI. The RMI specification is often intentionally vague on some issues, such as multithreading and connection usage, whereas the JRMP implementation is crystal clear in how things are managed, especially if you limit yourself to a particular version of the JRMP implementation.

In a perfect world, the separation between the specification, RMI, and the implementation, JRMP in this case, should be complete enough that there is no mention of the JRMP implementation in the RMI API classes. Unfortunately, the RMI classes currently contain some hard-coded hooks into the JRMP engine, which makes it difficult to replace it completely and transparently. Also, it is questionable as to whether some of the configuration parameters of RMI are really general and applicable to any RMI implementation or if they are specific to a particular implementation JRMP.

The separation between specification and implementation of RMI will hopefully improve in future versions. The introduction of custom socket factories is a good step in this direction, and there will most likely be more such changes down the road.

Which Version of RMI?

RMI has been around since JDK version 1.1 was released. However, since the initial versions, there have been a few interesting changes made to RMI. Some changes relate to minor practical details and bug fixes, whereas others are more important, such as semantical changes that directly affect how RMI works. Others yet are related directly to the general evolution of the JDK, such as how security is dealt with. Evolution of APIs is a very natural process, but when describing an API such as RMI, which has been around for a while, the question arises: Which version should be described? Should just the latest one be described, the first one, or should every version be described?

In this book, I have decided to limit myself to how RMI works in version 1.2.2 of the JDK, that is, the latest version as of this writing. The reasons for this are several. This book is primarily intended to provide an understanding of how it all works. If you really understand how it works in JDK1.2.2, it is quite easy to learn the differences in earlier versions if necessary. Furthermore, all the examples are created for JDK1.2.2, as it is a more convenient and mature platform in general. Having duplicates for JDK1.1 versions would merely complicate things. It is also important to consider in which scenarios RMI is best used. As you will see in later chapters, the RMI technology should not be used in cases where it is difficult to control the entire system including client setups. Therefore, if you consider using RMI only on those cases where you can control the system as a whole, it is a good idea overall to use later versions of the JDK and hence later versions of RMI.

I realize that this is a foggy subject, and not everyone will agree with my point of view, but here it is anyway. I want to emphasize again that this book is not only a "HOW-TO" book on RMI, but also that its aim is to explain how RMI works as well, because a fundamental understanding of any particular subject tends to make it easier to use in practice. This information will hopefully make RMI useful even for RMI programmers who are restricted to earlier versions of RMI.

The Principles of RMI

Before looking at how RMI is designed, it is a good idea to understand the fundamental design principles that have been used and the reasons for them. RMI was not created at random; there is a reason for every choice in the specification of RMI. What are those reasons? Well, as I am not a member of the RMI development team, the following reasons are only qualified guesses. However, I think it is safe to assume that their reasoning was very similar.

The main idea when designing a distributed client/server architecture is to make it as similar to normal Java programming as possible. This means that as many attributes as possible of Java should be preserved. Essentially, this concept had the following effect on the design of RMI:

- Java uses garbage collection to determine the lifecycle of objects. A distributed object architecture should therefore include garbage collection to control the lifecycle of the objects.

- Java uses the concept of exceptions to report errors that occur during computation. Because the introduction of a network in object communication is a source of errors, a distributed object architecture based on Java should use exceptions to report such errors to the user of the object.

- Java uses interfaces to expose implementation without exposing the exact source of the implementation. A distributed architecture that is based on delegating computation over a network to remotely accessible objects should therefore use interfaces to expose the functionality of the server objects. This can also be compared with Remote Procedure Calls (RPC) and Common Object Request Broker Architecture Interface Definition Language (CORBA IDL), where the interface is described independently of the implementation. However, in the case of RMI, a native Java interface is used to describe the interface of the remote object instead of some specific IDL language.

- Objects in Java are invoked by calling methods. Even though a network has been added between the client and the server, the use of proxies can provide the illusion that the Java object being called by the client is an ordinary Java object.

- Java allows advanced developers to use the *classloading* mechanism to provide classes that are not available on the system classpath. If objects instantiated from such classes create new objects, they should use the same classloader that was used to instantiate it. In order to allow this type of mechanism to be used in RMI, the state of marshalled objects that is sent between clients and servers has to include annotations about the location of its classes. RMI implementations can use this mechanism to allow custom classloading to be used. In RMI, this is known as *dynamic classloading*. This mechanism is explained in detail later in this chapter.

These are pretty straightforward principles, but they have a very direct impact on how RMI works. They also simplified the job for the designers of RMI because all they had to do was to focus on making RMI as transparent as possible. Unfortunately, it is not possible to make RMI entirely transparent, and there are some important differences between RMI programming and normal Java programming. These differences are explained in the next section.

How Does RMI Differ from Ordinary Java?

Although the design of RMI sure makes it easy to use remote objects, it is not completely transparent. But then again, perhaps that would not be desirable.

The following list contains some of the differences between RMI programming and normal Java programming.

- **Remote exceptions.** All methods that you want to call on remote objects must be in the remote interface. But because of the inherently faulty network between a client and a server, the method signature must include the `java.rmi.RemoteException`. This means that your client code must always be aware of the fact that it is a remote object that is being called, and it must also be able to gracefully recover from any RMI error that occurs.

- **Pass by value.** When you pass objects as arguments to a normal Java object method invocation, you only pass the reference to the object. If you modify the object in the called method, you are really modifying the original object and not a copy of it. In RMI, all objects that are not remote objects are copied during a method call. This means that any changes you make to nonremote objects are only local to the client. This also means that if the objects being sent are somewhat large, the serialization of them may become a performance issue. You should therefore try to limit the size of the objects you send through RMI.

- **Call overhead.** There is an added time overhead for every call because the parameters must be marshalled and sent over the network, and the result must be returned and unmarshalled before the call is completed. This overhead is something that you usually must account for in your design and implementation in order to get decent performance.

- **Security.** Because the call is sent over a network, you may have to consider the security aspects, especially if you do not control the network. For example, someone may listen in on the communication or change the contents.

All of these elements make it more difficult to design and implement RMI systems compared with normal Java applications, but they must be considered if you want to make your systems as effective as possible.

RMI/JRMP Architecture

Let's take a peek inside RMI and try to figure out how it all fits together. There are lots of little details that you need to examine before you can fully understand RMI, but let's begin by looking at the big picture of how RMI works. In Figure 2.1, you see a typical RMI scenario. The client and server parties have been included as well as the JRMP subsystem. Although it is not necessary to understand the JRMP runtime engine in order to use RMI for remote programming, it sure helps when you need to figure out exactly how things work. If nothing else, it is always good fun to get your hands dirty with the details, right?

As you can see, there are quite a few pieces in this puzzle, and yet only those that are directly relevant to the topic at hand have been included. For example, the JRMP engine, which is an implementation of the RMI specification, contains many more pieces in order to perform its work. Let's examine it by starting at the highest level and working inward. This means that you should start looking at the proxies of RMI, which are also known as *stubs*. Once you have some idea of how the stubs work, you can continue with an examination of marshalling in RMI, followed by a close look at the network communication management. You can then

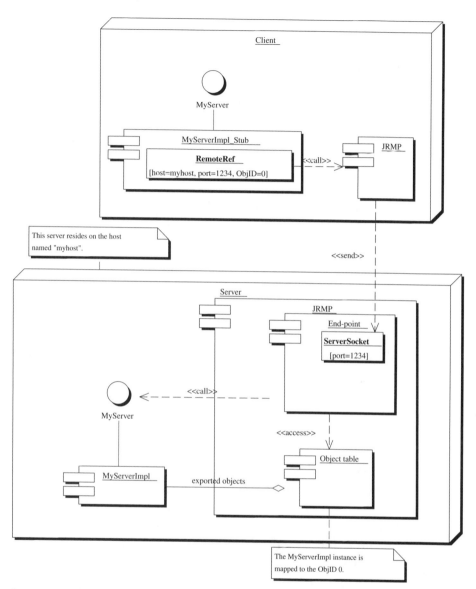

Figure 2.1 The RMI/JRMP architecture.

finish by looking at how naming is done in RMI, that is, how a client can acquire a stub to a server object.

All these issues are related to each other, and it is hard to find where it all begins and ends. It may be a good idea to revisit this part of the book occasionally to make sure you understand the flow of things.

Stubs

As explained in Chapter 1, when you are dealing with communication with remotely accessible objects, it is a good idea to hide all the details of network communication with a layer that looks like a regular Java object and has the same interface as the server object. This lets your applications focus on the particular problem to be solved, instead of meddling with the intricacies of distributed computing. In RMI these proxies are called *stubs*.

Stubs are proxies that implement a given set of RMI interfaces, which are also implemented by a remote object. If the remote object implements several RMI interfaces, then so does the stub (although it is fairly uncommon that a remote object implements more than one remote interface). When the stubs are invoked by some client, they delegate the calls to the JRMP engine, which forwards the calls to the server object. The server object performs some arbitrary computation, and the result is returned to the client. A specific tool that is supplied with the JDK, called *RMI compiler (rmic)*, typically generates the stub implementation classes. You should first figure out how to create the interface that is to be implemented by the server object and its corresponding stub.

The Remote Interface

Each server object or type of object that you want to access remotely must have a stub through which the client may talk to it by means of delegation. So, how do you create such a stub? The first step is to define the methods that you want to call on the remote object. You may only want to call some of the methods of an object, not all of them, so somewhere you have to tell RMI which methods should be callable from remote clients. These methods are collected in the object's *remote interface*. This interface has the following characteristics.

- It must extend the `java.rmi.Remote` interface, either explicitly or implicitly. The remote interface itself does not contain any methods, but instead works as a marker so that the RMI runtime knows what are regular objects and what are remote objects. This is important because remote objects are given special treatment during marshalling. It is okay if the interface does not extend the `java.rmi.Remote` directly, as long as it has `java.rmi.Remote` as one of its ancestors.

- The interface must be defined as `public` in order to let anyone access the methods in the interface. This is also important because you are going to generate stubs, that is, the RMI proxies, that will implement this interface. Had the interface not been defined as public, generating a stub that implements it would be impossible.

- The methods in the interface must be defined as `public`, and they must declare `java.rmi.RemoteException` or one of its superclasses, `java.io.IOException` and `java.lang.Exception`, in the throws clause. The exception requirement is necessary because the RMI runtime needs to be able to tell you as the client if any error occurs during the invocation. For example, if the runtime is unable to get a connection to the server, it throws a `java.rmi.ConnectException`, which is a subclass of `java.rmi.RemoteException`. You may of course also have any application-specific exceptions in the throws clause.

- At runtime, the method parameters and return values must be serializable. The reason for this is because the parameters that should be sent to the server upon stub invocation must be marshallable through the serialization mechanism. If you had no way of converting the parameters to a byte stream, how would you be able to send them over a network connection?

RemoteExceptions—Transparent or Not?

There has been some debate over whether `java.rmi.RemoteException` should be a subclass of `java.lang.Exception` or `java.lang.RuntimeException`. The difference for the RMI programmer is that a `RuntimeException` would not have to be declared in the remote interface, and any code that uses a remote object would not be required to catch `RemoteExceptions`.

This would provide cleaner interfaces and also make it easier to reuse code that had not been created to be used with remote objects. This would lower the effort needed to make a normal application remotely enabled.

However, this would give RMI programmers a false certainty, as networks are generally too unreliable to allow you to ignore the problems of network errors. Connections fail. Servers crash. Because special care has to be taken in order to correctly handle RMI exceptions, the RMI designers rightly chose to let `RemoteException` extend `Exception` instead of `RuntimeException`.

To understand what this means in practice, let's take a look at a few examples of remote interfaces. These are of course only a couple of simplistic examples of what is possible, but I hope that the general ideas explained previously are obvious.

```
public interface A
    extends java.rmi.Remote // Needs to extend Remote
{
    // Both Foo and Bar are serializable. Primitives, such as int,
    // are by default serializable.
    public Foo doSomething(Bar baz, int xyz)
        throws java.rmi.RemoteException, MyException;
}
public interface B
    extends A // Since A extends Remote, B is also a remote interface
{
    public void helloWorld()
        throws IOException; // Since IOException is a superclass of
                            // RemoteException we do not need to add
                            // RemoteException.

}
```

These two examples highlight the most common ways to construct remote interfaces. They both extend `java.rmi.Remote`, either explicitly such as A or implicitly such as B. They only have serializable parameters as method arguments and return values, and all methods throw `java.rmi.RemoteException` or one of its superclasses.

There is one other way of constructing a remote interface, and that is by extending an interface that is not a remote interface with one that is, as shown in the following code snippet.

```
public interface A // This is not a remote interface
{
    // Note that this method is a valid remote method
    public void doSomething(int xyz)
        throws IOException, MyException;
}
public interface B
    extends A, java.rmi.Remote // This makes B a remote interface
{
}
```

In this case, A is not a remote interface, whereas B is according to the rules that were defined earlier. But because the method in A is a proper remote method (note that it has to throw `java.rmi.RemoteException`, `java.io.IOException`, or `java.lang.Exception` for this to work), again according to the basic rules, it is now available in an interface that may be implemented by remote objects. By doing this, you have taken an interface that was not designed to be used in RMI and have added this capability without changing it. This is a powerful way to reuse interfaces that were created before the decision to use RMI was made, and it also makes the main interface, A in this case, unaware of the fact that it may be used in the RMI context. When designing this kind of system, you want to hide as much of the details of your architecture as possible, as this gives you greater freedom to change it at a later stage.

WARNING

Reusing interfaces that were not originally intended for RMI may sound promising at first, but in practice this can be very hard to achieve with good results because the interfaces may not take into account the changes that RMI introduces, such as pass by value of parameters and network overhead. Designing interfaces specifically to be used with a remote paradigm, such as RMI, is always preferred.

The Hello Interface

To show you a more hands-on way to build a remote interface, a version of the classic HelloWorld example is included in this section. I'll show you how to build a client/server system with RMI where the server consists of a remotely accessible object that has one method, `helloWorld`, which when called, does some computation and returns the result. The `helloWorld` method only has one parameter, which is a `java.lang.String` containing the name of the caller, and the result is also a string. The complete interface follows:

```
package masteringrmi.helloworld.interfaces;
import java.rmi.Remote;
import java.rmi.RemoteException;
public interface HelloWorld
    extends Remote
{
    // Public -----------------------------------------------------
    public String helloWorld(String name)
        throws RemoteException;
}
```

Notice that I have put it into a package whose name ends with "interfaces." I have found that it is good practice to put all classes that define what is called the *contract* between the client and server in a special package, which is separate from the package where the actual server is implemented. The content of such as contract usually includes the following types of classes:

- Remote interfaces of server objects.
- Application exceptions that may be thrown by any remote interface.
- Data holders. These are small classes that are only used to package data that should be moved between the client and server.

The general definition of contract classes is classes that may be used by both the client and server at some point in the application's execution, where application refers to both the client and server. By separating them, it becomes easier to package them later on, so that the client only gets the contract classes, whereas the server gets both the remote implementation and contract classes.

Moving on, you can see that I have let the simple interface extend `java.rmi.Remote`. Nothing fancy there. Also, `helloWorld` throws `java.rmi.RemoteException` because this is what the RMI implementation will throw if any error occurs during the invocation of the stub. For each call that is made, there are two possible sources of errors: the remote implementation itself and the RMI implementation. To the client this is transparent, as both types of errors appear as exceptions thrown from a method invocation.

Implementing the Remote Interface

Once you have defined your remote interface containing all the methods that you want to be able to access remotely, you need to create an object that implements this interface. This object will be a server object in your system. As with the remote interface, there are a couple of rules that you must follow in order to make everything work properly.

You first need to create a class that implements the interface. You must implement all methods that you have defined in the interface, so that the stub may delegate to these when the client calls it. How you implement these methods is entirely up to you. One thing that you could take advantage of to get cleaner code is that if your code does not throw `java.rmi.RemoteException`, you do not need to declare it in the throws clause of your method. Typically, remote method implementations only need to declare `java.rmi.RemoteException` in their throws clause if they in turn call another remote object and do not want to handle potential failures themselves.

You then need to decide how to make your object available to the RMI implementation. You need to, somehow, register your object with the RMI implementation, which creates an identifier that may be used by stubs later on when they forward calls to your server object. There are, essentially, two ways to register, or *export* in RMI lingo, your server object with the RMI implementation. You can either use the static method `exportObject` in `java.rmi.server.UnicastRemoteObject`, or you can subclass `java.rmi.server.UnicastRemoteObject`. What happens when you subclass `java.rmi.server.UnicastRemoteObject` is that the default constructor calls `exportObject`, so the difference is really quite small. One thing that is gained by subclassing `java.rmi.server.UnicastRemoteObject` is that you get implementations of the methods `equals`, `hashCode`, and `toString` (although it is a fairly common practice to reuse the source for these methods and include them in your own classes) that are appropriate for distributed use. If you do not plan on using your objects in hashtables or something similar, where proper implementation of those methods is crucial, you do not really need to subclass `UnicastRemoteObject`.

The fact that you are not required to extend `java.rmi.server.UnicastRemoteObject` along with the preceding method declaration trick, which lets you choose whether to declare `java.rmi.RemoteExceptions` or not, allows you to reuse objects that have not been created for remote access in RMI. Take a look at the following example.

```
public class HelloBean
{
   public String helloWorld(String name)
   {
      return "Hello " + name +"!";
   }
}
```

Because this example contains all the methods declared in the `Hello` interface, it is an implementation of this interface, although only implicitly as it does not yet have the implements `HelloWorld` statement. The only thing missing is the code to export it to be remotely accessible and for the class to implement the remote interface explicitly. You can easily add this by creating a subclass.

```
public class HelloWorldImpl
    extends HelloBean
    implements HelloWorld
{
    public HelloWorldImpl()
        throws RemoteException
    {
        UnicastRemoteObject.exportObject(this);
    }
}
```

The new constructor registers the object with the RMI runtime, so you now have a server object that can be accessed remotely through the `HelloWorld interface`.

What happens during export of an object? Not much really. The object to be exported is assigned an identification number, which is contained in a `java.rmi.server.ObjID` object and put into an object table, or object map, where the ID is the key, and the remote object is the value. RMI also creates a stub that can talk to your exported object. If `UnicastRemoteObject.exportObject(Remote foo)` is called, then RMI chooses any port number, but only the first time. Any subsequent calls to `exportObject` exports the remote object to the port number that was chosen the first time a remote object was exported. All such *anonymously exported* objects are then placed in the same object table.

You can also call the method `UnicastRemoteObject.exportObject(Remote foo, int port)`, which exports your object on the specified port. If there is no object table and server socket listener created for the given port, these are created automatically. Again, you can export any number of objects on the same port.

The stubs that are used to invoke methods on these exported objects contain not only the hostname and port number of the object, but also the generated identification number (contained in a `java.rmi.server.ObjID` instance). So, when a method invocation comes in on a particular socket port, the call contains the following information:

- Object identification number
- Method identification
- Method parameters

The identification number is used to retrieve the correct object from the internal object table. The method identification is used to select the methods to invoke, and the parameters are then used to invoke the method on the particular object. In Chapter 3, you will trace a call through the RMI architecture, so if it is still fuzzy as to how all of this works, hang in there.

Creating the Stubs

Once you have defined your remote interface, containing all the methods that you want to be able to access remotely, and have implemented it in a server class, it is time to generate the stub so that some client may actually call objects of that class remotely. To do this, you use the *rmic* tool, which is a part of the JDK installation. The rmic tool takes a given class and introspects it to find which methods should be remotely accessible. It then generates a class that is a subclass of `java.rmi.server.RemoteStub`, containing all the found remote methods, and also explicitly implements the remote interfaces of the server object.

The implementation of those methods simply delegates the call to the underlying RMI implementation. Because it explicitly implements the remote interfaces of your server class, you can cast an RMI stub to those interfaces. If a client has acquired a stub that implements a specific interface, it is important to remember that you may not cast it to the server implementation class. The stub is a representation of the server, but it is not the server. The only thing that the stub and the server classes have in common is the remote interface, so trying to cast the stub to the server implementation will generate a `java.lang.ClassCastException`.

Normally, rmic deletes the generated source code after it has generated the stub class. However, you can tell rmic to save the source code by using the `-keepgenerated flag`. You should try this at least once, and browse through the generated source code to get a feel for how it works. The following code snippet contains a generated stub that implements the `HelloWorld` interface.

```
public final class HelloWorldImpl_Stub
   extends java.rmi.server.RemoteStub
   implements masteringrmi.helloworld.interfaces.HelloWorld
{
 . . .
public java.lang.String helloWorld(java.lang.String $param_String_1)
   throws java.rmi.RemoteException
```

```
    {
  try {
      Object $result = ref.invoke(this, $method_helloWorld_0, new
  java.lang.Object[] {$param_String_1}, 1565891452170378145L);
      return ((java.lang.String) $result);
  } catch (java.lang.RuntimeException e) {
      throw e;
  } catch (java.rmi.RemoteException e) {
      throw e;
  } catch (java.lang.Exception e) {
      throw new java.rmi.UnexpectedException("undeclared checked excep-
  tion", e);
  }
    }
  . . .
  }
```

The important details to notice in the preceding code are that the generated stub extends `java.rmi.server.RemoteStub`, that it implements the `HelloWorld` interface, and that it contains an implementation of the `helloWorld` method, whose method body simply delegates the invocation to the RMI runtime through the `ref.invoke` call. The RMI runtime then performs its magic by forwarding this call to the server and invoking the method on the server object. This involves two important processes: the method parameters and result value must be marshalled in order to be transferred to and from the server, and some kind of network connection must be used to transfer these marshalled values. These are the next topics to be covered, and as you can see, they map very well to the basic concepts that were defined in Chapter 1.

Marshalling

The marshalling of method invocation parameters and the result values are the trickier parts of RMI. As explained in Chapter 1, marshalling is all about how to transform a graph of in-memory objects into a stream of bytes that can be transferred through network connections. The bytes must then be transformed back into a similar object graph, or unmarshalled, at the other end. This is shown in Figure 2.2.

Figure 2.2 Marshalling and unmarshalling.

Serialization

The basic enabling technology for marshalling and unmarshalling is called Java Serialization. Serialization is a specification for how to perform the marshalling and unmarshalling of Java objects. The actual algorithms that perform these processes are implemented by the `java.io.ObjectOutputStream` and `java.io.ObjectInputStream classes`. Typically, these classes are used by calling `writeObject` on the output stream, and then `readObject` on the input stream at the other end.

What is needed to allow this magic to happen? What are the requirements, and is there a way for you as a programmer to control it somehow? Let's start with the requirements. The first thing to do is to let any object that should be serialized implement the `java.io.Serializable` interface. As with the `java.rmi.Remote` interface, the `java.io.Serializable` interface does not contain any methods, but only functions as a marker stating that, "yes, objects of this class are serializable." If you try to serialize an object whose class is not serializable, the `writeObject` method throws a `java.io.NotSerializableException`.

TIP

When you begin working with RMI or serialization in general, it often happens that you forget to tag the class as serializable, and then this exception is raised. The recommended action is to remain calm, add the java.io.Serializable interface to your class, and watch the problem disappear.

Okay, so now you have marked your class as serializable, and you are serializing an object through the `java.io.ObjectOutputStream` class. What actually happens during this process? Well, the `java.io.ObjectOutputStream` does one of two things. First it checks whether the object in addition to the `java.io.Serializable` interface also contains an implementation of the following method:

```
private void writeObject(java.io.ObjectOutputStream stream)
    throws IOException
```

If so, this means that the class wishes to control the serialization of its objects on its own. The method is thus invoked, and the object may use the supplied stream to write any content it wishes that represents its state.

However, if this method is not implemented, it means that the `java.io.ObjectOutputStream` should instead apply the default algorithm in order to serialize the object. This algorithm introspects the object, and for each instance field it does the following:

- If the field is marked as `transient`, do nothing.
- If the field is marked as `static`, do nothing.
- If it is a primitive field, serialize the value (primitive values, such as ints and longs, are always serializable).
- If it is another object, serialize that object recursively.
- If it is an array, serialize all objects that it contains.

To make a long story short, it flattens out the object to a byte stream (taking into account multiple usage of the same object and circular references). This stream may then be transferred through network communication streams, sent to a file for persistent storage, or whatever.

During the deserialization of the bytestream through the use of the `java.io.ObjectInputStream`, the reverse process is applied. The class of the object to be deserialized is first checked for the following method:

```
private void readObject(ObjectInputStream stream)
    throws IOException, ClassNotFoundException
```

If this method is found, it is invoked, and the implementation of this method should typically do the reverse of the `writeObject` method. If it is not found, then the default algorithm is applied. This is, simply put, the reverse of the one used while doing serialization. One important thing to remember is that because transient attributes are not transferred, they are set to their default values in the newly deserialized object. Similarly, any static fields will not be transferred through the serialization mechanism. The focus is on object state only, not class state.

TIP

Transient fields are typically used to contain temporary calculations or objects that only make sense within a particular JVM, such as network connections or file objects. Because of this, you will typically want to recalculate or reacquire these fields in the readObject method. However, these values are also typically initialized in the constructors of the class, so you may want to factor it out to a separate method that both the readObject and constructor methods can call.

The following simple code snippet shows how to serialize and deserialize objects. Let's first define two serializable classes that you can experiment with.

```
class A
    implements java.io.Serializable // A is hence serializable
{
    // Static values are not serialized
    static long someValue = 1;

    // This attribute is serialized
    int foo = 10;

    // Transient attributes are not serialized
    transient String bar = "Hello World!";

    // If baz points to a B instance,that object is also serialized
    B baz;
}
class B
    extends A // Since A is serializable, so is B
{
    // This is transient -> not serialized
    transient long lastRead;
    int serializationCount = 0;

    private void readObject(ObjectInputStream in)
        throws IOException, ClassNotFoundException
    {
        // First call the default algorithm in order
        // to restore the correct value of serializationCount
        in.defaultReadObject();

        // Increase the count
        serializationCount++;

        // Set the transient value
        lastRead = System.currentTimeMillis();
    }
}
```

Notice that A does not really do that much in order to be serializable. B does a little more to fine-tune the deserialization process. It defines the readObject method, which is called when ObjectInputStream. readObject is called. The first thing it does is call the default deserialization process, which restores serializationCount to the value it had when the instance was serialized. This value is then incremented. You can then check this value to see how many times this particular object has been serialized and deserialized. Note that if you did deserialization again using the same byte stream as input, you would have two identical objects.

Now that you have two classes whose instances would be serializable, let's try them out.

```
// Create streams to serialize object
ByteArrayOutputStream bout = new ByteArrayOutputStream();
ObjectOutputStream out = new ObjectOutputStream(bout);

// Create some objects and change some values
A object = new A();
object.foo = 11;
object.bar = "Goodbye World . . . ";
object.baz = new B();
object.baz.lastRead = -1;

// Serialize the object
out.writeObject(object);

// Create streams to deserialize object
ByteArrayInputStream bin =
    new ByteArrayInputStream(bout.toByteArray());
ObjectInputStream in = new ObjectInputStream(bin);

// Deserialize the object
object = (A)in.readObject();

// Test object values
System.out.println(object.foo); // Should print 11
System.out.println(object.bar); // Should print null
System.out.println(object.baz.serializationCount); // Should print 1
```

In this simple example, the serializer and deserializer is the same object, and the only intermediary medium is a byte array. Typically, and especially in an RMI context, you use a network stream to transfer the serialized object to somewhere else. Serialization is also a good way to store objects in files.

TIP

The default serialization algorithm uses dynamic introspection methods to perform this transformation. If you have classes that are sent often, you will probably want to provide your own readObject and writeObject methods as this speeds up the process, even though your custom serialization may do exactly the same thing. If such objects are sent often enough, the performance difference may be quite substantial.

I will not go into the details of serialization, so if you want to find out more about the serialization process, I recommend that you read the Java Object Serialization Specification (Sun Microsystems, 1997) and the javadoc documentation of the `java.io.ObjectInputStream` and `java.io.ObjectOutputStream` classes. For the purposes discussed in this chapter, it is only important that you understand the basic concept, and in practice, it is often enough to simply mark classes with the `java.io.Serializable` interface.

However, there are some aspects of marshalling and serialization that are given special treatment in RMI, specifically how remote objects are marshalled and how class loading is done. These topics are covered in the next section. When you deal with class loading, it is also important to consider the security issues that are involved and how classes are versioned.

Remote Object Replacement

Marshalling in RMI uses regular serialization to a great extent, but there is one exception, namely how remote objects are handled. For example, if a method parameter or result value of a method invocation in RMI is an object that is a remote object, that is, it implements a remote interface and is exported by the RMI implementation, you would not want it to be serialized. If it was serialized, then the object would be transferred to a new location, and the remote property of the object would be lost.

What you really want to do is to send the stub instead of the remote object, which can then be used at the other end to call methods on your remote object. One way to do this is to get the stub yourself and return it. The following is an example of how a remote method call returns the stub to another remote object.

```
public MyRemote getTheRemote()
{
    // Acquire the server object somehow
    MyRemote remoteObject =  . . .
    // Explicitly locate and return the stub
    return (MyRemote)java.rmi.server.RemoteObject.toStub(remoteObject);
}
```

The client can now invoke a method on the return value of this method, which is a stub that implements the MyRemote remote interface, and the call will be delegated through RMI to the server-side object remoteObject.

This works, but it is a bit impractical. It would be much better if you could simply return `remoteObject` and have RMI automatically replace it with the stub. And this is indeed exactly what happens in RMI.

RMI/JRMP internally uses a subclass of `java.io.ObjectOutput-`
`Stream` called `sun.rmi.server.MarshalOutputStream`, which,
upon serialization of an object, checks if it implements a remote interface. If it does, and it has been exported, the object is replaced with the
stub. By doing this, RMI keeps the remote objects located in the server
JVM, and at the same time, makes it very convenient to pass them
around. Implementations other than RMI/JRMP are not required to use
the `sun.rmi.server.MarshalOutputStream` because it is specific
to the JRMP implementation. However, they must provide the same
behavior because it is mandated by the RMI specification.

One interesting point is that if an object that implements a remote interface is not exported, then it will be serialized in the usual fashion, at least
if JDK1.2.2 or later is used. In Chapter 8 you will see how this can be
exploited to add some nifty functionality on top of RMI.

Dynamic Classloading

The other major issue that is handled differently in RMI compared with
normal serialization is classloading. I will begin by describing the problem that must be solved and continue by explaining how RMI has solved
this problem.

Let's look at an example. You have a remote interface that has a method
that returns an object that implements the A interface, as shown in the
following code snippet.

```
public MyRemote
   extends Remote
{
   public A doSomething()
      throws RemoteException;
}
```

Because A is an interface, you cannot return instances of it. Instead you
have a class B that implements this interface. However, to make it interesting, class B is only available in the server's classpath. This is quite
okay for the client because it is only concerned with getting objects that
implement A. Now, let's say that `doSomething` is implemented as follows:

```
public A doSomething()
{
   return new B(); // No casting needed since B extends A
}
```

What will happen? Because this is a remote method invocation you are dealing with, the result is marshalled by RMI and transferred through a network connection to the client that invoked the method. On the client, the B object is unmarshalled, so that the client may use it. But wait! This does not work because the client has no knowledge of the B class, and hence it cannot reconstruct the object. Remember, the A interface is included in both the client's and the server's classpath, but the B class is only available to the server. The remote call therefore results in an exception being thrown, specifically a subclass of `java.rmi.Remote-Exception` called `java.rmi.UnmarshalException`.

What you want is for the client to be able to access the classes that the server used to construct the return value. The same reasoning applies to parameters that are sent to the server from the client. The solution for this in RMI is called *dynamic classloading*.

What happens is that during the marshalling process, the server, in addition to the serialized parameters or return values, adds information about the marshalled objects classes. Part of this information is where the class was loaded from. If the class was loaded by the system classloader, then the value of the system property *java.rmi.server.codebase* is used. The value of this property should be set to a URL from which the class can be loaded. Typically, it points to an HTTP URL (i.e., something like http://myhost:8080/myclasses/), which means that you have to set up a Web server that can provide these classes. If the class was loaded by an instance of `java.net.URLClassLoader` (or any subclass thereof), then the URLs of that classloader are written to the stream.

TIP

Because it is generally overkill to use a full-featured Web server for dynamic classloading purposes, JavaSoft has created a mini Web server that can be used to provide classes in RMI.

I have extended this server somewhat in order to make it easier to use. The modified Web server can be found on the accompanying CD. It is used by some of the examples in this book, so check them out to see how you can easily integrate this Web server with your own application.

TIP

System properties can be set in two ways. First, you can do as follows in your code:

```
System.getProperties().put("someproperty", "somevalue");
```

However, this often leads to hard-coded values of properties and generally should be avoided.

Second, provide the system properties when you execute the JVM through the -D flag:

```
java -Dsomeproperty=somevalue myapp.Main
```

This sets the "someproperty" property to "somevalue". This is more flexible and is easier to change without recompiling, but on the other hand, it requires that the executor of your app know which parameters must be set.

A good compromise is to use a standard Java properties file (see the javadoc of java.lang.Properties for details on format), which contains these settings and is loaded during application startup. The properties file can be loaded with the following code:

```
ClassLoader cl = Thread.currentThread().getContextClassLoader();
InputStream in =cl.getResourceAsStream("system.properties");
System.getProperties().load(in);
```

This code reads all the property settings from the resource named "system.properties", which is a text file that is accessible through the classpath, and adds these settings to the current system properties. This solution does not require that the users of your program know which flags must be set, and it is easy to avoid hard-coded values. All examples provided on the CD use this approach, so take a look at them for more details.

When the client starts to deserialize the objects and at some point finds an object whose class is not available, it uses the provided URL from where it tries to load the needed class or classes. How does it do this? By using a `java.net.URLClassLoader` (or a subclass thereof), which has been initialized with the URL. If the class can indeed be loaded from the given URL, it is then associated with that classloader.

TIP

Given the dynamic classloading algorithm, how would you go about having several RMI objects with different codebases in the same JVM? Simply make sure that they are loaded with a java.net.URLClassLoader! When they are exported to RMI, the stub classes will be loaded primarily from the classloader of the exported object. So, if you have several classloaders with varying sets of URLs, then you can have as many codebases as you want within a single JVM.

One caveat with this is to make sure that the remote objects implementation class is not loaded by the system classloader. To avoid this, you should simply not include the class in the system classpath.

To fully master this kind of trick, you need to understand on a fundamental level how classloading, and in particular the classloader delegation model, works. This is beyond the scope of this book, but any decent general Java book should cover this topic.

Figure 2.3 illustrates how dynamic classloading works. In this scenario, you have one RMI server, one RMI client, and one Web server, which holds, in this case, the stub class of the RMI server.

The remote interface `MyRemote` is available to the client, or else you would not have been able to compile if the client used `MyRemote` in the code. However, the generated stub is not in the client's classpath. So, when the stub of the server object is transferred to the client, possibly through a naming lookup (which is described later in this chapter (see the section on "Naming")) during the deserialization process, it will want to create an object of the type `MyRemoteImpl_Stub` (i.e., the name of the stub). But because this class is not available, it will try to use dynamic classloading. Because the server properly set the codebase system property (or the class was loaded by a `java.net.URLClassLoader`

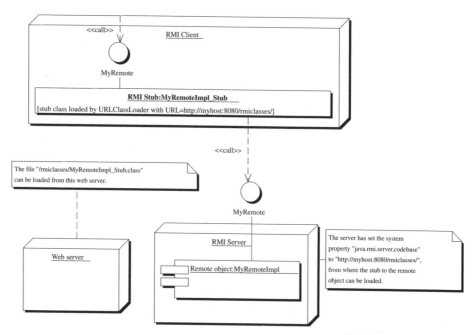

Figure 2.3 Dynamic classloading.

instance), the value of that property was transferred during the call. The client, or rather the RMI implementation, uses this value and creates a classloader that can load classes from URLs (as described earlier). What happens if the client sends the object to yet another client? Well, because the class was loaded by a `java.lang.URLClassLoader` instance, the URLs used to load the class will be properly propagated to the second client.

The most common use of dynamic classloading is to load only the stub class. However, because this algorithm is applied to all method parameters and result values, you can use it for any other classes that are not initially available on the receiving end. For example, in Chapter 8, dynamic classloading is used to upload objects to the server where they may perform some computation. The classes of those objects are not available to the server before the objects are uploaded. This is a very powerful way to customize the behavior of the server.

WARNING

There are a number of ways to make dynamic classloading fail. The most common errors are the following:

- If the client already has the class to be loaded dynamically, it is loaded through the default classloader, and the URL is not associated with the class through a java.net.URLClassLoader. If the object is then sent to another RMI client and the first client has not set the codebase property to the same as the initial codebase, then the second client is not able to load the class.
- The codebase URL may not be properly formatted. For example, if a URL does not end with "/", it is assumed to be a JAR file. This means that the following URL is treated as a URL to a JAR file: http://somehost/rmiclasses, whereas this URL is treated as pointing to a directory: http://somehost/rmiclasses/. Usually the latter is desired.
- Packages are not considered properly. Let's say your stub class is called MyRemoteImpl_Stub.class and is located in the "myapp" package. If your codebase is http://somehost/rmiclasses/, then the stub class is expected to be found at http://somehost/rmiclasses/myapp/MyRemoteImpl_Stub.class.
- Because loading classes from URLs are a potential security risk, dynamic classloading is not enabled if there is no security manager installed. Even if a security manager is installed, you may run into trouble if the security policy does not allow you to access files from the annotated URL. This is described further in the next section.
- If you want to use dynamic classloading with a remote object that is bound to an RMI registry, then both the remote interface and the stub class must be available for downloading by the registry; providing only the stub class will not be sufficient.

Security Issues

Because you are dealing with a distributed environment, there are a number of security issues to consider. One of the issues is which server a client should be able to connect to and from where should it be able to retrieve classes by means of dynamic classloading. All of these issues are dealt with by using the Java2 security framework. This topic is not directly related to RMI, and full coverage of this topic would likely require a book of its own. However, I will try to give you some idea of the basic framework and what you need to do to enable basic security in your applications.

In Java2, there is a notion of *permissions*. Permissions can be granted to code depending on where it was loaded from and who has written the code. Code that wants to protect itself may then check whether the caller of the code has a particular permission. For example, applets running in a browser are not allowed to access the local file system. This is implemented by letting all I/O classes check whether the caller has the `java.io.FilePermission`. In addition, the applet runtime environment is set up so that no applets have that particular permission. Because of this, all attempts by an applet to perform file I/O will generate security exceptions.

Permissions are typically given to code by modifying a *policy file*. This file contains declarative statements that tell the Java runtime which classes should have which permissions. The default policy file, which is located in the /lib/security directory of your Java2 installation, contains the following snippet:

```
grant codeBase "file:${java.home}/lib/ext/*" {
permission java.security.AllPermission;
};
```

This snippet means that all classes that are loaded from the extension directory, that is, /lib/ext, should be granted the `java.security.AllPermission`. The `java.security.AllPermission` permission is a special permission that implies all other permissions. So, if a piece of code checks for the `java.net.SocketPermission` and the caller has the `java.security.AllPermission`, the check will pass.

The use of permissions is only relevant if you have a security manager installed. A security manager is an instance of the class `java.lang.SecurityManager` (or a subclass thereof). If you have not installed a security manager, all permission checks will pass. Clients must install a security manager if they want to use dynamic classloading as described in the previous section. There is no obligation to install one on the server unless the server itself wants to allow clients to send objects to it whose classes must be accessed by using dynamic classloading.

WARNING

If you do install a security manager on the server, be sure to set the security permissions properly for dynamically downloaded classes. If you don't, the following scenario could occur: A rogue client that wants to crash the server could upload an object whose class is, for example, a subclass of java.util.Vector. The server will load this class and think that it is safe because it is just a plain old Vector—nothing strange. However, when a method is called on the Vector, it could create some side effect that is unwanted, such as deleting files on the server computer or connecting to a system that the client normally cannot connect to. The dynamically loaded class acts as a Trojan through which damage can be done to your server system.

Because of this, you should either consider not installing a security manager on the server, or take great care when deciding what permissions dynamically loaded classes should have.

For more information about the Java2 security architecture, read the documentation available at the Java Security API home page (http://java.sun.com/security/).

So, how does the Java2 security affect you when you write RMI applications? The most important thing to consider is the permissions that affect how you can handle sockets. Specifically, because RMI uses sockets to communicate with the server, you need to have a `java.net.SocketPermission` that allows you to talk to the server.

If the client is an applet, there is one standard rule that applies: The applet may only connect to the server from where it was loaded. In general, this is not a problem for RMI applications, but there is one thing in particular that may go wrong. If the applet was loaded using a hostname xyz and the host has the default name foo in addition to the name xyz, you are in trouble because the applet runner thinks that the applet is trying to connect to some host foo, which it is not allowed to do. In fact, it may connect because it is the same host, so you somehow need to fix this. The solution is to use the system property *java.rmi.server.hostname*. You should set this to the hostname that you want the RMI clients to use when connecting to the server.

TIP

One very common case where this happens is with local testing of RMI applets. Let's say that you have created an applet that uses RMI. You typically access the HTML page that contains this applet by issuing the following command:

```
appletviewer http://localhost/myapplet.html
```

You have an RMI server running on your host, which you want the applet to access. When it does this, you return an RMI stub that contains the Domain Name Service (DNS) hostname of your computer. This is not equal to "localhost". So, when you start calling your RMI stub, you will get exceptions stating that you are not allowed to access the server. This is easily fixed by setting the hostname system property to "localhost".

Because most of the examples on the CD use applets as clients, they perform this workaround. If you want to access these examples from clients other than your own computer, you must remove this setting. However, as you do this, you must be careful not to access the applet through the "localhost" hostname.

If the client is an application and you do not want to use dynamic class-loading, you are not obliged to use a security manager at all, in which case no security checks will be performed. All code will be able to perform all actions without any trouble. However, if you want to use dynamic classloading, you have to install a security manager, in which case you must deal with how security permissions are granted to the applications classes. Applets always have a security manager installed because the browser or applet viewer automatically installs one.

It all boils down to creating the proper security policy file. In most cases, you probably won't want to bother with it, and instead use a policy file that contains the following lines:

```
grant {
        // Allow everything for now
        permission java.security.AllPermission;
};
```

As stated, this allows all classes to perform any action and is a very convenient setting to use during development. Once you have developed your application, you may want to narrow permissions down a bit, so that not all classes are allowed to do whatever they want. For a full explanation of how to create a proper security policy file, check out the documentation at the Java Security API home page.

Once you have defined your security policy file, you need to tell your application to use it, and also install a security manager that will use the policy file to enforce the permission requirements. To make your application use your custom policy file, add the system property *java.security.policy*, which should be set to the name of your policy file. To install a security manager, you may either call `System.setSecurityManager(new SecurityManager())`, or use the system property *java.security.manager*. Unfortunately, this last system property is only checked at JVM startup, so setting it in your the application will not do any good. Either set it by using the -D flag, or use the `System.setSecurityManager()` call. The latter is preferred because it makes it easier to invoke your application.

Again, note that setting a security manager is required in order to do dynamic classloading. This applies to both the server and the client. Remember that the server can be a client in some sense, so all rules apply to all involved parties. Using dynamic classloading on an RMI server is required if you want your RMI clients to be able to upload objects whose classes are not initially available on the server. Dynamic classloading is explored further in Chapter 8.

Class Versioning

Once you have written your application and have deployed your clients, everything is fine. Your app runs as it should, the clients perform their work without problems, and your users are happy.

But then it happens. You need to do a bug fix or add some functionality. Making this fix in your own development environment is usually easy, but you now have the problem of updating your deployment environment. The servers are usually easy as there are relatively few, and more often there is just one. However, the real problem is with the clients. If you have used applets, the fix is simple. All you have to do is update the applet on your Web server. However, if you have chosen to use a standalone application as your client, you might run into some trouble. The problem is that if you update your application classes on the server, the client may not be able to call your server. For example, if your server, as a response to some request, returns an object whose class you have changed, the client may not be able to reconstruct the object during the unmarshalling process. The most common problem is that you might have removed some attribute in the class, and when the client wants to unmarshal an object of this class, it looks for an attribute that is no longer being sent as part of the object's state. Therefore, the unmarshalling fails.

The solution to this problem is twofold: either stay away from using stand-alone client applications as much as possible and use applets instead, or use the versioning system that serialization uses. Basically, each class has a *serial version UID*, which is a number that represents its current version. This can be set programmatically by including the following attribute in your class:

```
private static final long serialVersionUID
```

The value of this number should be set to the version of your class. Typically, you would begin with 1, and increment the value each time you make a change that makes it incompatible with the previous version. When objects are deserialized, the version of the deserialized object is compared with the version of the class that is loaded in the JVM. If the versions are the same, the state to be deserialized and the current class are compatible.

If you do not set this value, Java assigns it automatically to the hash value of the class. If you are not worried about versioning, for example, if you will always be able to update all parties in your system with the latest classes, this is the recommended strategy.

RMI Threading and Network Connection Management

By now you should have a pretty good idea about how the proxy and marshalling concepts are implemented in RMI. The next major step to examine is how threads and network connections are managed.

In a client/server architecture, the threading and connection management is perhaps one of the most important building blocks to achieve a good infrastructure for dynamic computing. If done right, you get very good performance, and if done wrong, your system will probably be very slow regardless of how clever the rest of the system is.

As stated previously, because threading and connection management is a very important piece of the puzzle, you would not want to restrict the ways to implement it too much. For this reason, the RMI specification

Threads and Sockets in Java

In Java, threads and sockets are closely tied together. Currently, it is only possible to get data from a socket by using a thread that is dedicated to a particular socket. The reason for this is the lack of nonblocking I/O in Java. Basically, the only way to retrieve data from a socket is to get its input stream and call any of its read methods. This call blocks until data is available.

Some other languages, such as C++, support so-called nonblocking I/O, which means that they do not have to have a thread block on a read call. Instead, the application is asynchronously notified when data comes in on the socket, at which point, it can allocate a thread to read from the socket. This is a much more efficient way to do network programming as fewer resources are used. A couple of threads can typically serve thousands of active socket connections, instead of having one thread per socket.

Support for nonblocking is currently being added to the Java platform, and when this happens, any APIs that perform networking, such as RMI, will benefit immensely.

does not provide much information on how it works. The implementation should have a fair degree of freedom in order to optimize how RMI calls are handled.

However, there are a few short lines in the RMI specification that are worth noticing. The first few sentences in section 3.2 ("Thread Usage in Remote Method Invocations") states the following:

"A method dispatched by the RMI runtime to a remote object implementation may or may not execute in a separate thread. The RMI runtime makes no guarantees with respect to mapping remote object invocations to threads."

This statement is a tad cryptic if you ask me. What this really means is that if any of your server objects calls another server object, there is no guarantee that this invocation is made using a separate thread, as would always be the case if a client in a separate JVM called a server. Basically, this allows the stub of the remote object to be called to skip the network layer and marshalling process and directly call the server object. This only works if the two objects reside within the same JVM, but it may be a significant optimization regarding performance and resource usage.

The next sentence reads:

"Since remote method invocation on the same remote object may execute concurrently, a remote object implementation needs to make sure its implementation is thread-safe."

This innocent little statement has profound implications for the RMI programmer. Basically, it means is that the RMI runtime accepts incoming calls and delegates them to your server objects as fast as possible with no regard for whether some of the requests are coming in concurrently. This is important because in your server object code, you will either have to deal with the possibility of having several threads working on the object simultaneously or use the standard Java synchronization primitives to ensure that only one thread at a time is using your objects. If you do not consider this issue, then your implementation may crash spontaneously depending on how clients access your server objects. Some of the later examples in this book show you some scenarios where this factor is important and how to solve it.

Network Connections

For network connections, RMI uses *socket factories*. Socket factories are used to acquire socket connections on the client and on the server. There is one interface `java.rmi.server.RMIClientSocketFactory` that contains a method for acquiring socket connections on the client, and there is one interface `java.rmi.server.RMIServerSocketFactory` that contains a method for acquiring server-side sockets that listen for incoming requests. The default implementation for both interfaces is provided by the class `java.rmi.server.RMISocketFactory`.

When you export a remote object so that it becomes available for incoming calls, you may provide the socket factories that should be used by RMI to receive calls to your object. By doing so, you can use socket implementations that do encryption or client authentication, or whatever nice feature you can come up with. This possibility is explored in Chapter 5. However, if you do not specify your own socket factories, which is the usual case, the JRMP runtime uses the default `java.rmi.server.RMISocketFactory` factory to create socket connections. This provides a good default implementation, which uses plain sockets in the normal case and also tries to use SOCKS or HTTP tunneling if necessary. These last two options are mostly relevant in a scenario where firewalls are being used. Custom connection management is discussed further in Chapter 5.

Threading Model

As for threading, there is no thread factory or anything similar, at least not one that is defined through a public interface, so you cannot affect it as you can with socket factories. An RMI implementation may manage threads any way it wants. In particular, the JRMP implementation simply creates threads as new connections are made to a server and associates the new socket connection with the thread. The relationships between the JRMP implementation, sockets, and threads are shown in Figure 2.4. Note that this figure only shows the server-side of the story. You will look at the client's perspective in Chapter 3.

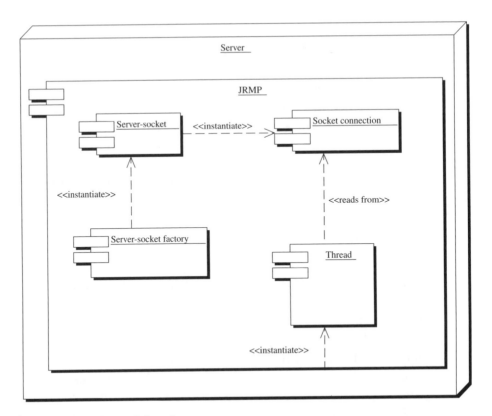

Figure 2.4 Socket and threads.

Let's examine exactly what this figure means. The JRMP implementation uses server-socket factories to create server-sockets, that is, subclasses of `java.net.ServerSocket`. After that the server-socket is asked to accept incoming requests. When a connection is made, the RMI implementation is notified of this by handing over the newly created socket connection object, which must be an instance of a subclass of the `java.net.Socket` class.

In the case of the JRMP implementation, a new thread is instantiated for each connection, which starts checking for incoming calls from the client that are being sent over the socket connection. Once the thread receives a call, it looks up the server object that is being called (remember that each call contains the ID of the object to be called) in the internal object table and forwards the call to it. Essentially, this is done in two steps. The call method and parameters are unmarshalled, as described earlier, and then the object is invoked on the specified method using the parameters. The object then performs its work and returns some kind of result. The thread that invoked the object marshals the result and sends it back to the client using the socket connection.

As far as the server in the scenario is concerned, the call has been completely handled when this is done. The thread then listens to the socket connection for the next remote call from the client. This process proceeds until either the server is stopped or the JRMP implementation decides that the connection is not needed.

As for client threads and connections, they are even more unspecified in the RMI specification as to how they should work. The thread part is quite straightforward. The call is made using the thread that invokes an RMI stub. There is no need to spawn a new thread and let that process the call. As for connections to the server, those are a bit trickier. Because the RMI specification does not mandate how connections are managed, this depends on the particular implementation.

As usual, if you look at how the JRMP implementation handles this, it uses a rather simple model. Each client connection may only process one call at a time. Connections between the client and the server are then established "on demand." For example, if the client part of the JRMP implementation has one connection to a particular server and two calls are made concurrently, the JRMP implementation automatically creates a new connection in order to serve the two calls. If you have many concurrent threads in a client VM, you may have lots of connections to a particular server. This is a scalability issue, in that, your server may not be able to serve that many clients, which is best solved by using some other RMI implementation.

For example, the WebLogic Application Server uses its own implementation of RMI, which does not use the same connection model as the JRMP implementation. Instead, it multiplexes concurrent calls onto one connection, so that a client never has more than one physical connection to a server. The side effect of this is that the server can handle many more concurrent clients as its resources are more moderately used for each client. If there are multiple concurrent calls from a client, the calls are multiplexed to make sure that one call is not blocking all the other ones.

Distributed Garbage Collection

This chapter began by enumerating a couple of principles that normal Java programming uses, which should be used as transparently as possible in a distributed context, such as RMI. One of those principles was garbage collection. Unlike many other languages, you, the programmer that is, never has to bother with memory management. You create objects in your code, and the JVM takes care of removing them once they are no longer used, that is, it collects the garbage so to speak.

In RMI, it is not possible to use the JVM garbage collection to keep track of objects as both servers and clients are spread over multiple JVMs. Because the users of the server objects are clients that possibly reside in other JVMs, RMI has to add some framework for keeping track of live references to server objects. To accomplish this, the RMI architecture includes Distributed Garbage Collection (DGC).

Basically, when a client receives a stub that points to a live remote object, it sends a message to the server stating that it now has a live reference to the server object. The server makes a note of this and expects the client to continually send notifications that it is still using the object. The client is said to have a **lease**, which it must renew at given intervals.

TIP

The interval between lease renewals can be set explicitly by modifying the system property *java.rmi.dgc.leaseValue*. This denotes the interval in minutes between client renewals of remote object leases. If the server does not receive a renewal of a lease within this period of time, it considers the lease expired.

A common scenario for setting this value is when you want your remote objects to be garbage collected as soon as possible after the client has stopped using them. Remember that if the client crashes, the leases are not renewed. A way to detect that a client has crashed is to detect when DGC has no more live clients using the remote object. To help the DGC determine this as fast as possible, set the lease interval to a low value. For example, if you set the value to 1, the DGC will detect a client crash within a minute.

If the lease is not renewed or if the client explicitly tells the server that it no longer holds a reference to the server object, then the client is removed from the list of clients using the particular object. Once the number of references reaches zero, the remote object is valid for local JVM garbage collection.

In newer implementations of RMI, the JRMP implementation holds remote objects through weak references. This means that the remote object is in the JRMP object table as long as there are references other than its own reference to it. Once all in-VM references have been dropped and all remote references have timed out, the object can finally be removed and garbage collected.

The Unreferenced Interface

Sometimes it is necessary for your remote object to find out whether anyone is using the object or not. For example, if you have a remote object that represents a client of your application, an indication that your client has crashed is that there are no references to it anymore. In RMI, the interface that can be used to detect that there are no more remote references to a particular object is called `java.rmi.Unreferenced`. This interface should be implemented by any remote objects that want to detect that there are no clients referencing it. The interface has a single method, `unreferenced`, which is called by the RMI implementation once it detects that there are no more references.

WARNING

There are some subtle problems to consider with the java.rmi.Unreferenced interface. Typically, you would want unreferenced to be invoked exactly when the client drops its last reference to the object. Unfortunately, this is not the case. If a client crashes, the RMI implementation waits for the duration of the lease time before considering the remote reference gone. So, if you have a high lease value and the default is 10 minutes, you will not detect client failures very rapidly.

The best way to solve this is to have the client explicitly notify your remote object that it is finished with it or lower the lease time. That way the java.rmi.Unreferenced interface becomes more of a safety net than the default way of detecting that no clients are using it.

Also, if you have bound your remote object in the RMI registry, which is described in the "Naming" section, this counts as a reference. So, even if there are no clients holding any stubs to the object, the unreferenced method will never be called. Any remote objects bound to the RMI registry should therefore not implement the Unreferenced interface.

Naming

You now have all of the basic components of a remote object framework in place. You can manage network connections, marshal remote method invocations over these connections, and hide the details of marshalling by using stubs. The only thing missing is the answer to the question of how to acquire these stubs in the first place. How does a client find a stub so that it can call the remote object that it points to? One way to do this is to construct it manually on the client. If you know the object identifier that a remote object was assigned when it was exported, you can create this stub. Unfortunately, this is more than a bit awkward because those object identifiers are often assigned randomly, hence making it difficult to accomplish this. It would be nice if all you had to know was, "I want to talk to server X. Gimme a stub to server X, please," and then have some easy method to do this. So far you have done quite a good job hiding all the gory details of remote invocations, so why stop now?

The first thing you should be aware of is that because stubs are just serializable Java objects, you can use any method you want to allow clients to acquire these stubs: serialize, transfer to the client, and then deserialize. That is all there is to it. One way to do this is to serialize a stub to a file and have that file be accessible through a Web server. A client could then access it by knowing only the URL to the file. For example, let's say that server X wants to be easily accessible to a client, has serialized its stub to a file "x.ser," and that file is located at the document root of a Web server. A client could then load this stub by retrieving the file from the server by accessing the URL www.somehost.com/x.ser. The client could then deserialize this stub, and voila, it now has a stub to the server that it can start invoking methods on. When a method on the stub is invoked, it automatically uses the underlying RMI implementation to forward the method call to the server object.

If you read the RMI documentation or any RMI tutorial, you will be told that there is a tool called *rmiregistry* that you should use to perform naming in RMI. What it does is start a naming service that you can use to bind stubs to names, and then look up these stubs using the known names. The RMI registry itself is actually an RMI object, and it has a remote interface that contains the methods necessary to do these basic naming operations. The rmiregistry tool is simply a native application that creates and exports an RMI registry object, so that you can call it in your application.

How to use the RMI registry is discussed in Chapter 3. You are walked through all the steps of creating a simple RMI application. Once you have some idea of how naming works using the RMI registry, you look at hiding the RMI registry behind the Java Naming and Directory Interface (JNDI API), which is a generic naming API.

There is one piece of magic associated with the RMI registry that should be explained right away. If the registry itself is a remote object, how do you get a stub to it? Won't you have the same problem as with other remote objects when it comes to locating stubs? Well, remember that all exported remote objects are assigned a unique object identifier. In the case of the RMI registry as well as the DGC mechanism, both have predefined object identifiers, which allow a client to construct a stub manually. So, there is no magic. However, you can cheat. Because stub construction is a fairly complex task, this process has been hidden behind a class called *java.rmi.Naming*, which you can call to create stubs to remote registries.

Summary

In this chapter, you examined how the basic client/server concepts in Chapter 1 mapped to the RMI architecture. The chapter began with a general description of what RMI is, and what it is not. The discussion continued with a look at why you would want to do all of this in Java anyway. As you saw, there are quite a few good things about Java that make it suitable for networked applications.

You then took a closer look at the RMI specification and how it is implemented with JRMP. You also looked at how proxies are implemented by stubs in RMI. The stubs hid all the details of acquiring network connections and marshalling remote method invocations.

You learned how marshalling is performed by the RMI implementations through the use of standard Java Serialization. You also looked at the fine nuances of remote object semantics, because remote objects when marshalled are automatically replaced with the corresponding stubs. Also described was how dynamic classloading is used in RMI to automatically distribute classes to different parts of an RMI application. Because of the security implications of moving code around, you looked at how security is handled in RMI, and what you need to do in order to make proper use of dynamic classloading. You will continue to explore this further in later chapters. The issue of class versioning is always important in a highly distributed environment because applications evolve, and you looked at different ways of dealing with this.

The third part of the RMI architecture overview looked at the network connection management in RMI and the associated threading issues. The RMI specification does not provide much information on the subject, so you had to explore the specifics of the JRMP implementation in order to get any useful view of how they worked.

Because RMI supports the notion of garbage collection in order to manage objects' lifecycles, you looked at DGC and how it helps you to keep track of how remote objects are used.

Finally, you took a brief look at how naming is supported in RMI. The specific practical details of naming is covered in more detail in later chapters, but the basic lesson is that "anything goes." Any way you can think of to deliver your stubs to a client is allowed.

So, now that you have an idea of how RMI performs its magic, let's put it into practice. The next chapter walks you through a simple example and explains all the required steps. If you have understood everything in this chapter, it will not be that difficult. However, because this chapter really contains the essence of RMI, you might want to make sure that you have all the details covered before going forward. If you do move on right away, you might find it practical to come back to this chapter and remind yourself of how the underlying implementation performs the job for you.

PART TWO

Building RMI Applications

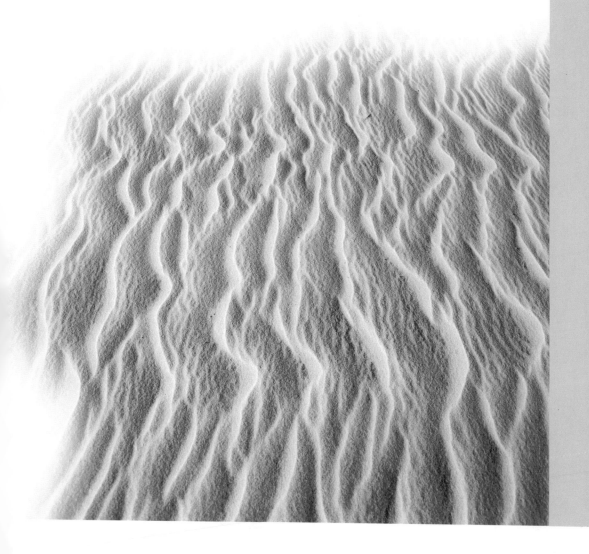

Part One talked about the theory and concepts behind remote object invocation and took a close look at the RMI framework and the standard implementation JRMP. Now that you have a clear picture of the different pieces of RMI and how they work together, it is time to build a small application to put this information into practice.

Chapter 3 starts by demonstrating the classic HelloWorld application. It highlights the basic steps that are required to build a simple RMI application. To keep things simple, advanced features such as dynamic classloading or activation are not used. The example provided is in a bare bones form to give you a rough idea of what you need to do in order to successfully create your first RMI application.

Chapter 4 progressively enhances the basic RMI application by introducing dynamic classloading using applets as clients and JNDI as an abstraction layer for naming.

Chapter 5 introduces you to one of the more advanced concepts called custom connection factories, which allows you to control the communication between the clients and the server.

Chapter 6 describes the powerful feature called activation, which enables remote objects to be activated on demand and also provides stubs that can be used over an extended period of time. The final application provides a good base from which you can start developing your own applications.

After completing Part Two, you should have a pretty good idea of how to make RMI applications. However, there is more to making RMI applications than just coding. In Part Three of this book, you will look at a couple of larger RMI projects and learn how to deal with different types of common problems. Part Four then introduces you to related technologies that you will most likely be interested in if you feel that RMI is not enough for you—for example if you need to build secure transactional systems or ones where flexible fault tolerance is of high importance.

CHAPTER 3

The HelloWorld Application

The first part of this book introduced you to the concepts of distributed computing and client/server architectures in general. It also showed how Remote Method Invocation (RMI) works on the inside. Now that you have a view of the internal workings, you can put them into practice.

Let's begin by looking at what you want your application to do. You can then define the remote interface that your remote object, which is a server in this application, will implement. Next, you will look at how that implementation is constructed and how to package it in order to make it as flexible as possible. The last part of this simple application is to create a basic client that can locate and use your server.

Application Overview

In this chapter, you will create the most basic of applications: the HelloWorld application. It consists of one simple remote object, which has one simple method that you can call from a client. The method takes the name of the client as input and creates a greeting in response. For example, entering "World" as the name would yield the response "Hello World!".

Why make such a silly application? Would it not be a better idea to make something more useful? The point of this simple example is that you can easily identify the basic required steps that are needed in order to make a complete RMI application. Once you have done that, you can make more useful applications that make better use of the features in RMI.

You first need to design the application. Because this is such a bare bones example, the design is rather trivial. Figure 3.1 shows the classes and how they relate to each other.

The server consists of two classes: the implementation of the `HelloWorld` interface and a `Main` class, which functions as the manager of the remote object. Often, it is a good idea to split the implementation of the remote interface and the management of remote objects into separate parts. The reason for this is that your remote object may be used in ways that you had not considered when you wrote it. For example, you may want to create one server that holds several different remote objects, or you may want to use some other naming service to access it. In these cases, you would have to rewrite your remote object to accommodate the new requirements if this functionality was contained within the remote object itself. By moving it outside of the object, you have immediately made the object more reusable.

The client is a stand-alone application that simply looks up the object using some naming mechanism, calls it, and prints out the result.

The remote interface `HelloWorld` is the glue between the client and the server in this scenario and is often referred to as part of the contract. A contract is the set of classes that both the client and server must share in order to communicate. It is more or less the same as when people use a language to communicate. If they did not agree on what words and grammar to use when they talk to each other, it would be hard to make

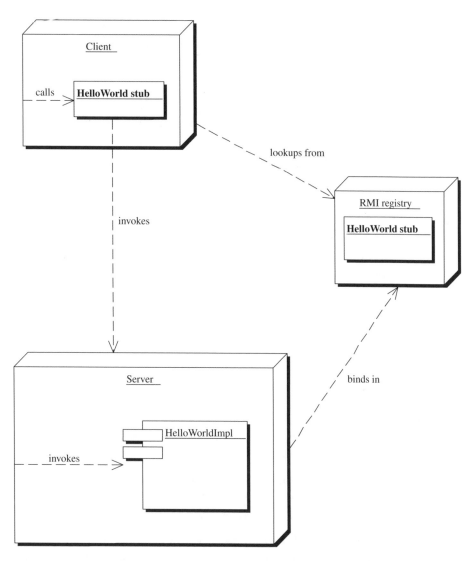

Figure 3.1   The HelloWorld application design.

any sense of a conversation. The same principle applies to a contract. The client and the server must agree on how to communicate with each other. So, what is included in an RMI contract? The following types of classes are commonly considered part of a contract.

- **Remote interfaces.** All remote interfaces that you are using in your application.

- **Exception classes.** All exceptions that can be thrown from your remote interfaces. Note that many of those exceptions are typically core Java exceptions, that is, they are located in the `java.*` packages.

- **Data-holder classes.** As you will see, it is often useful to have certain classes contain data in order to make it easier to transport them around the network between clients and servers. These data-holder classes are typically very small and usually only contain get and set methods.

What should you do with this knowledge once you have identified which classes make up the contract in your application? There are two things to consider. First, because these classes are needed by both clients and servers in your application, you will most likely want to package them in such a way that you can separate them from your client and server. For example, your client will consist of any classes that implement your client and the contract, and similarly, your server will consist of your server implementation and the contract classes. By making sure that you can easily package the contract classes separately for both the server and the client, you have made your life much simpler.

TIP

I usually use Java packages to perform this separation. One way to do it is to use the following package structure:

myapplication.client — Put all client classes in this package.
myapplication.interfaces — Put all contract classes in this package.
myapplication.server — Put all server classes in this package.

By doing this, you can then easily package myapplication.client and myapplication.interfaces into a client and package myapplication.server and myapplication.interfaces into a server.

Second, because contract classes define the rules of engagement between several parts of your application, you will most likely not want to change them often. Again, let's compare this with a real-life counterpart situation. If you started changing the language you use to communicate too often, it would make it very difficult to understand each other. The same principle applies in a contract. For this reason, you should think long and hard when defining your contract classes because they tend to stick around for a very long time once you have deployed your application.

If you, for some reason, really need to make changes to the contract, these changes should preferably be extensions, that is, pure additions to the old contract. Removing or modifying contracts may lead to strange results if you are not able to update all parties that depend on the contract. In Chapter 7, where we develop a chat application, you will see how the effects of this can be minimized.

The Remote Interface

It is now time to create the very first part of your application: the remote interface. This defines which methods a client will be able to invoke remotely on a server. As stated in the overview section, you want to be able to send a name to the server and have it compute a greeting in response. The interface is constructed as follows.

```
// Follow the packaging guidelines and put the interface
// in a separate package suffixed "interfaces"
package masteringrmi.helloworld.interfaces;

// Import RMI-classes
import java.rmi.Remote;
import java.rmi.RemoteException;

/**
 *    This is the remote interface of the remote object.
 *
 *    It has one method which can be invoked remotely.
 *
 *    @see masteringrmi.helloworld.server.HelloWorldImpl
 *    @author Rickard Öberg (rickard@dreambean.com)
 *    @version $Revision:$
 */
public interface HelloWorld
    extends Remote // This marks our interface as a remote one
{
    // Constants ------------------------------------------
    // Declare the name which we will use to locate a server
    // implementing this interface.
    public static String NAME = "helloworld";

    // Public ---------------------------------------------

    /**
     *    Send the name of the caller, and return a greeting.
     *
```

```
 *    Tip: Send "World" as name to get "Hello World!" back.
 *
 * @param    name  a name
 * @return      a greeting
 * @exception   RemoteException  thrown if something goes wrong
 *              in the RMI-implementation
 */
public String helloWorld(String name)
   throws RemoteException;
}
```

There are three things to consider in this construction. First, you put the interface into a package suffixed with "interfaces." This makes it easier to package later on. Second, the interface extends `java.rmi.Remote`. As explained in Chapter 2, this is necessary for the RMI implementation to understand that objects implementing this interface should not be serialized during marshalling of a call, but rather it should be replaced with its corresponding stub object. Third, your only method, `helloWorld`, must throw `java.rmi.RemoteException`.

The Server

As discussed in the overview, the server consists of two classes because you want your remote objects to be more reusable in different applications. Let's take a closer look at these two classes and see what they actually do.

The Remote Object

The source for the remote object, or "server," in this scenario is as follows.

```
package masteringrmi.helloworld.server;

import java.rmi.RemoteException;
import java.rmi.server.RemoteServer;
import java.rmi.server.UnicastRemoteObject;

import masteringrmi.helloworld.interfaces.HelloWorld;
```

As you can see, the server has been placed in a package that is separate from the remote interface. This allows you to easily package your application and also hides the implementation details from the client, which should only be exposed to the `HelloWorld` interface. Your server class is declared as follows.

```
public class HelloWorldImpl
   extends RemoteServer
   implements HelloWorld
{
```

It extends `java.rmi.server.RemoteServer`. To be precise, this is not necessary, but it is recommended. By inheriting `RemoteServer`, you gain implementations of the `equals` and `hashCode` methods, which are useful in a distributed application. More concretely, they use the unique object identifier that was assigned to the remote object during the export process to perform these methods.

```
// Constructors ─────────────────────
public HelloWorldImpl()
   throws RemoteException
{
   UnicastRemoteObject.exportObject(this, 1234);
}
```

The constructor needs to export this object, and you export it on port 1234 (the choice of port is more or less arbitrary). This means that the RMI implementation creates a listener socket that is bound to port 1234. Note however, that this does not mean that other objects cannot also be bound to port 1234. If other objects want to use the same port for incoming calls, that is okay. Remember that each call contains the unique object identifier, so the listener can easily figure out which object is being called when a request comes in.

If you had extended `java.rmi.server.UnicastRemoteObject` instead of `java.rmi.server.RemoteServer`, then the default constructor of `UnicastRemoteObject` would have performed this export call itself. The reason I did not do this was to give you some insights into what is going on under the hood. Once you are comfortable with how the export process works, you could extend `UnicastRemoteObject` instead and allow its default constructor to perform this step for you.

Because export is a process that may potentially fail, you have to throw `java.rmi.RemoteException` from your constructor. If you want to create remote objects that are also JavaBeans, that is, they have default constructors with no parameters and do not throw any exceptions, then I suggest that this export call be made by some external manager of the object. It does not matter who does the call. As long as the call is made, the object will be available for remote use. Finally, the implementation of the remote interface is as follows.

```
public String helloWorld(String name)
{
    return "Hello " + name +"!";
}
```

The method takes a string as an argument and returns a greeting containing that name. Because you are not doing anything that could potentially lead to any remote exceptions being thrown, you do not declare any *throws* clause. Because of the standard Java rules, the preceding code is still a valid implementation of the `helloWorld` method in the remote interface.

The Manager

Now you have a class whose instances can be called remotely. But you need something that creates those instances and also makes sure that clients can access this remote object from some naming system. To do this, you create a separate class whose task is to perform these operations and manage the remote object.

The source of this class is as follows.

```
package masteringrmi.helloworld.server;

import java.io.IOException;
import java.net.MalformedURLException;
import java.rmi.Naming;
import java.rmi.AlreadyBoundException;
import java.rmi.RemoteException;

public class Main
{
```

The manager class is located in the same package as the HelloWorld remote object class because it also is part of what you will call the server in this application. Next, you import the classes and exceptions that you intend to use. After this follows the application bootstrap code and constructor.

```
public static void main(String[] args)
    throws Exception
{
    new Main();
}

// Public ------------------------------------------------------
public Main()
{
    try
    {
        // Create remote object
        HelloWorldImpl server = new HelloWorldImpl();

        // Register server with naming service
        // Use rebind instead of bind
        // This is useful if this is a restart of the server,
        // since we then will overwrite the old binding
        Naming.rebind(HelloWorldImpl.NAME, server);

        System.out.println("Server has been started and registered");
    } catch (MalformedURLException e)
    {
        System.out.println("The server name was incorrect");
        e.printStackTrace(System.err);
    } catch (RemoteException e)
    {
        System.out.println("The object could not be created");
        e.printStackTrace(System.err);
    }
}
```

The static main method is called when this application is started. The first, and only, thing it does is to instantiate an instance of this class. In the constructor, you perform all the operations that this manager should take care of. First, you create the remote object. A side effect of this is that the remote object gets exported, so that any remote client may call it. Second, you bind it into the RMI registry. The RMI registry is the naming system that you want to use in this initial application. It is a convenient tool that is always available as it is distributed with the Java Development Kit (JDK) installation.

Note that it is not actually the remote object that is bound in the registry, but rather its stub. Why is this? Because the registry itself is a remote object, the bind invocation issues an RMI call to the registry. As discussed in Chapter 2, the marshalling of method invocation arguments uses plain Java serialization, but with one important exception: Remote objects are automatically replaced with the corresponding stub. So, because the server object is indeed a remote object that has been exported, it is replaced with its stub before it is sent to the registry. The registry then makes a note of this binding, so that a client may retrieve it at a later time.

There are a couple of problems with this approach to managing remote objects. If you look in the preceding code, you will see that there are some assumptions that have been made. First, you assume that a naming system is available when the manager starts, so that you can call bind right away. This may of course not be the case in real life. It might have been started, but later crashed, or it may not have been started at the time the manager was started. Also, even if the naming system was started prior to the manager performing its operations, what happens if the naming system goes down? It will most likely forget all the bindings that have been made, so that when it comes back online, it will be empty. Ideally, the manager should recognize that this has happened and reregister your remote object. Unfortunately, this kind of fault-tolerant behavior is hard to do without any help.

But, there is help! It is called Jini, which is a set of application programming interfaces (APIs) that have been built on top of RMI to handle these kinds of situations. Jini and its uses are discussed in Chapter 9. For now, you will have to settle with this simpler behavior.

The Client

The client is in this case is a stand-alone Java application that wants to use the service that the remote object, or server, provides. It must first locate the server using some naming system. When it has acquired a stub that points to the server, it can invoke the stub to call the remote object that is used to implement the server.

Let's take a look at the code for this client.

```
package masteringrmi.helloworld.client;

import java.io.IOException;
import java.net.MalformedURLException;
import java.rmi.Naming;
import java.rmi.NotBoundException;
```

```
import java.rmi.RemoteException;
import java.util.Properties;

import masteringrmi.helloworld.interfaces.HelloWorld;
```

To begin with, this client is placed in a package separate from both the contract classes and the server classes. This helps to identify which classes belong to the client. Also, the classes and exceptions that are needed are imported. The last import statement tells you that you want to use the `HelloWorld` remote interface. Because you want to use instances of objects implementing the interface directly, you must package it with the client. Note however, that you do not import any classes from the server package. Those classes are hidden by the abstraction provided by the remote interface. This is where the concept of a contract comes in. You can now see that only the contract is relevant for both parties. The server does not need to know what the client looks like, and the client does not need to know how the server is implemented, but both must be aware of the contract between them.

```
public class Main
    implements Runnable
{
   public static void main(String[] args)
      throws Exception
   {
      new Main().run();
   }
```

You declare the client as `Runnable` and provide a `main` method, which is invoked when you start the application.

Now comes the important part of the client.

```
public void run()
{
   try
   {
      // Locate remote object
      HelloWorld server = (HelloWorld)Naming.lookup
                    ("rmi://localhost/"+HelloWorld.NAME);

      // Call it
      String result = server.helloWorld("World");

      // Print result
      System.out.println(result);
```

```
    } catch (NotBoundException e)
    {
      System.out.println("The server could not be found");
      e.printStackTrace(System.err);
    } catch (MalformedURLException e)
    {
      System.out.println("The server name was incorrect");
      e.printStackTrace(System.err);
    } catch (Exception e)
    {
      System.out.println("The object could not be created");
      e.printStackTrace(System.err);
    }
  }
}
```

The first thing you do is to use the default RMI naming system, which uses the RMI registry as implementation to look up the server that your manager has bound into it. As noted earlier, this call returns a stub that implements the `HelloWorld` interface, and not the server itself. The server is most likely running in a separate Java Virtual Machine (JVM), so your only way of communicating with it is to go through the stub.

The Remote Call

After you have located the server, you invoke it using the method that you declared in the `HelloWorld` interface. You send a parameter, and then print out the result. Not very hard, right? But be aware that under the surface a lot has happened. Just to show you how much has happened, let's try to trace this call and see what parts of the RMI system have been used to invoke this simple method. The sequence diagram in Figure 3.2 shows the flow of the call from the client's point of view.

As you can see, the first thing that happens is that the client invokes the stub. The stub then uses the internal object reference to forward the call. A live connection to the server is acquired from the Java Remote Method Protocol (JRMP) engine. If a connection is available, you will get that one, and if the pool of connections to this particular server is empty, a new connection will be created for you to use.

Once you have a connection, you can start sending the call. The object ID, method, and arguments are serialized and written to the connection

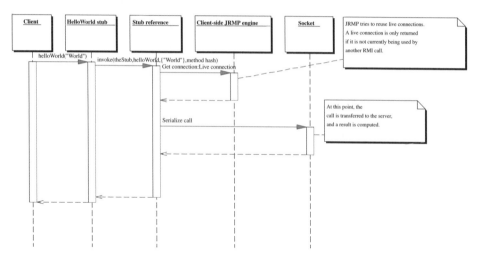

Figure 3.2   A client's view of a remote call.

through an output stream, and then you wait for the server to return a result. The result may either be an exception, in which case you should throw it from the stub, or a computed result, in which case you simply return it as the result of the stub invocation.

Now that you have an idea of what happens on the client side, let's take a look at the server's point of view for the same call. The diagram in Figure 3.3 shows what happens on the server.

The beginning of this call might seem a little magical because the code begins with a thread reading from a socket. How did you get there? What happens is that when you export an object for remote access, a server socket starts listening for incoming connection requests. When a request comes in to create a new connection, a new thread is spawned, and this thread starts listening for incoming calls to remote objects using that server socket. As described in Chapter 2, one server socket may serve several, possibly all, remote objects, so the connection is not coupled with any particular remote object.

Once a call comes in, the thread deserializes it in order to produce the pieces of information it needs to call a remote object. Once this is done,

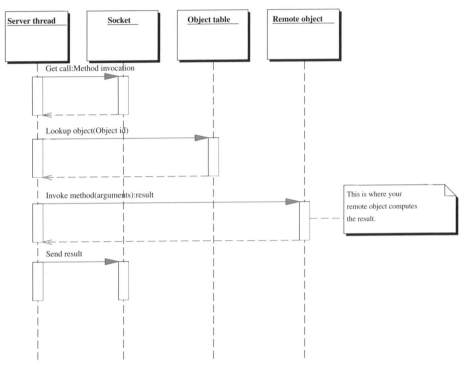

Figure 3.3 A server's view of a remote call.

you need to look up the object to be invoked. This is done by asking the internal object table if any object corresponding to a given object ID, which was sent in the call, has been put in the object table. If so, then it is returned to the server thread. The thread then has all it needs to invoke the object and does so by using the reflection API that was introduced in Java 2.

Your remote object now gains control and can compute whatever it needs, returning some result or throwing an exception if anything goes wrong. The server thread takes the result, even if it was an exception, and sends it back to the client by serializing it to the socket.

This section illustrated a rough outline of what happens during a remote method call. There are many more details concerning how the connection management is handled, how marshalling of arguments is performed, and how invocation is finally made. However, those are only details. At this point, if you have some visual understanding of how remote calls flow between clients and servers, you know everything you need in order to use RMI effectively.

The Application

Now that you have all pieces of this simple HelloWorld application written, you need to put them together. This requires a couple of steps, which you will look at in the following sections.

Packaging

You should first package the different parts, so that you can easily execute them separately. This is done by putting the classes and additional files, such as property files, into Java ARchive (JAR) files. A JAR file is a bundle of files that have been compressed using the popular Zip format. Additionally, it contains a special manifest file that holds a description of the contents of the file. Creating JAR files can be done by using the *jar* tool, which is bundled with the JDK. See the documentation in your JDK installation for information on this tool.

TIP

One of the biggest problems with creating Java applications is how to manage the classpath, that is, the list of directories and files where classes and resources should be loaded. Prior to JDK 1.2, you had to specify the classpath either as an environment variable or by using the -classpath option of the "java" command. Using the environment variable made it complex to have several applications running on the same machine, and you usually ended up creating shell scripts that set up the environment prior to starting a Java application. Similarly, using the -classpath quickly became difficult as the number of paths to be added increased, which made it more complex to use the application unless you used shell scripts to hide the awkward detail.

This problem was dealt with in Java 2 by allowing the classpath to be defined in the manifest file of JAR files. By simply adding the line "Class-Path: foo bar xyzzy" to the manifest file, you can now easily extend the classpath of the classes loaded from that JAR. Read the JDK documentation for more details on how to use these settings in the manifest file. You can also look at all the examples in this book because they all use this approach to deal with classpath settings.

Starting the Naming Service

Once you have packaged all the classes, you can start the naming service. Because your application uses the RMI registry for naming, you should start the *rmiregistry* tool that comes with the JDK. Locate it under the bin directory of your JDK installation, and execute it.

WARNING

The application example does not use dynamic classloading. This means that if you want to use the stub of the application, you have to have the stub and remote interface classes installed in order to use them. Because the RMI registry is implemented as an RMI object, this applies to it as well. What this means is that you must make sure that the RMI registry has these classes in its classpath prior to binding any of your servers' stubs in it. If you do not do this, you will get exceptions because the registry will be unable to deserialize the stubs in its own virtual machine (VM).

There are two ways to get around this: either start the RMI registry as part of your own server or use dynamic classloading. You could also consider using some other naming strategy that does not require that the naming implementation have access to these contract classes. In later examples, you will investigate these different possibilities.

Starting the Server

Next, you should start your server. Because you have packaged your application in JAR files, you can start the application by using the following shell command from the bin directory:

```
>java -classpath server.jar masteringrmi.helloworld.server.Main
```

This command executes the manager that you created by using the classes available in the server.jar file and classes that it points to with its `Class-Path` manifest header.

In this particular example, another manifest header called `Main-Class` has also been utilized. It denotes the class that contains the main-method that should be called on startup of the application. Consequently, the following command will also work:

```
>java -jar server.jar
```

This command is essentially used as a shorthand way of starting the application.

TIP

When you install a JDK or a Java Runtime Environment (JRE) on a Windows system, the .jar file extension is typically associated with the Java runtime. This allows you to simply double-click on JAR files to execute them, provided that they have used the Class-Path manifest header properly.

If you do not have this association, you can add it manually by associating the .jar extension with the command "java -jar %1".

Once the manager has created the remote object and has bound it into the naming service, it will notify you. You can then execute any clients of this service.

If you do not start the naming service before the server, you will get errors because the manager object will not be able to bind the created remote object into the registry.

Starting the Client

The final piece of the puzzle is the client, which you should start next. You do this by issuing the following command:

```
>java -jar client.jar
```

The client.jar file contains all the client and contract classes, and the manifest points out the class masteringrmi.helloworld.client.Main as the main class, which it will then be called.

The client performs its work by first locating the server stub using the naming service, and then invoking it. The output is as follows:

```
Hello World!
```

This completes the first basic example of an RMI application.

Summary

In this chapter, you made your first RMI application, the HelloWorld application. It was composed of three components: a server, a naming service, and a client. The server was in turn created by having one remote object whose sole purpose was to serve client requests and one manager object that created the remote object and made sure that it was accessible through the naming service. A remote interface was created to form the basic contract between the client and the server.

Once you had all the parts of your application in place, you traced a remote call from the client to the server to see how it was dealt with by different parts of the application as well as the RMI implementation. You saw that all basic client/server architecture concepts were being utilized on every remote call.

Lastly, you handled some of the more practical issues of how to package the application, and then how to execute it. For packaging, you used JAR files, which not only provided clearly defined application binaries, but also helped in defining the classpath of the application—something that is normally rather difficult to get right. When you executed the application, you saw that it was important to start the respective components in the proper order: first the naming service, then the server, and lastly the client. If you did not follow this order, you would get errors because the dependencies were not satisfied.

In the next chapter, you will learn how to improve this example by adding a generic access to the naming service and using dynamic class-loading.

CHAPTER 4

Improving the
HelloWorld Example

The last chapter walked you through a simple example of how to build an RMI application. The functionality was not very advanced and neither was the structure. You did not use any special features, such as dynamic classloading or generalized naming.

The example in this chapter shows the exact same functionality, but this time, you are going to do some of the steps a little differently. You will look at a couple of techniques that will help make your RMI application a bit more robust and flexible.

Let's begin by looking at how things were accomplished in the previous example, and how you might want to change them. Then, you will look at how to implement some new techniques.

The Improved Application Overview

One of the most fundamental decisions that was made when designing the HelloWorld application was that the client was a stand-alone application. This gives you great flexibility as it allows you to have a client that is not restricted in what it can do. Applets—Java applications that can be embedded in Web pages—are restricted in what they can do. However, the benefit of applets is that they are loaded on demand from the server, so they do not have to be preinstalled on the client. If you choose to use Java applications, you will have to come up with a strategy for distributing and updating your client applications, or you will be in trouble. Java applets, on the other hand, are automatically updated because they are loaded from the server when a user accesses the Web page that the applets have been embedded in. This allows the client to be updated on the server, and the user automatically gets the right version the next time the page is accessed. Hence, by changing your client to be an applet, you avoid many hassles that come with system upgrades.

One of the other decisions that was made in the previous example was to use the RMI registry for naming. This is convenient, as the registry is a tool that is provided with the JDK and is somewhat easy to use. However, it does have a fair share of problems. It is hard to manage properly, it requires access to the stub classes and remote interfaces (either through dynamic classloading or through its classpath), and it does not support hierarchical names. Because of these problems, you want your RMI application to be designed so that you can easily use another naming system if you want to without having to change the code. All the application is interested in is using a naming service. Which naming service it uses is not that relevant as long as it works reasonably well.

The way to introduce an abstraction for the naming service is to use Java Naming and Directory Interface (JNDI). This is a generalized naming API that can be used to access a wide range of naming services. You should change the server manager to use JNDI when binding the server into a naming service, and you should also change the client to use JNDI to look up the server. This allows you to use another naming service rather than the RMI registry later on. If you use JNDI, you do not have to make any changes to your source code to make use of another naming service implementation. Which naming service you use will then only be a configuration detail of your system.

The server in the first version of the HelloWorld example was divided into parts in the sense that it really consisted of a naming service and the actual remote object, which were running as two separate applications in two different Java Virtual Machines (JVMs). This time around you can integrate the two into one. This gives you a nicer package and allows you to be sure that all parts of the server are started properly and in the right order. The way you do this is to simply create the RMI registry through an API that is available for that purpose.

One of the most interesting features of RMI is dynamic classloading. As explained in Chapter 2, it allows an RMI client to not have the contract classes (including stub classes) installed beforehand. These may instead be loaded from a Web server. You can update your RMI application to use this feature. In this particular example, it is not that useful because your client, by virtue of being an applet, can access the classes from the server anyway. In the case of a Java application, the use of dynamic classloading makes it easier to package your application, as you do not have to package all contract classes with the client. Figure 4.1 outlines the system design of the improved example.

The core of the server, the `HelloWorldImpl` and `Hello` remote interface, are the same. Because the basic service is the same, there is no need to change these. The client has been replaced with an applet, which during runtime, is executed within a Web browser or an appletviewer.

As you can see, from an architectural point of view, you have not changed that much. But from a design and implementation point of view, your new approach is much cleaner.

The Server

Let's take a look at the new classes and see what has changed. Although the `HelloWorldImpl` class still provides the same service, I have decided to change it slightly in order to show you another way to implement the RMI export process.

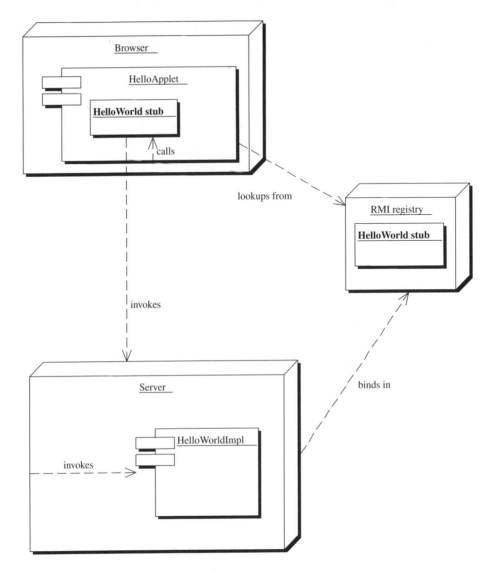

Figure 4.1 The HelloApplet system design.

The Remote Object

The source for the remote object is as follows.

```
// The imports are the same
package masteringrmi.helloapplet.server;

import java.rmi.RemoteException;
import java.rmi.server.UnicastRemoteObject;
```

```
       try
       {
java.rmi.registry.LocateRegistry.createRegistry(Registry.REGISTRY_PORT);
       } catch (java.rmi.server.ExportException ee)
       {
           // Registry already exists
       } catch (RemoteException e)
       {
           throw new ServerException("Could not create registry", e);
       }
   }
```

You use the `LocateRegistry` class to create a new registry, which runs on the default port. As you can see, you are able to use another running registry if one is available, that is, a `java.rmi.ExportException` is thrown when you try to create your registry. Why? Because you cannot export two remote objects with the same object identifier, and the registry always has the same one. If you had not used dynamic classloading, this would have been a problem, as the registry would not be able to bind your stubs because the classes might not be in its classpath.

If you really want to use your own registry, you should propagate the `ExportException`, which is an indication that another registry is already running on the given port.

As the last part of your startup sequence, start and bind your service. This code is as follows.

```
    protected void startService()
       throws RemoteException
    {
       // Create remote object
       server = new HelloWorldImpl();

       // Register server with naming service
       // Use JNDI to hide away the fact that we are using the registry
       // This allows us to easily change the naming service later on
       try
       {
          new InitialContext().rebind(HelloWorldImpl.NAME,server);
       } catch (NamingException e)
       {
          throw new ServerException("The server could not be bound"+
                            " into the naming service", e);
    }
}
```

You begin by simply instantiating your remote object. Because it now extends `UnicastRemoteObject`, there is no need to explicitly export it. That is taken care of by the constructor of `UnicastRemoteObject`.

Next, create a new JNDI context, and bind the server into it. JNDI will choose the implementation and location of the service by looking for configuration information in a file called `jndi.properties`, which must be in classpath. It also adds any information that is contained in the system properties. Your `jndi.properties` file should contain the following lines.

```
java.naming.factory.initial=com.sun.jndi.rmi.registry.RegistryCon-
textFactory
java.naming.provider.url=rmi://localhost
```

The first line tells JNDI which naming service provider you want to use. The `RegistryContextFactory` is a JNDI wrapper for the RMI registry, which can be used to access the registry. The second line tells you the location of the naming service provider, which in this case is `local-host`. In other scenarios, you might want to use one naming service provider for a set of computers, in which case all of your applications would point to this global server. Note that because of a security restriction in the RMI registry, it only allows clients on the same machine to bind into it. This makes it impossible to use one RMI registry for a set of computers running RMI servers.

The Client

Now let's look at the new client. The difference between this version and the first one is that you are using an applet. The basic reason for this is that it is much simpler to distribute an applet rather than an application to a client. As described earlier in this chapter, applications have to be preinstalled on the client and must be updated if the application changes. Applets, on the other hand, are loaded over the Web at runtime and thus do not require any special administration. Your client users only have to surf to the Web page that holds the applet, and it is loaded automatically.

The code for the client is as follows.

```
package masteringrmi.helloapplet.client;

import java.applet.Applet;
```

The Java Plug-In

In the beginning of Java technology's life, applets were supported by having each browser include its own implementation of a JVM. This approach was rather problematic as the applets were far too often error prone and were not kept up-to-date with the current version of Java. Anyone who has written applets for the early versions of the most popular Web browsers can tell you that it was a pure nightmare in terms of quality assurance and testing.

Instead of having each browser vendor implement a JVM, Java functionality has now been added through a standard plug-in. This plug-in is installed just as any other browser plug-in and works with most popular browsers. The new approach allows the JVM of a browser to be updated as often as needed, and several plug-ins can be used concurrently, allowing applets for different versions of a JVM to be used.

```
import java.awt.Label;
import java.rmi.RemoteException;

import javax.naming.InitialContext;
import javax.naming.NamingException;

import masteringrmi.helloapplet.interfaces.HelloWorld;
```

The imports are similar to those of the first example. The most significant differences are that you make use of the `java.applet.Applet` class and the JNDI API classes. The client will extend from `Applet`, and it will use JNDI to look up the server stub.

```
public class HelloApplet
   extends Applet
{
   Label response = new Label();

   public HelloApplet()
   {
      // Setup GUI
      add("Center",response);
   }
```

The client extends `Applet`, allowing it to be embedded in a Web page, and creates a `java.awt.Label` into which you can put a text message. You can use this to show the reply from the server, or in case of an exception, an error message.

Next, you need to override the initialization method from the Applet class. This will perform the lookup and call to the server.

```
public void init()
{
    try
    {
        // Create URL to remote server
        String url =
"rmi://"+getCodeBase().getHost()+"/"+HelloWorld.NAME;

        // Locate remote object
        HelloWorld server = (HelloWorld)new
InitialContext().lookup(url);

        // Call server and show response
        response.setText(server.helloWorld("World"));
    } catch (NamingException e)
    {
        response.setText("The server could not be found");
        e.printStackTrace(System.err);
    } catch (RemoteException e)
    {
        response.setText("The object could not be called");
        e.printStackTrace(System.err);
    } catch (Exception e)
    {
        response.setText(e.getMessage());
        e.printStackTrace(System.err);
    }
}
}
```

A URL to the server object is constructed by using the name of the code-base server, which is `localhost` in this example, and the name to which you have bound the server stub. Next, use this name to look up your server. As you can see, the process used is very similar to using the RMI registry access class `java.rmi.Naming`. The difference here is that you are not directly exposed to the fact that you are using the RMI registry to implement this name to stub mapping.

The call to the server is performed in the same way as in the last example. No changes there.

Next, you must create an HTML page that uses your applet. The markup code that you are going to use is as follows.

```
<OBJECT classid="clsid:8AD9C840-044E-11D1-B3E9-00805F499D93"
    width="200" height="200" align="baseline"
```

```
     codebase="http://java.sun.com/products/plugin/1.2.2/jinstall
-1_2_2-win.cab#Version=1,2,2,0">
 <PARAM NAME="code" VALUE="masteringrmi.helloapplet.client.HelloApplet">
 <PARAM NAME="type" VALUE="application/x-java-applet;version=1.2.2">
 <PARAM NAME="scriptable" VALUE="true">
 <COMMENT>
     <EMBED type="application/x-java-applet;version=1.2.2" width="200"
        height="200" align="baseline"
        code="masteringrmi.helloapplet.client.HelloApplet"
        pluginspage="http://java.sun.com/products/plugin/1.2/
plugin-install.html">
     <NOEMBED>
     </COMMENT>
           No JDK 1.2 support for APPLET!!
     </NOEMBED></EMBED>
 </OBJECT>
```

The tag contains information that can be used with both Netscape and
Internet Explorer. Netscape uses the <EMBED> tag, and Explorer uses
the surrounding <OBJECT> tag. The tags tell the Java plug-in which
class to use as the applet class. If the plug-in is not installed in the client's
browser, it will be downloaded automatically.

This code is placed inside `index.html`, which is available from your
internally created Web server. Because the Web server can access any
file in classpath, all you have to do is add index.html to your package.

The Application

This example did not teach you that much about the specifics of RMI,
but you did acquire a set of good principles that will help you create
applications that are more flexible. Now let's look into some tricks
regarding the practical aspects of your application, such as packaging
and running it.

Packaging

As in the previous example, you want to package your application so
that it is easy to distribute and use. Again, you should be using JAR files
to contain your classes and additional files.

One of the biggest changes from the first example is that you are now
using an applet whose class files and wrapping HTML should be acces-

sible from your server. For this reason, you need to package these with your server. Because the DynaServer allows you to load any of these from the server classpath, all you have to do is bundle them in the JAR, and that's it.

Another difference is that you now have a set of external libraries that you want to use. Traditionally, this meant editing the classpath environment variable or setting the `-classpath` JVM startup flag. The new way to handle classpaths, as described in the previous chapter, is to have a manifest header `Class-Path` that enumerates the libraries that you depend on. This, together with the `Main-Class` header that is used to tell the VM which class to use as the main application class, leads to the following manifest file.

```
Main-Class: masteringrmi.helloapplet.server.Main

Class-Path: ../lib/ext/dynaserver.jar
```

You execute this JAR file from the /bin directory, and because the external library containing your Web server is in the /lib/ext library, the relative path is ../lib/ext.

However, the preceding manifest file only works on JDK 1.3 and later. If you were to try this on a JDK 1.2 VM, you could get exceptions because those VMs do not contain the JNDI API nor the JNDI provider for the RMI registry. To ensure that your application works on JDK 1.2 as well, modify the manifest file to the following.

```
Main-Class: masteringrmi.helloapplet.server.Main
Class-Path: ../lib/ext/dynaserver.jar ../lib/ext/jndi.jar
   ../lib/ext/providerutil.jar ../lib/ext/rmiregistry.jar
```

This ensures that your application can run on any Java 2 platform. You also have to bundle these libraries with your application in order to be sure that the application will work.

Starting the Server

Next, start your server. The process is the same as in the first example, so you can start the application by using the following shell command from the bin directory.

```
>java -jar server.jar
```

Once the manager has created the remote object and has bound it into the naming service, it will notify you of this, and you can then execute any clients of this service.

Because your manager in the server creates an RMI registry internally, there is no way for the server to start prior to the naming service. Also, because the registry will be run in the same JVM as the server, it will automatically have access to the stub classes; so binding a remote object in it will never lead to any `ClassNotFoundExceptions`. Creating the registry internally in this fashion is often the most painless way to handle naming.

Starting the Client

It's time to start your applet, which is the client in this example. You could use a Web browser with the Java 2 plug-in installed, but for simplicity let's use the appletviewer, which is a JDK tool that can be used to execute applets. Issue the following command.

```
>appletviewer http://localhost:8080/index.html
```

The appletviewer accesses the HTML page containing your applet. It finds your applet in the page, and executes it. The applet starts loading classes from the server by using the DynaServer that you embedded in your server. Note that although you have enabled dynamic classloading in your server by setting the codebase, your client will not make use of dynamic classloading. Why not? Well, because the applet itself is being loaded from the same place as the stub classes, they will seem to already be packaged with the applet, so there is no need to use any other way to access these classes. Had your client been a stand-alone application this would not be the case. One way for you to test that this really works is to start the RMI registry before starting the server with its internal RMI registry. The server then uses the registry you already started. This registry has to load the stub classes through dynamic classloading when the server is bound into it, and hence, you will get some confirmation that this works as intended.

The applet locates the server stub by using the naming service, and then invokes it. The output is as follows:

```
Hello World!
```

And thus, you are finished with this example of how to create RMI applications.

Summary

The previous chapter showed you how to create a simple RMI application. In this chapter, you used the same basic example, but enhanced it in various ways.

Instead of using the RMI interfaces for using naming services, you used the standardized JNDI API. This allows you to switch naming services later on should the need arise and also gives you access to a more advanced naming model.

You were then introduced to dynamic classloading by letting all classes be served by an internally maintained Web server. This lets your clients access the server without having all the classes beforehand. If an object is sent to the client whose class is not available on the client, this class is loaded automatically from the server.

Next, instead of using an external RMI registry for naming, you created a registry inside your server application. This gives you greater control over the lifecycle of the registry and also removes some potential bug sources. Because the registry is created internally, it automatically has access to all the stub classes, which removes any classpath problems that can occur if the registry is run separately.

After having made the server more flexible, you updated your client. In the previous chapter, you used a standard Java application as a client, and in this chapter, you changed this to an applet. The reasons for this were several. First, the user only needs a browser with the Java plug-in installed. Second, this gives you an easy way to upgrade clients because applets always load their code from the server on startup.

In the next chapter, you will look at how you can control the connections between the client and the server as well as what functionality you can add by doing this.

CHAPTER 5

Custom Connection Management

So far you have only looked at how to make your objects remotely accessible. Clients have been able to find and use remote objects that a server exposes, which makes all sorts of functionality available for clients. However, some aspects of your remote objects may not be directly related to the actual function that they perform, but rather various aspects of how they are accessed. For example, if your remote objects are being used over the Internet, you might be concerned with the security of such calls. Someone may be listening to your communication, someone who is not authorized to do so may be accessing your system, or perhaps you are moving so much data that the system becomes terribly slow.

This chapter looks at custom connection management, which is a technique that can be used to address many of these problems. After completing this chapter, you should be able to introduce a wide range of connection oriented functionality into your RMI applications.

Overview of Custom Connection Management

When a client accesses a remote object on a server, it needs to use some kind of network connection to do so. If you do not do anything, RMI uses the default socket connections that are used by the particular RMI implementation. Most likely, this is good enough for most applications, but in many occurrences, you may want to have more control over this process.

For example, if the communication is being made over a particularly slow network or if large amounts of data are to be sent, then it is a good idea to use network connections that automatically compress the data, so that the actual use of the physical network is minimized. Another likely scenario is that you'll need to be able to identify and authenticate the clients that access the services provided by a server. If the data contained on the server is sensitive (that is, if it is critical that only authorized users access the functionality), then you want to use a protocol that ensures that the communication is being done in a secure way.

For these situations, RMI has introduced a mechanism called *connection factories*. This lets you choose your own way to manage the connections used to talk to remote objects. The basic technique is to define a connection factory that is used by clients to create sockets to talk to the server, and then create another connection factory that is used by the server to accept incoming connection requests. These factories can then be used when exporting remote objects. All communication with the exported object is done using these factories, which is shown in Figure 5.1.

As you can see, at least four new parts need to be implemented if you want to make your own connection management:

- **Server socket factory.** The socket connection factory to be used on the server side is responsible for creating an instance of `java.net.ServerSocket`.

- **Client socket factory.** The client's socket connection factory is used whenever a stub wants to talk to the remote object through

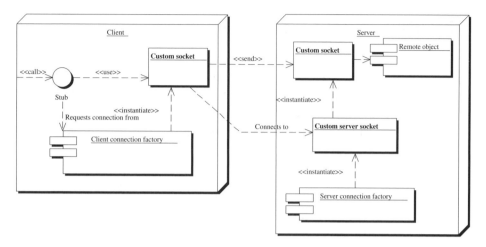

Figure 5.1 Custom connection management.

your custom connection. It creates instances of `java.net.Socket`, which are connected to the server.

- **Custom server socket.** Server sockets listen on a particular port for incoming connection requests and create instances of `java.net.Socket` when such a request is received from a client.

- **Custom socket.** The custom sockets are the objects that perform the actual communication between the client and the server. They implement whatever special features you want to have when communicating with your remote objects. Note that both clients and servers use sockets, although they are used for communication in opposite directions. The simplest case is to have one implementation with functionality for both the client and the server. It might also be a good idea to split the custom socket into two parts: one custom socket that implements the server's communication protocol and one that is used on the client.

Later in this chapter, you will see a complete example of custom connection management, but let's begin with the RMI interfaces that you are required to implement.

The RMIServerSocketFactory Interface

The first interface that RMI defines for the purpose of custom connection management is `java.rmi.server.RMIServerSocketFactory`. Implementations of this interface are used to create server sockets that are used to accept incoming connection requests. The interface is defined as follows:

```
public interface RMIServerSocketFactory
{
    /**
     * Create a server socket on the specified port (port 0 indicates
     * an anonymous port).
     * @param  port the port number
     * @return the server socket on the specified port
     * @exception IOException if an I/O error occurs during
     *            server socket creation
     */
    public ServerSocket createServerSocket(int port)
        throws IOException;
}
```

As you can see, you only need to define one method. In this method, you should instantiate your own version of a `ServerSocket`. How you implement this server socket is up to you and should of course reflect the functionality that you want to introduce. In the example in this chapter, I will show you one possible way to implement this factory interface and the server socket.

The RMIClientSocketFactory Interface

The interface used by RMI clients wanting to access your remote objects is as simple as the following:

```
public interface RMIClientSocketFactory
{
    /**
     * Create a client socket connected to the specified
     * host and port.
     * @param  host   the host name
```

```
 * @param  port   the port number
 * @return a socket connected to the specified host and port.
 * @exception IOException if an I/O error occurs in socket creation
 */
public Socket createSocket(String host, int port
throws IOException;
}
```

In `createSocket`, you should instantiate your version of `java.net.Socket`, which connects to the given host and port. As with the server factory, I will show you an example of how to implement this interface and the sockets it returns in this chapter.

However, two details related to implementing this interface are not shown by simply looking at it. First, an instance of the implementation of this interface is sent along with the stub to your remote object. This means that you must make your implementation serializable. In the simplest case, this only means that you must implement the `java.io.Serializable` interface as well. If your implementation requires more control over the serialization, then the normal rules of serialization apply. The second issue is that the client side of the RMI implementation tries to reuse connections created by this factory. The way it does this is to store the factory in a hashtable and check whether two separate stubs with client connection factories actually use the same connection factory. If they do, then the two stubs are able to share the connections that have been created. As noted previously, the comparison between connection factories is done by using a hashtable.

So how should you modify your implementation to take advantage of connection equality? The answer is to override the `equals` and `hashCode` methods from `java.lang.Object`. The hashtable then uses these methods to compare two connection factories to determine if they are indeed the same. The implementation of these methods is of course dependent on how equality between network connections is defined in your particular implementation. In some cases, all connections created by a particular kind of connection factory are equal, whereas in other cases, they may all be different. If they are all equal, which is the most common scenario, the `equals` method may simply check whether the class of the other connection factory is the same as its own. The example provided in this chapter uses this algorithm.

A Sample Connection Factory

Now that all the necessary components that you need in order create your own connection factory have been identified, let's walk through a simple example. You first need to choose the kind of functionality you want your custom code to implement.

I have, quite randomly, chosen to make a connection management implementation that lets you identify the name of the user calling the server. The idea is that the server should be able to detect the user's name in order to make some decisions based on the user's identity.

The example only deals with the identification of the user. It does not try to authenticate the user, that is, determine if the user actually is who he says he is. This is a separate problem that requires more thought and is not really necessary in order to show how connection factories work. Consider it as an exercise for the reader to add authentication to the example.

Let's begin by taking a look at which classes are needed:

- **IdentityServerSocketFactory.** This class is responsible for creating custom server sockets.

- **IdentityClientSocketFactory.** This class is responsible for creating custom sockets that clients use to call the remote object.

- **IdentityServerSocket.** This is your implementation of `java.net.ServerSocket`. You use it to accept client connections whose user identity should be made available somehow.

- **IdentitySocket.** This class is responsible for creating custom sockets that are used by both clients and the server to communicate. I have chosen to put both the server and client socket code in this class, but you could just as well split this into two separate classes.

In addition, the `IdentitySocket` internally uses custom stream implementations to exchange the user identity information between the client and the server.

To make use of this custom connection factory, I have modified the HelloWorld applet. Because the functionality of the HelloWorld client and server is almost unchanged, I will not detail that too much; although I will show you how I have modified it to use the new custom connections.

The IdentityServerSocketFactory Class

Let's begin with the server socket factory implementation. This class implements the `java.rmi.server.RMIServerSocketFactory` interface. When you export your remote objects, you tell the RMI implementation to use this factory instead of the default.

The implementation of this factory should simply create and return your custom variant of the `java.net.ServerSocket` class. The code for this class is as follows:

```
public class IdentityServerSocketFactory
   implements RMIServerSocketFactory
{
   public ServerSocket createServerSocket(int port)
      throws IOException
   {
      return new IdentityServerSocket(port);
   }
}
```

As you can see, this class is about as trivial as it gets. The only thing you do is pass on the port number to the constructor of your custom server socket.

The IdentityClientSocketFactory Class

Moving on, you come to the client side of things, which is the implementation of the `java.rmi.server.RMIClientSocketfactory` interface. This class is responsible for creating connections that the client uses to connect to the remote objects on the server. As discussed in the interface description, this class is a little more complicated.

```
public class IdentityClientSocketFactory
   implements RMIClientSocketFactory, java.io.Serializable
{
   public Socket createSocket(String host, int port)
      throws IOException
   {
      return new IdentitySocket(host, port);
   }
```

To begin with, because objects of this class are going to be sent to the clients along with the stub, they need to be serializable. You have no state to maintain though, so all you have to do is implement the `java.io.Serializable` interface.

You then have the implementation of the socket factory. As with the server side of things, you simply create an instance of your custom socket, and pass on the initialization parameters to the constructor.

TIP

If you send an RMI stub whose remote object uses a custom socket factory and then send that stub back to the server, the stub is still registered as though it is in a remote JVM. The DGC mechanism then starts sending usage notification calls to the server by creating a connection through the client socket factory. Because of this, the socket factory makes a connection from the server JVM to the server JVM. You may want to detect this case somehow and supply a socket implementation that is optimized in case of JVM local usage.

As described in the "The RMIClientSocketFactory Interface" section, the RMI implementation tries to reuse socket connections from equivalent connection factories. This is done by using a hashtable, so your factory should implement the methods `equals` and `hashCode`:

```
public boolean equals(Object obj)
{
    return obj instanceof IdentityClientSocketFactory;
}

public int hashCode()
{
    return getClass().toString().hashCode();
}
```

The `equals` implementation simply checks whether the other object is the same kind of socket factory and the `hashCode` implementation uses the hash value of the class name. By doing this, the RMI implementation is able to detect whether two RMI stubs are using the same connection factory and if so, reuses the connections that have been created with either of them.

The IdentityServerSocket Class

The next class is the custom `java.net.ServerSocket` subclass, which you use to accept incoming connection requests. This class is also very easy to create. All you have to do is make sure that it delivers your custom socket when a client connects to it.

```
public class IdentityServerSocket
    extends ServerSocket
{
    protected IdentityServerSocket(int port)
        throws IOException
    {
        super(port);
    }
```

The class must extend `java.net.ServerSocket`, and the constructor simply saves the port that should be listened to by sending it to the superclass.

```
    public Socket accept()
        throws IOException
    {
        Socket socket = new IdentitySocket();
        super.implAccept(socket);
        return socket;
    }
}
```

The RMI thread that is used to handle incoming connection requests calls the accept method. In this method, you create an instance of your own socket and delegate it to the low-level accept functionality in `ServerSocket`. This accepts and creates the physical connection to the client, which is then sent to your own socket. Hence, your socket is more of a wrapper around the default socket implementation rather than a completely new implementation of sockets. Typically, this is done in most cases because you want to augment standard sockets rather than replace them with something completely different.

The IdentitySocket Class

The last class is the subclass of `java.net.Socket`, which is the work-horse of the HelloWorld example. All interesting functionality, which is related to actually identifying clients, is contained in this class. You have probably noticed that none of the other classes really has any code that is specific to this particular example. They are rather general and can therefore easily be reused.

Because this is a slightly larger class, let's walk through it step-by-step.

```
public class IdentitySocket
   extends Socket
{
   String client;
   boolean isClient = false;


   static ThreadLocal clientIdentity = new ThreadLocal();
   public static String getClient()
   {
      return (String)clientIdentity.get();
   }
}
```

The first requirement is, of course, that you subclass `java.net.Socket`. This gives you access to the standard implementation of sockets, which is what you would typically want. Next, you declare two variables. The first one, `client`, is the name of the client and is used to store the name of the client. The second one, `isClient`, is used to determine whether this socket is used by a client or a server. If a client uses it, you want to send your identity to the server, and if the server uses it, you want to get the identity from the client.

You then declare a thread local variable, which holds the name of the client calling. What happens is that you associate each RMI thread that uses your custom sockets with the name of the calling client. Any remote objects may then use the `getClient` method to determine the name of the client.

```
public IdentitySocket()
{
   isClient = false;
}
public IdentitySocket(String host, int port)
   throws java.net.UnknownHostException, java.io.IOException
{
```

```
    super(host, port);
    isClient = true;
}
```

The server and the client use the preceding constructors, respectively. You store this information so that you can let your succeeding code do different things, depending on whether it is being used by the client or the server.

```
public InputStream getInputStream()
    throws IOException
{
    if (!isClient && client == null)
    {
        // Get the name of the client
        DataInputStream din =
            new DataInputStream(super.getInputStream());
        client = din.readUTF();
    }

    // Associate this thread with the client name
    clientIdentity.set(client);
    // Return the stream so that it may be used
    // by the RMI implementation
    return super.getInputStream();
}
```

In the preceding code, you return the input stream to the socket. If this code is used on the server, then the first thing you do is receive the name of the client. The name is then associated with the current thread by using the thread local variable `clientIdentity`. Then return the standard input stream.

In the code, you have an example of a custom socket, which performs an initialization handshake procedure. The preceding custom code is only performed when the socket is first created. Thereafter, special communication between the server and the client does not occur.

If you want to continually modify the data that is being sent, for example, by encrypting it, then you should return your own implementation of `java.io.InputStream`, which filters the standard stream.

The following corresponding code creates the output stream from a socket:

```
public OutputStream getOutputStream()
    throws IOException
{
```

```
        if (isClient && client == null)
        {
            // Send the name of this client
            DataOutputStream dout =
                new DataOutputStream(super.getOutputStream());

            // Get the name from system properties
            // This is the login name
            client = System.getProperty("user.name");
            dout.writeUTF(client);
        }

        // Return the stream so that it may be used
        // by the RMI implementation
        return super.getOutputStream();
    }
}
```

Begin by checking whether a client of a remote object is calling this code and also, if this is the first time the stream is being requested. If so, send the value of the system property user.name. This property is the name of the user that started the JVM. The server then knows your identity, which it can associate to this connection. After that, simply return the standard output stream to this socket.

Putting the Custom Connection Factory to Use

Now that you have created all parts of your custom connection factory, let's put it to use. To use a connection factory, you must specify it to be used when you export an object. If your remote object subclass is java.rmi.server.UnicastRemoteObject, then you must use the constructor that takes a connection factory as a parameter. The following example is based on the HelloWorld example that does explicit export. It provides the following code:

```
server = new HelloWorldImpl();
UnicastRemoteObject.exportObject(server,
                                 1234,
                                 new IdentityClientSocketFactory(),
                                 new IdentityServerSocketFactory());
```

Instead of using the simpler export method, you can now use one that takes four arguments: your remote object, the server port number, the client-side connection factory, and the server-side connection factory.

The RMI implementation puts your remote object in the exported object table, so that it can be invoked. It also creates a new thread that calls the `accept` method on the server socket that you provide through the factory.

Now that you are using this neat connection factory, you can modify the HelloWorld example so that it identifies the clients that call it. The following is a modified HelloWorld remote object:

```
public String helloWorld()
{
   // Get the name of the client and include it in the greeting
   return "Hello " + IdentitySocket.getClient() +"!";
}
```

Instead of supplying the name as a method argument, you can retrieve it from your custom connection. This enables you to always find out who the caller is without having to supply it as an explicit method argument all the time.

The client itself is only modified so that it does not send a name as a parameter to `helloWorld`. Other than that, the usage of this factory is completely transparent to the client. The only thing that you need to worry about is that the client must have access to the new connection factory classes or at least the ones that are used by the client. You can either use dynamic classloading to load these from the server, or you can bundle them with the client. As always, by using dynamic classloading, it is much easier to update the classes later on, or you can easily use another connection factory altogether without having to redistribute your client application.

Summary

This chapter showed you what was needed in order to introduce custom connection management, which is a good way to add functionality to your RMI application. The custom connection management functionality does not directly relate to what the application does, but rather it relates to how the communication between the clients and the server is handled. For example, you can add encryption to the communication, you can compress the data that is sent, or you can identify the client's name (as shown in the example in this chapter).

In order to create your own connection factory, you discovered that you needed a client and a server connection factory as well as a custom server socket and a custom socket implementation. The custom socket is used by both the client and the server, so it has to have some way of knowing which way it is being used. The way to identify these cases is to look at which constructor is being used.

After you implemented all parts of your custom connection factory, you modified the HelloWorld example to use it. This was relatively simple. All you had to do was change how it was exported. The HelloWorld remote object itself was then modified to take advantage of the new functionality, which made it possible for you to find out the caller's identity without explicitly sending it to the server.

The last important feature of RMI that you should know about is activation, which is the subject of the next chapter.

CHAPTER 6

Activation

You have now looked at more or less all the main features of RMI. You know how to make remote objects and how to access them, and you have looked at how to gain more control over how connections between the clients and the servers are managed. With the information you have so far, you should have no trouble creating some rather complex applications.

However, if you have paid attention to the examples, you have noticed that there is a recurring order to the process.

1. The naming is started.
2. The remote object is created on the server.
3. The server is bound in the naming service.
4. The client looks up the server and starts calling it.

What happens if, for example, the server crashes after the client has looked it up? Well, with what you know so far, the client will get an exception when it tries to talk to the server. Even if the server is restarted properly, the client must get a new stub to the server after it has been rebound into the naming server in order to start talking to it again.

This property of remote systems is not desired, especially if you intend to run these services for a very long time, in which case, you will definitely want to restart the server now and then. (For example, if you have fixed some bug in the code, you will then want to restart.)

So, what is it that the client must do then? Well, for each call, it must be prepared for the server to have ceased, in which case, the client must try to get a new stub from the naming service. If the server has not been restarted, the client will get the old stub, which is of course invalid at this point. And even if the server has been restarted, the stub will not work because the communications port may have changed, or the object ID is different this time around.

This kind of client code is very tedious to write, and it is very hard to get right because there are so many possibilities at each point. Most developers would probably do it the easy way and simply say "restart the whole client if something goes wrong." Well, that will work, but wouldn't it be nice if this was not necessary. (Also, remember that the client, in some cases, may be another server that needs to access functionality from another server. In this case, restarting the client may not be a good idea or may even be possible.)

To make this situation better, there is a function in RMI called *activation*. Activation helps you make the stubs a little more persistent by not breaking as easily, and it also helps you manage your remote services. After completing this chapter, not only should you be able to make a rather complex RMI application, but you should also be able make it stay alive for a considerable amount of time without too many hassles.

Activation Overview

The basic idea behind activation is to let you assign persistent object identifiers to your objects, so that even if your server with the remote objects crashes, a client will be able to talk to it if it comes back up. Keep in mind that with standard remote objects, they may be assigned new object identifiers each time the server is run.

Activation also helps you with the life cycle of your remote objects. If a client wants to talk to a remote object that is not yet started, the activation system can create and register the activatable remote object for you. By using activation, you minimize the amount of system resources that are used by not having to run all services all the time. Instead, you can have some or all of them activated on demand—hence the name activation.

There are two main concepts in activation: *activation groups* and *activatables*. Activation groups are essentially groups of activatables, and there is at most one activation group per JVM, or rather, there is one JVM per activation group. An activatable is a remote object that has been exported to the RMI runtime through the activation interfaces.

Let's start by looking at how a system using activation would typically be set up. (See Figure 6.1.)

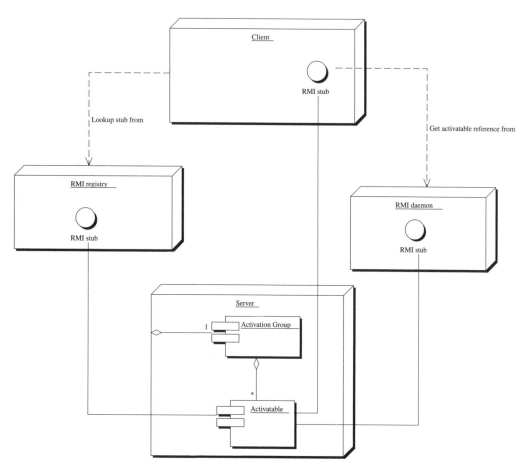

Figure 6.1 Activation overview.

Besides the standard client, server, and registry, there is also an RMI daemon in this figure. What is its purpose? Well, the daemon is the bookkeeper in activation. It keeps track of what objects can be activated, and if an object is activated, it knows where it is, and so forth. It is also responsible for the creation and management of JVMs in which it can activate remote objects if necessary.

The initialization process of a system that is using activation is a bit different from the usual process. Previously, you would start something you have called a server in which you would create and export a remote object whose stub you would bind into a naming service, so that clients could obtain it. The process for using activation is somewhat different. Instead of explicitly starting up remote objects, you perform a kind of setup phase where you tell the RMI daemon what kind of object you want to be able to activate and how it should do that. For example, you might say that you want to be able to activate an object of class Foo, and that it should be communicating on port X using connection factory Xyzzy. But you do not create and export this object yourself; this is the job of the RMI daemon.

During the execution of this setup, you are given a stub to the activatable object that you have registered with the RMI daemon. This stub can then be bound into an RMI registry so that clients can locate it. But, remember that at this point there is no existing remote object! All that exists is a stub in a registry and your description of your object within the RMI daemon.

When the first client retrieves the stub from the registry and starts calling it, in the same way it would with any remote object, this is when the activation part kicks in. You see, the stub contains three components: a live reference to the remote object, the activation ID of the object, and a reference to the RMI daemon. When the client makes the first call, the stub does not contain a live reference, and hence it must ask the RMI daemon to provide one for the given activation ID. The daemon looks in its tables and comes to the conclusion that it does not yet have that object running. It then creates a new JVM in which the remote object is created. The RMI daemon then returns the live reference to the remote object, and the client call can proceed. The remote object has been activated.

In the same way, if the server crashes for some reason, the live reference in the client's stub will fail. The client can then ask the RMI daemon for a new one. The RMI daemon recognizes that the server has crashed, spawns a new JVM for the activation group with the activatable in it, and all is well again.

The remote object may also be removed in an orderly fashion, in which case, the activation group can decide to exit the JVM in order to preserve resources. The same re-creation process as previously described applies if a client wants to access the activatable object at some later point.

Activation Groups

As noted in the overview, there is one JVM per activation group in which all activatable objects for that activation group are created. When an activatable object is created, it is registered with the activation group as being active, which in turn notifies the RMI daemon of this so that stubs needing a live reference can get it.

When an activatable is first registered with the RMI daemon, it must also be associated with an activation group in which it should live. To allow this, a description of the group is created to which the activatable object is later associated. This description is an instance of the `java.rmi.activation.ActivationGroupDesc` class. It contains the set of system properties that JVMs that are spawned for it should have. In addition, a description of the parameters used to start the JVM is given.

When the activation groups description is registered with the RMI daemon, it is assigned a unique identifier. This identifier is of the class `java.rmi.activation.ActivationGroupID`. It is an internal identifier that the RMI daemon uses to keep track of the groups and the objects that are registered with each group.

Note that several activatable objects can be registered with the same activation group. This allows several activatable objects to share the same JVM. If you want to use this feature, you must store the group ID when the group is registered with the RMI daemon, so that you can use it for all activatable objects that you want to have in the same group. The group ID is serializable, so the easiest way to store it is probably to serialize it to a file.

Activatables

With standard remote objects, you use `java.rmi.server.Unicas-tRemoteObject` to export them to the RMI implementation. With activation, you use the base class `java.rmi.activation.Activatable` instead. As was the case with the `UnicastRemoteObject` class, there are two ways to use it: Either subclass it and use the implicit export done by the constructor in the `Activatable` class, or call a static method in it to explicitly export remote objects to use the activation mechanism. So the basic idea is pretty similar.

Typically, you do not create and export your activatable objects yourself because this is one of the primary purposes of the RMI daemon. Instead, you create a special constructor that is used by the activation system when the object is activated. The implementation of this constructor in the `Activatable` class exports the remote object, which was also the case with the default constructor of `UnicastRemoteObject`. So, similarly, if you do not want your remote object to extend the `Activatable` base class, then you must explicitly export your remote object in this special constructor. The specifics of what this constructor looks like is shown in the section "The Server Class."

During the setup phase of activation, you register a description of your activatable with the RMI daemon. It is at this point that the persistent object identifier is assigned to your remote object. This is the ID that your remote object has as long as it is registered with the activation system. This identifier is then embedded into all stubs to your remote object, so that a stub always can acquire a live reference to it. The identifier is of class `java.rmi.activation.ActivationID`. The identifier itself contains an instance of `java.rmi.server.UID` and a stub through which it is possible to talk to the RMI daemon (yes, the RMI daemon itself is also a remote object). The description, which you use to register the activatable, is of class `java.rmi.activation.ActivationDesc`. It contains the activation group identifier (so that the RMI daemon knows where to create the object), the classname of your remote object (so that the RMI daemon knows which class to use during activation), the codebase of your remote object (so that the RMI daemon knows where to get the remote objects class), and any initialization data you want in the form of a `java.rmi.MarshalledObject`. After you have registered this information with the RMI daemon, it then has everything it needs in order to activate your object on demand.

To Activate or Not to Activate

At first glance, activation may seem very usable-and it is, but it does have a rather significant impact on the design of your application that in some cases is unwanted. The reason is as follows.

Activation does two things for you: It provides persistent object identifiers to your remote objects, and it provides a way to activate them on demand. The first feature is very useful in many cases, but the latter is not. The reason is that if you use activation, the RMI daemon is in complete control of how the JVM is managed. If you need to construct fairly coarse servers that utilize additional services, such as logging or database connections, you may want to manually control how JVMs start as well as what environment they run in. In that case, activation is not for you, as it requires quite a bit of control to be handed over to the RMI daemon.

Also, even if you decide to use activation, you may not want to use it for all of your objects, but only for root objects that define a rather coarse grained interface to your service-sort of the entry point.

Of course, exactly how you do this is completely dependent on your individual situation. The previous conditions may be important to consider when deciding if and how to use activation in a system.

An Activation Example

Now that you have examined activation from a rather theoretical perspective, let's put it into practice by modifying the HelloWorld example to be an activatable object. This can be done in three steps:

1. Change your manager program to perform the setup phase of activation.

2. Modify the remote object to allow it to be activated on demand.

3. Alter the client to take advantage of this new functionality.

The remote interface is unchanged from the previous examples. Let's walk through these steps one at a time. The last step is not strictly required, but allows you to easily see what happens with your activatable object.

The Setup Class

One of the main differences between the setup class and the previous manager class is that the setup is only run once, and once it is done, it does not stay running. In contrast, the manager class of the previous examples not only creates and hosts the remote object, it also manages the additional services, such as the RMI registry and the Web server.

Because of this difference, all the additional services are now run as stand-alone applications. Hence, the setup class only holds the code that is related to the registration of the activatable remote object. The code is as follows.

```
package masteringrmi.helloactivate.server;

import java.io.IOException;
import java.net.MalformedURLException;
import java.rmi.MarshalledObject;
import java.rmi.RemoteException;
import java.rmi.ServerException;
import java.rmi.AlreadyBoundException;
import java.rmi.activation.ActivationGroupDesc;
import java.rmi.activation.ActivationGroupID;
import java.rmi.activation.ActivationGroup;
import java.rmi.activation.ActivationDesc;
import java.rmi.activation.Activatable;
import java.util.Properties;

import javax.naming.InitialContext;

import masteringrmi.helloactivate.interfaces.HelloWorld;
```

The setup is contained in the server package because this is a server only class. The imports have changed slightly to include the activation classes. You also include the JNDI class `javax.naming.Initial-Context,` so that you can bind the activatable with the naming service.

```
public class Setup
{
    public static void main(String[] args)
        throws Exception
    {
        new Setup();

        System.exit(0);
    }
```

The application startup method, main, is similar to the previous manager code. The primary difference is that you explicitly exit the setup application once it has completed. If you did not do this, the application would not exit because the RMI subsystem and its threads start, which effectively stops the JVM from exiting without explicit intervention.

```
public Setup()
   throws Exception
   {
   // Load system properties from resource file
   System.getProperties().load(
      Thread.currentThread().
      getContextClassLoader().
      getResourceAsStream("system.properties"));

   System.setProperty("java.security.policy",
      getClass().getResource("/server.policy").toString());
```

The preceding code is the constructor of your setup application in which all the work is done. You begin, as usual, by loading the system properties of the setup. The main setting you are concerned with is the RMI codebase to be used for dynamic classloading. This value is used in two ways. First, because the RMI daemon needs to know where to find the classes of the activatable you have created, you use this codebase for that. Second, when you bind the stub into the naming service, the RMI registry in your case, you need to have it set so that the RMI registry can access the classes of the stub. If it cannot do that, you will receive ClassNotFound exceptions when you try to bind the stub into the registry.

You also set the security policy to be used. Why is this needed? Well, when you create an activation group later on, a security manager is automatically set. This causes security checks to be performed for certain operations. Because you will perform some of these restricted operations (talking to the RMI registry for example), you need to set a security policy that allows you to do that. The server.policy file contains permission grants to allow you to do anything including talking to the registry.

Because the security policy is contained in your JAR, you locate its URL by using the resource mechanism. By doing this, you do not have to hard code the location of the policy in your code, and it thus becomes much less error prone. Using the resource mechanism in this way is a good way to locate files without having to resort to using the java.io.File class. It is also very powerful because it allows you to easily access files that are contained within a JAR file.

Now let's take a look at the activation group definition and creation.

```
// Create activation group description
Properties cfg = null;
ActivationGroupDesc.CommandEnvironment ace = null;
ActivationGroupDesc helloGroup = new ActivationGroupDesc(cfg, null);

// Register group with activation system
ActivationGroupID agi =
   ActivationGroup.getSystem().registerGroup(helloGroup);

// Create the group
// This is necessary since the activation description created
// below will use this group
ActivationGroup.createGroup(agi, helloGroup, 0);
System.out.println("Activation group created");
```

The code performs three functions. First, you create a description of your group. A description of an activation group contains two items: the system properties that you want to set for the JVM associated with the activation group and the command-line options for the JVM. There are no special requirements on these options, so use null for both.

WARNING

If you choose to provide settings for either of these two parameters, then you also need to grant the RMI daemon permission to use these settings. Supplying a security policy file to the RMI daemon can do this.

You can also turn off these restrictions in the RMI daemon by supplying the following parameter to the RMI daemon when you start it:

```
-J-Dsun.rmi.activation.execPolicy=none
```

Note that this only works with Sun's RMI daemon implementation. Check the RMI daemons documentation for more information about these issues.

Second, when a description of the group has been created, you register it with the RMI daemon. This gives you a unique activation group identifier in return. In the future, this ID will be used to refer to this particular activation group.

Third, you immediately use this ID to create the activation group manually in the current JVM. This is necessary because the activatable object that you are about to register should reside within this activation group.

Next, you perform the registration of your activatable object.

```
// Use the same codebase as this class
String location = System.getProperty("java.rmi.server.codebase");

MarshalledObject data = null;
ActivationDesc desc = new

ActivationDesc("masteringrmi.helloactivate.server.HelloWorldImpl",
               location, data, true);

// Register object with activation system
HelloWorld hello = (HelloWorld)Activatable.register(desc);
System.out.println("Registered server with activation system");
```

The activatable object description contains four items:

- The fully qualified classname of your implementation class
- The codebase where the implementation class can be found
- Any custom initialization data in the form of a marshalled object
- Whether or not to activate this object immediately when the RMI daemon is started

Using this information about the remote object, the RMI daemon will be able to perform its magic.

TIP

Because a significant feature of activation is its capability to activate objects on demand, you may ask why I have set the restart flag to true. Does this not counter the lazy loading aspect of activation? Yes it does, but I have chosen to do so because of how I want to handle crash recovery. After this setup has completed, there will be a stub to the activatable in the RMI registry that clients can access and use to communicate with the activatable.

However, if you need to restart the RMI registry, this binding will be lost. There are two main strategies to deal with this: Either store the stub in a file somewhere and have a special version of the setup program that only reads this stub and places it in the registry, or let the activatable place itself into the registry every time it is activated.

To keep it simple, I have chosen the latter alternative, which means that if I need to restart the RMI registry, I also restart the RMI daemon. Because I set the restart object flag to true, it will immediately be restarted too and will then bind itself into the registry. Clients will then be able to access the stub again.

The last thing you do is make the initial binding of the stub into the naming service by using its JNDI interface.

```
// Register objects stub with naming service
new InitialContext().rebind(HelloWorld.NAME, hello);
```

Rebind is used instead of bind to override any earlier registrations of this name. The setup phase of this system is now complete. Next, you will learn how to change the remote object server.

The Server Class

As described previously, there are two ways you can modify the server to be activatable. Either subclass the class `java.rmi.activation.Activatable` and use its special activation constructor to register your remote object as being activated, or do this manually in your own constructor.

Let's do this manually just to make the process explicit. The following code shows what the special constructor should look like.

```
public HelloWorldImpl(ActivationID id, MarshalledObject data)
    throws RemoteException
{
    Remote stub = Activatable.exportObject(this, id, 0);
```

The constructor should have two arguments. The first argument is the activation ID that was assigned to this object during the registration process, and the second argument is the custom initialization data that you provided in the activatable object descriptor. As noted earlier, this constructor is not called by you, but by the activation system.

You then explicitly export the object. The export method takes three arguments: the remote object to export for remote invocation, the activation identifier to associate it with, and the port to use. A port value of zero means that the activation system may choose any port that is available.

The stub is stored so that you can bind into the RMI registry. This is because of the crash recovery strategy that I chose for this example. Every time the object becomes active, you bind into the registry to make sure that there is always a binding in the registry so that clients can get the stub.

```
try
{
    Properties cfg = new Properties();
    cfg.load(this.getClass().
            getResourceAsStream("/jndi.properties"));
    new InitialContext(cfg).rebind(HelloWorld.NAME, stub);
} catch (Exception e)
{
    throw new ServerException("Could not bind server", e);
}
}
```

Because you are using JNDI, you need to provide some properties. Specifically, you need to tell JNDI which initial context factory to use. Because the `jndi.properties` is available through the codebase that was used to load this class, you can easily access it by using the preceding code. These settings are loaded into a `java.util.Properties` object, which is then supplied to JNDI. You then associate the JNDI name of your remote object with the stub.

The server has now been modified to allow it to be used for activation. The last piece that you need to change is the client.

The Client Class

The client is now an application with a GUI. But instead of only calling the server once, a button has been added to allow you to repeatedly call the server to see what happens when the activation kicks in. Let's begin with the imports of the new client.

```
package masteringrmi.helloactivate.client;

import java.awt.Frame;
import java.awt.Label;
import java.awt.Button;
import java.awt.event.ActionListener;
import java.awt.event.ActionEvent;
import java.awt.event.WindowAdapter;
import java.awt.event.WindowEvent;
import java.rmi.RemoteException;

import javax.naming.InitialContext;
import javax.naming.NamingException;

import masteringrmi.helloactivate.interfaces.HelloWorld;
```

This client class imports a number of classes that are related to the Abstract Windowing Toolkit (AWT), which is used to construct the GUI. The toolkit is not discussed in any detail because it is only used to call your server, and this is a book about RMI, not how to construct GUIs.

Let's take a look at the main client code.

```
public class HelloClient
    extends Frame
{
    /**
     *    The response will be shown in this label
     */
    Label response = new Label();

    /**
     *    Press this button to say hello again
     */
    Button helloButton = new Button("Say hello again!");

    /**
     *    Keep track of how many times we have called the server
     */
    int iteration = 1; // Always call one time

    /**
     *    A reference to the server
     */
    HelloWorld server;
```

The client now extends `java.awt.Frame` so that you get a window into which you can show the GUI. You have a `java.awt.Label` that shows the replies from the server, and also a button that you can push. When the button is pushed, the server is called. An attribute has also been added, which keeps track of how many times the server has been called. Finally, there is a reference to the server's stub, which you use to communicate with the server.

The main method of this application is as follows.

```
public static void main(String[] args)
{
    new HelloClient();
}
```

No surprises in this method. You simply instantiate the client.

The next code snippet shows the constructor, which sets up the security manager, initializes the GUI, looks up the server's stub, and makes an initial call to it.

```
public HelloClient()
{
    System.setProperty("java.security.policy",
                        getClass().
                        getResource("/client.policy").toString());
    System.setSecurityManager(new SecurityManager());

    // Setup GUI
    add("Center",response);
    add("South",helloButton);

    helloButton.addActionListener(new ActionListener()
    {
        public void actionPerformed(ActionEvent evt)
        {
            // Call server again and show response
            sayHello();
        }
    });

    addWindowListener(new WindowAdapter()
    {
        public void windowClosing(WindowEvent evt)
        {
            System.exit(0);
        }
    });

    pack();
    show();
```

Why is a security manager needed? The reason is that you want to use dynamic classloading to access the class of the RMI stub. So, you first set the policy to be used (which, in this case, grants all permissions to all code), and then install a security manager to enforce it.

You have now also created the GUI for this client. You have a label to show responses with and a button to call the server with. You have also defined that any attempt to close the window will also exit this client.

```
try
{
    // Locate remote object
    server =
        (HelloWorld)new InitialContext().lookup(HelloWorld.NAME);

    // Call server and show response
    sayHello();
} catch (NamingException e)
{
        response.setText("The server could not be found");
        e.printStackTrace(System.err);
} catch (Exception e)
{
    response.setText(e.getMessage());
    e.printStackTrace(System.err);
}
}
```

The lookup is a bit of magic, courtesy of JNDI. As you can see, the only thing you need is the name of the object that you have bound. But where should you look for it on the network? There is no mention of where to find it! The answer is that JNDI automatically looks for the `jndi.properties` file in which you have defined the property `java.naming.provider.url`. In this case, the property has the value `rmi://localhost`. So, in reality, the full name is not only the value of `HelloWorld.NAME` (which is `helloactivate`), but rather `rmi://localhost/helloactivate`.

The last part of the client takes care of what happens when the button in the GUI is pushed. The code is invoked from the action listener that you defined in the constructor of the client.

```
public void sayHello()
{
    try
    {
        response.setText(server.helloWorld("World ("+iteration+")"));
        iteration++;
    } catch (Exception e)
    {
        response.setText("The object could not be called");
        e.printStackTrace(System.err);
    }
}
```

As you can see, all the preceding code does is call the server and show the response in the GUI. If an error occurs, then an error message is shown. One important aspect in this code snippet is that if the server fails, you will get exceptions upon calling the server, and normally, you would have to perform some kind of reconnect logic. Because you are using activation, the object identifier that is contained within the remote object stub is persistent in the sense that when you restart the RMI daemon, it assigns this identifier to the activatable remote object. Your calls will then automatically start working by virtue of the reconnect functionality contained in the activatable remote references. Practical, right?

Running the Example

Now that you have all the classes, you need to know how to start this system. Although most of this is fairly straightforward, and all the necessary details are contained in the scripts included in the example on the accompanying CD, I will go through the steps because it is interesting to see exactly what happens at each step.

The first step is to start the RMI daemon, which is the execution manager in an activation scenario. This is done by executing the tool *rmid*, which is located in the /bin directory of the JDK or the Java Runtime Environment (JRE) installation. When you do this the first time, it creates a log directory in which files containing information about all the registered activatable objects are kept.

You can specify where this log directory should be located by using the -log switch. If you want to have several RMI daemons running, you need to use the -port switch to differentiate between them. Refer to the JDK documentation for more details.

Note also that the name "log" is slightly misleading. It is not really a log of events that is placed in this directory, but rather it is where the RMI daemon places the persistent information about the registered activatable objects and activation groups. Perhaps the name "state" would have been better.

Next, start the RMI registry by executing the tool *rmiregistry*, which is also located in the /bin directory of the JDK or JRE installation. Once you have the two main modules of the system running, the last important piece of the puzzle is to start the Web server to be used for dynamic classloading. You may of course use any Web server you want, but one has been provided on the CD, which is sufficient for most uses. You start it by issuing the following command (from the /bin directory of the supplied example).

```
java -jar ../lib/ext/dynaserver.jar
```

This Web server allows a client to access any class in the Web server's classpath. The configuration file for the Web server, /lib/ext/dynaserver.properties, has been set to add the file /bin/setup.jar to the classpath, and because all the necessary classes are provided in this JAR, you have everything you need.

At this point, you have a working base system, but it is not yet coupled to your specific application. The next step is to run the setup application in order to register the activatable object with the RMI daemon. Execute the following command to complete this step.

```
java -jar setup.jar
```

The setup.jar file is constructed to execute the setup class you created. When this is done, the activatable remote object identifier is created and registered with the RMI daemon, and a copy of the stub pointing to this object is placed within the RMI registry. Because the registry requires the classes that were used to create the stub, it acquires these from the Web server because you have designated it as the RMI codebase.

Note however that at this point, the object has only been registered, not created. Although the activatable description says that the object should be reactivated when the RMI daemon is restarted, it does not mean that the activatable object should be created upon registration. This subtle feature makes it mandatory for your setup to also register the activatable objects stub into the registry—something that otherwise could have been done automatically when the object was created.

Because the setup class receives a stub to the activatable object, an alternative solution would be for your setup class to call a dummy method on the activatable in order to cause it to be created. This would force it to be registered in the RMI registry because this is done in your constructor code.

After the setup has finished, it is possible to start the client, which is done by executing the following command from the /bin directory of the example.

```
java -jar client.jar
```

This command starts the client, which locates the stub in the registry and makes a call to it. At this point, the stub does not have a live reference to the activatable, so it has to ask the RMI daemon for a reference. Because this is the first time the activatable remote server object is being asked for, it has not yet been created. Hence, this is then done. But because the activation group that the object has been associated with is not currently available, a new JVM is spawned to host it. Once this has been done, the activation group creates the remote object and registers it as active with the RMI daemon, which is then able to return a live reference to the client. The stub is then able to complete the call to the remote object.

The entire scenario is shown in Figure 6.2.

Summary

This chapter dealt with the concept of activation of remote objects. Primarily, activation solves two issues: It provides persistent object identifiers, and it allows remote objects to be activated on demand. By using activation, an RMI application becomes much more fault tolerant and is easier to maintain over time. Stubs do not become invalid simply because the server stops.

You looked at the pieces of the activation system, at the heart of which are activation groups and activatables. Activation groups represent all activatable objects within a particular JVM, and an activatable is simply a remote object that can be activated through the activation system. You were introduced to the RMI daemon, which is responsible for dealing with the registration and actual management of the activatable objects.

After having looked into the details of the activation system, you converted your previous constructed example into one that used activation. As previously shown, there are two steps necessary to do this. First, you

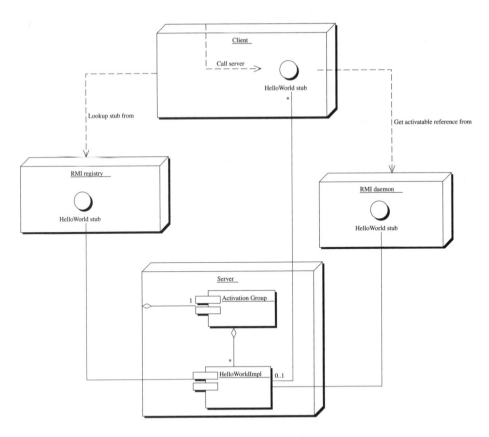

Figure 6.2 Activation example overview.

changed the remote object to include a special constructor that was to be used by the activation system. In this constructor, you exported the object to use activation instead of normal RMI, and you also bound the remote objects stub into the RMI registry in case the registry had previously shutdown. Although this particular strategy used explicit exporting of your remote object, you could instead have inherited the class `java.rmi.activation.Activatable` to accomplish the same thing.

Second, you changed the manager application. This result was quite different from how it used to work. First of all, you called it a setup application because it was only run once and did not stay alive for the duration of the remote object. Neither did it run any of the additional services that you needed in your system. These were instead run as stand-alone applications. The setup application primarily did two things: It created an activation group within which you could create activatable objects, and it created a descriptor of your activatable remote object, which was registered in the activation group. Both of these were then associated with the RMI daemon, so that they could be activated automatically later on. In the last part of the setup application, you also registered the stub of the activatable object in the RMI registry, so that any clients could access it and cause the object to be activated when called. Lastly, you looked at some of the practical aspects of running this system.

And this is pretty much all there is to say about activation. Now that you have quite a good understanding of all the features of RMI, it is time to put them to work by constructing some interesting examples. This is the topic of Part Three of this book and will cover many important tricks involved with RMI.

Creating Real Applications

In the previous parts of the book, client/server architectures in general and the specific features of RMI were discussed. Now let's put this knowledge to use in this third part by creating a couple of complete applications.

Chapter 7 walks you through the creation of a complete chat application including a chat server and a chat applet. The main topics focus on RMI callbacks, how to build robust and extensible client/server contracts, how to handle errors, and how to solve a couple of performance problems. These are some of the main design issues that you are most likely to run into once you start working with larger RMI applications. Some common distributed design patterns are demonstrated as well as some techniques and practices that are useful to your projects.

Chapter 8 is dedicated to creating a system for mobile agents, which are objects that can move between servers in order to perform some task. Some interesting uses of the RMI framework are shown, such as advanced dynamic classloading and special uses of the RMI serialization semantics.

After this part, not only will you know how to use RMI, but you will also know how to use it intelligently. As you will notice in these chapters to come, there are many ways to do things, and these chapters will only show you a limited number of them. As with all design patterns, they have their benefits and consequences, but the ones discussed in these chapters do not have any major drawbacks.

CHAPTER 7

Developing a Chat Application

L et's begin this excursion into applied RMI by creating a chat application. The purpose of the chat is to let various users talk to each other in real time by sending messages to various topics. All users who are watching a topic then receive the messages that are sent to that topic. This is illustrated in Figure 7.1.

For example, all messages sent to the topic "Some topic" are sent to all listeners registered with that particular topic, which in this case is Client 1 and Client 2. This is the basic idea, and you will explore one of the possible designs of such a system in this chapter.

This application is a somewhat more complex example of what you can do with RMI, and it allows you to highlight some interesting issues. As you will see, there are a couple of design principles that often can be applied that make your application perform better and make it easier to maintain. Using RMI as an abstraction to the network services makes it very easy to implement this system, and as you will see, the final source code for this system is quite small. Ease of development and maintainability are sometimes more important features than pure performance, but you will see how you can achieve all of these features.

Now, let's take a look at the overall design of the system. What components are there, and how do they relate to each other?

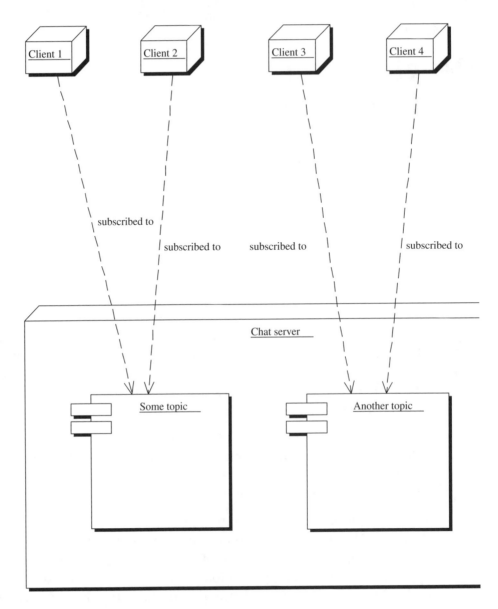

Figure 7.1 Chat scenario.

Overview of Chat Design

There are, as usual, two main parts involved: the client and the server. These two, and the parts they contain, are depicted in Figure 7.2.

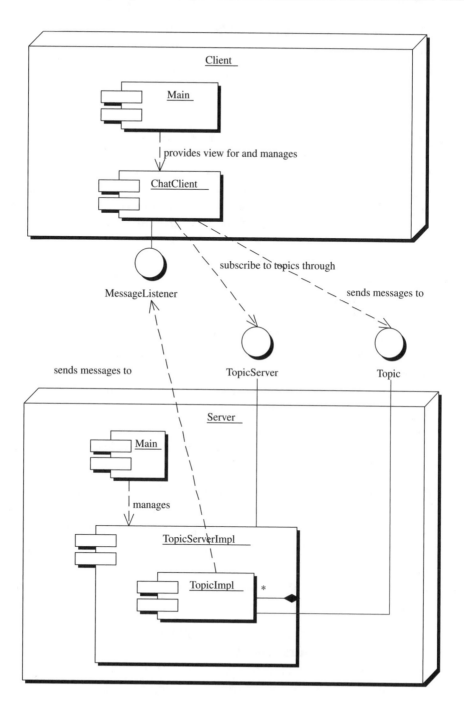

Figure 7.2 Chat system design.

The server has a manager class, `Main`, that is responsible for setting up the environment that the chat server is going to need (for example, start registry and Web server for dynamic classloading) and also loads any configuration that has been set.

TIP

As in all the previous examples, by putting this kind of code in a separate class, it becomes easier to adapt the system to change. For example, later on you might want to run the chat server together with other functionality in the same JVM, or you might want to use some other way to configure it. Then, all you have to do is change or replace the manager. The core of the system implementation can remain unchanged, allowing you to use it with both the new and the old way to manage it.

The server also has a couple of classes that implement the actual chat server. There is one class, `TopicServerImpl`, that represents the server as a whole. For each topic, there is an instance of the class `TopicImpl`, which manages the list of clients that are listening to it and makes sure that messages are properly sent to them. The class `Listener` is used to encapsulate all information that the server has about a user. There is also a class called `MessageQueue`, which holds all messages that are pending for delivery to clients. What queues are, how they work, and why you would want to have them is explained in the section "The TopicServerImpl Class." Lastly, the server uses a class called `Worker` to help it with delivering messages. Workers are also explained in "The TopicServerImpl Class."

The client consists of only two classes: `ChatClient` takes care of the client's interaction with the server. It also manages a model of the server state. The class `ChatGUI` is an applet that takes care of the client GUI and also uses the `ChatClient` to talk to the server. The idea is that if you want to provide another graphical representation of the client, you can simply change or replace the `ChatGUI` class without having to change the `ChatClient` class.

Now you have both the server and client, and the only significant part that is left is the contract between the two. The contract is defined in the classes `ListenerInfo`, `TopicInfo`, and `Message` and the remote interfaces `TopicServer`, `Topic`, and `MessageListener`.

The `ListenerInfo` class encapsulates information that describes the client, such as the user's name. The `TopicInfo` class is used to encapsulate information about each topic, such as its name and description.

The `Message`class is the core information packet in this system and is used to send messages between clients and topics.

The remote interfaces are used for defining the remote objects' contracts. The `TopicServerImpl` class, naturally, implements the `TopicServer` remote interface through which clients can access the server as a whole in order to list available topics and subscribe to them. The `TopicImpl` class implements the `Topic` remote interface and is used by clients to send messages to the topic as well as to get information about the other listeners subscribed to that topic. Finally, `ChatClient` implements the `MessageListener` interface, which lets the server send messages to the client. So, in this scenario, you have remote objects both on the server and on the client. The reason for this is explained later, in the section "The MessageListener Remote Interface."

Now let's take a closer look at these classes and interfaces, one at a time. Let's begin with the contract classes, which are the remote interfaces and data classes, after which you will look at the server classes, and finally round off with the client. All contract classes and interfaces are located in the package `masteringrmi.chat.interfaces`, the client classes are located in the package `masteringrmi.chat.client`, and the server classes are located in the package `masteringrmi.chat.server` package. Note that package and import listings have been omitted from the code listings for brevity.

The TopicServer Remote Interface

The topic server is a remote object, which is going to be accessed by RMI clients. To be able to do this, you need a remote interface that it, and its stub, can implement. This is the purpose of the `TopicServer` interface, which is shown as follows.

```
public interface TopicServer
   extends Remote
{
   // Public ---------------------------------------------------
   public Collection getTopicInfos()
      throws RemoteException;

   public void addListener(ListenerInfo info, MessageListener callBack)
      throws RemoteException;

   public void removeListener(ListenerInfo info)
      throws RemoteException;
```

```
    public Topic subscribe(TopicInfo topic, ListenerInfo info)
        throws RemoteException;

    public void unsubscribe(TopicInfo topic, ListenerInfo info)
        throws RemoteException;
}
```

To start off with, the interface extends `java.rmi.Remote`, as is expected because this is how RMI identifies remote objects. The next method, `getTopicInfos`, is used to retrieve a collection of `TopicInfo` objects that describe the topics that are available. Next, there are methods for adding and removing message listeners, that is, chat clients. A `ListenerInfo` object contains information about the client, such as the name of the user, as well as a reference to the client. The callback is a remote stub to the client that is used by the server to send messages to the client.

The last two methods in the `TopicServer` interface allow clients to subscribe to the various topics on the server. By doing this, the topic server associates the client with the topic. Any messages sent to the topic are distributed to all clients that have subscribed to the topic.

As usual, all the methods in this interface throw a `java.rmi.RemoteException`. As it happens, none of the implementation methods throw this exception or any of its subclasses, so if it is thrown from the stub, it is only due to communication problems in the RMI layer.

The Topic Remote Interface

One of the core concepts in this application is that of a topic. Because you model these as remote objects that clients can communicate with, you now introduce a remote interface for that purpose.

Once a client has connected to the chat server and has decided which topic to use, it acquires a stub to a topic, which is a remote object that implements the `Topic` interface. The code for the `Topic` interface is shown as follows.

```
public interface Topic
    extends Remote
{
    public void publishMessage(Message message)
        throws RemoteException;
```

```
public Collection getListenerInfos()
   throws RemoteException;
}
```

The `publishMessage` method is used to publish a message to the topic, which is to be sent to all other clients that have subscribed to that particular topic. The `getListenerInfos` method can be used to retrieve information about the other clients. This method can be used by a GUI to show a listing of the other participants that have subscribed to the topic.

TIP

One of the most important design strategies for how remote interfaces are designed can be noted at this point. The publishMessage method only takes a Message object as a parameter. What if it instead accepted all attributes of a Message as input? How would that impact your design? The most important point is the question: What if the contents of a message change? If you designed your remote interface to take the attributes as parameters, you would have to change the interface, the object that implements this interface, and all clients that use this interface. In addition, if this system was already in use, you would have to re-create stubs according to the new interface and redistribute them to the clients (unless dynamic classloading was used).

But, because this is not the case, you do not have to change anything other than how messages are created and used in the end. The way they are sent throughout the system remains unchanged. By using data objects that encapsulate this information, you have made your interface significantly more stable and long lived. This line of reasoning has also been used for the listener information and topic information objects and how they are passed between the client and server.

This notion of data objects is extremely useful in distributed systems and should be used as often as possible.

The MessageListener Remote Interface

A remote object in the client implements the `MessageListener` remote interface so that the server can send messages to it.

Hang on a minute, the client has a remote object? Well, yes, the thing is that in this scenario not only does the server have a remote object; the client also has one, so that the server can call it when it needs to send a message to it.

It used to be the case that you could state that the part of the system that held a remote object was a server, but it is not that simple anymore. In this case, what you call the server will also be a client to what you have defined as client. So, both the client and the server are clients and servers. This goes back to the way the words "client" and "server" were defined in Chapter 1. Both use services provided by the other.

When a client registers itself with the server like this, the stub to the client's remote object is said to be a *callback*. The server can then use it to call back to the client if necessary. In this particular case, you could have chosen a design that does not need a callback by letting the client continuously ask the server if there are any new messages for it. This type of process is called *polling*, but should in general be avoided because it is a rather costly way to get messages. The method you are using in this example is called *push* because the server actively pushes the messages from a topic to a client by using the callback to the client. I will show you what the callback looks like when we design the client implementation in the section " The ChatClient Class." The code for this remote interface follows.

```
public interface MessageListener
   extends Remote
{
   public void messagePublished(Message message)
      throws RemoteException;

   public void messagePublished(Collection messages)
      throws RemoteException;
}
```

The first `messagePublished` method of the remote interface is used by the server to send a single message to the listener, which in this case is the chat client applet. Because the message object encapsulates all relevant information, there is no need for any additional parameters. The second `messagePublished` method is used to send a collection of messages to the client. The reason for this method is mainly to increase server throughput, that is, the rate at which the server handles messages. This topic is discussed further when you deal with the message queue implementation in the section "The MessageQueue Class."

TIP

As you can see, I have used the java.util.Collection interface as method parameter instead of the actual implementation class that the message queue is using. The reason for this is that by using an interface for the contract between the client and

Polling versus Pushing

The two principles that you can use to allow clients to receive messages from the server are called push and poll. With pushing, the server actively sends messages directly to the client, similar to what the postman does to deliver messages to your mailbox. With polling, the client continuously checks the server for new messages, similar to what you do every morning when you check your mailbox. Although the purpose of these two principles is the same ("You got mail"), their characteristics are quite different.

Pushing does not utilize much processing resources because it only does things when it is absolutely necessary, that is, when there really are messages to deliver. However, usually it is not possible for the server to establish a socket connection to the client, for example, if the client is an applet, which means that the client has to create the connection to the server through which the messages will be delivered. The drawback of this is that if you have many clients, for example, 100 000, then there will be an equal number of open connections to the server, and because they each use up a certain amount of memory, the server will most likely crash from out of memory problems. If you have a limited number of clients or if you can cluster the server so that the connections are not all made to the same physical machine, then the situation is much better.

Polling has the opposite characteristics. The continuous checking by the client utilizes both processing resources on the server as well as network bandwidth. This is typically solved by using a sufficiently powerful server CPU and a big fat network connection. If the client polls too often and the server is not that powerful, it may be the case that the server never gets anything, but instead says, "No, there are still no messages for you." The length of the poll interval is hence crucial and often takes quite a lot of testing to get right. On the other hand, the connections between the client and server are only established during the time of the poll, so the server will not crash because of too many simultaneous connections.

These are the general characteristics of these two callback principles. Which one you should choose in your particular system is dependent on the previously mentioned factors, so be sure you understand the preceding information and make an educated decision in each case.

To illustrate how complex this can be, many of you may remember the somewhat disastrous "Web push" technology a couple of years ago. The idea was to push Web content to clients without having them actively seek it out. The callback principle used was poll (not the one that the technology name implied), but the early implementations failed miserably. Why? Because the HTTP 1.1 transfer protocol was used, which had the neat feature that it allowed Web server connections to be long lived, so that you could get several Web pages through one

continues

> socket connection. This was great for regular surfing, but for a poll system, it did not work well when thousands of people wanted active content. In effect, you got the CPU and network characteristics of poll as well as the memory usage characteristics of push. The result was obviously not so good.

server, I can choose the implementation of Collection that best fits the server implementation. If I later change the implementation of how message queues deliver messages in terms of what Collection class is used, the remote interface remains unchanged.

You should try to use interfaces in this way as much as possible to ensure that you do not have to change it if your implementation of the interface changes.

As usual, this interface extends the `java.rmi.Remote` interface, and the methods throw `java.rmi.RemoteException`.

The ListenerInfo Class

The `ListenerInfo` class is one of the data objects in the contract between the client and the server. As stated earlier in this chapter, the data object pattern is very useful, so you can apply it in this code. The `ListenerInfo` class encapsulates all information that a client needs to register with the server when it logs on. The code is as follows.

```
public class ListenerInfo
    implements java.io.Serializable
{
```

First of all, it needs to be serializable. Why? Because you are going to transfer it between the client and the server, and because it is not a remote object, it has to be transformed to a series of bytes, that is, serialized.

```
String name;
```

In this version of the chat system, the only information that is kept about the client is the name of the user. If you want to, you can easily extend this to include an e-mail address, a phone number, or whatever. Because all interfaces have been designed to accept `ListenerInfo` objects, any such changes will have a minimal impact on the code. That is why I have chosen to create a `ListenerInfo` class instead of simply using a `java.lang.String` to pass the user name. It does take more effort initially, but it will pay off when I want to expand the system to hold more information about the user.

```
public ListenerInfo(String name)
{
    this.name = name;
}
```

This is the constructor of this data object, and it simply assigns the attributes of this object.

```
public String getName() { return name; }
```

You provide an accessor to the attribute. Note that once the object has been created, there is no way to change its attributes; there are no "set" methods. This makes the object immutable. An immutable object is one that is read-only. The only way to change it is to create a new object with new values.

```
public String toString() { return name; }

public boolean equals(Object obj)
{
    return ((ListenerInfo)obj).getName().equals(name);
}

public int hashCode()
{
    return name.hashCode();
}
}
```

The `equals` and `hashCode` method implementations are necessary because this object is used in a hash table to keep track of all the connected clients. Hash tables, in general, use the `hashCode` method to determine the general location of a key within the table, and then use the `equals` method to find its exact location.

The TopicInfo Class

The `ListenerInfo` class was used by the client to identify itself with the server, and similarly, the `TopicInfo` is also a data object that is used by the server to hand out descriptions of the topics that are available.

It contains all the relevant information about a topic, such as its name as well as a brief description of the topic. The code is as follows.

```java
public class TopicInfo
    implements java.io.Serializable
{
    String name;
    String description;
```

This class is also used as a data carrier and must therefore be serializable. It contains two attributes, which can be used by the client GUI to present information about this topic to the user.

```java
public TopicInfo(String name, String description)
{
    this.name = name;
    this.description = description;
}
```

The constructor simply takes all the attributes as parameters and assigns them accordingly.

```java
public String getName()
{
    return name;
}

public String getDescription()
{
    return description;
}
```

As with the previous data classes, you provide accessors to the fields, but with no set methods because the information is immutable. It would not make much sense if a client tried to change a `TopicInfo` object because the client only holds a copy of it, and hence the values would be unchanged at the server.

```java
public String toString()
{
    return name;
}

public boolean equals(Object obj)
{
    return ((TopicInfo)obj).getName().equals(name);
}
```

```
public int hashCode()
{
    return name.hashCode();
}
}
```

Finally, you provide implementations of the `toString`, `equals`, and `hashCode` methods. As you can see, you are using the name of the topic to identify it; hence, these methods delegate to the respective methods in `java.lang.String`.

The Message Class

The `Message` class is by far the most central class in this example. It is the main information carrier that is used by both the client and the server components to communicate.

This warrants some extra thought as to the design and implementation of the class. Specifically, you would want to make sure that it is transferred as fast as possible because you will be sending around instances of it quite a lot. It would also be desirable to be able to update the chat system with new functionality without having to change such a core class.

Let's begin with the structure of the message. Each message has three attributes: the sender, which is the name of the user that sent it; the type, which indicates the semantics of the message; and finally the content of the message. The content can be any object, but in most cases is a string. What that string means is determined by looking at the type of the message.

The type of the message has been chosen to be a simple string. The reason for this is to make it as extensible as possible. The idea is that the available set of types can be changed if necessary. For example, the standard type is "Text," which is what all chat messages will use. Then there are the types "UserJoined" and "UserLeft," which are used by messages sent by the server itself to denote that someone just joined or left the topic that the client has subscribed to.

However, the client should only deal with those messages that it understands and throw away the rest. To exemplify this, I have let the current client GUI introduce a custom message type "IsTyping." A message of this type is sent as soon as the user starts typing in a message to be sent.

Other clients can then let the GUI show this message by, for example, marking that particular user's name in a different color. Clients that do not have this ability, for example, text-only clients or similar simpler clients, can safely ignore messages of this type.

You can use this technique to introduce new types of messages, but because it is such a flexible system, it is not critical that all users' clients are upgraded to understand the new messages. This is a useful example of how you should think when designing your system. Always design so that you have the option to add new features later on. You will thank yourself later on if you do and curse yourself if you do not.

Without further ado, the code for the `Message` class is as follows. Let's then dissect it in order to make sure all issues are addressed properly.

```
public final class Message
    implements java.io.Serializable
{
    private static final long serialVersionUID = 1L;
```

As usual, the class implements the `java.io.Serializable` interface to denote that objects of this class can be serialized into byte streams, and then transformed back into `Message` objects when needed.

The serial version UID is new though. This is basically a versioning system where the number denotes the version of this class. When you send serializable objects, the version number is automatically computed for you. Although the overhead for this computation is not great, it can be substantial if it is frequently done. Because this is the case in messages, it has been assigned manually for use by the serialization process. I have simply designated it as version 1, but you can also use the tool *serialver*, which is provided in the JDK, to compute the version of a class. This tool basically inspects your class and creates a number based on the attributes and methods in the class. If you later make a compatible change to the class, that is, you add a field or method, then running the tool on the new class will yield a version number that denotes it as being compatible with the old one. By doing this, you will be able to serialize objects with the old class and deserialize them with the new one. A means of upgrading the object, so to speak.

Because I have used a design that allows me to add new semantics to a `Message` without changing the actual class, I have decided to simply use my own versioning system and set the version to 1.

The following are a couple of predefined senders and message types.

```
// Predefined name for messages sent from the system
public static final String SYSTEM = "System";

// Predefined types of messages
// This is the most common type: a text message
public static final String TEXT = "Text";

// Predefined types for control messages
public static final String TOPIC_CREATED = "TopicCreated";
public static final String TOPIC_REMOVED = "TopicRemoved";

public static final String USER_JOINED = "UserJoined";
public static final String USER_LEFT = "UserLeft";

public static final String GREETING  = "Greeting";
```

The preceding code begins with defining a special username "System," which is used by all messages to clients that did not originate from another user, but originated from the system itself. These are typically treated differently from other messages as they usually have a special meaning.

You then define a couple of special types of messages. As discussed earlier, the "TopicCreated" and "TopicRemoved" types are used by the server to notify clients when topics have been created or removed. The type "Greeting" is used by the server to send a greeting to the client when it first connects to the server. All of these messages are sent with the sender set as "System."

```
String sender;
String type;
Object content;

// Constructors -------------------------------------------------
public Message(String sender, String type, Object content)
{
    this.sender = sender;
    this.type = type;
    this.content = content;
}
```

As you can see, the three attributes are the sender, the type, and the content in the form of an object. The constructor simply assigns these values respectively.

```
public String getSender()
{
   return sender;
}

public String getType()
{
   return type;
}

public Object getContent()
{
   return content;
}
```

The usual accessors are added, making the object immutable. Note that the client has to cast the content to its specific class depending on the type of the message. If you want, you can, for example, modify this chat system to send pictures of the users or icons to be inserted into the text. Because the class of the content is not strictly defined, this allows for quite a bit of freedom in what to send.

```
private void writeObject(java.io.ObjectOutputStream out)
   throws java.io.IOException
{
   out.writeUTF(sender);
   out.writeUTF(type);
   out.writeObject(content);
}

private void readObject(java.io.ObjectInputStream in)
   throws java.io.IOException, ClassNotFoundException
{
   sender = in.readUTF();
   type   = in.readUTF();
   content = in.readObject();
}
}
```

The preceding code is the optimized serialization code. Instead of letting the serialization process figure out on its own what attributes to serialize, you do it explicitly as was described in Chapter 2. This is significantly faster, but because it adds some code, you should only do it with those classes where it really counts. The `Message` class definitely falls into that category because of its frequent use.

You are now finished with the contract classes and can move on to the classes that are used by the chat server.

The Listener Class

The Listener class is simply used to contain all information about a client: its user information, the callback, and the message queue. It can be used internally to keep track of each client.

```
class Listener
{
    ListenerInfo info;
    MessageListener listener;
    MessageQueue queue;

    public Listener(ListenerInfo info, MessageListener listener)
    {
        this.info = info;
        this.listener = listener;
        this.queue = new MessageQueue(this);
    }

    public ListenerInfo getInfo()
    {
        return info;
    }

    public MessageListener getListener()
    {
        return listener;
    }

    public MessageQueue getMessageQueue()
    {
        return queue;
    }
}
```

You keep track of all the client related information including creating a new queue onto which you can post messages to be sent to the client. The constructor simply assigns the attributes. You also have accessors so that you can use this information.

The TopicServerImpl Class

The main server object is the class TopicServerImpl. As the name implies, it is a remote object class that implements the interface Topic-Server. There is only one instance of this class in the server, that is, it is a singleton, and it has the following responsibilities:

- **Manages topics.** Topics can be created, and clients are able to get a listing of available topics.

- **Manages topic subscriptions.** A client can subscribe to a topic so that it will receive messages sent to the topic. When a client wants to change to a new topic, it first unsubscribes from the current topic before subscribing to the new one.

- **Manages clients.** The topic server manages a list of active clients. The first thing that happens when a new client connects to the server is that it is registered with the topic server. This allows the server to send generic messages to the client that are not directly related to a particular topic, such as the greeting that has been set for the server.

- **Sends messages to clients.** When a client sends a message to a topic, that is, publishes a message, the topic asks the server to deliver the message to all clients that have subscribed to that topic. The server then takes care of the actual forwarding and delivery of the message.

Now that you have covered the high-level design of the server, let's take a look at the implementation of the server. You will also want to read the sidebars as they contain important conceptual explanations of the techniques that I will be using.

Let's start looking at the implementation of the TopicServer, which will then lead to worker threads and message queues.

```
public class TopicServerImpl
    implements TopicServer
{
```

You begin by stating that the class is implementing the TopicServer remote interface, hence, denoting objects of this class as remote objects. However, note that because this class does not inherit from java.rmi.server.UnicastRemoteObject, it is not automatically exported to RMI, so this is something that you have to do explicitly. This is not necessarily a bad thing. This allows you to keep all things related to managing the server, including exporting it, in a separate class.

```
Map topics = new HashMap();
Map listeners = new HashMap();
```

Message Queues

Sending messages to clients requires a detailed explanation as this is the most complex part of the server. There are various algorithms that can be used to distribute a message to all clients, and they have very different characteristics in terms of performance.

The first, most simplistic way to do this is to immediately redistribute an incoming message to all listeners, so that when the client's call to the server returns, the message has been sent to all the other clients subscribed to that topic. But what happens then? Basically, the client that sent the message has to wait while the message is being delivered to everybody else. If any of the other clients have a relatively slow connection to the server, then this could take quite some time. The client that sent the message will probably start to wonder why such a simple operation as sending a message is taking so long. Therefore, this is not a very good idea.

So, what do you do? Well, the common solution is to add *queues*. When a message comes in from a client, it is put on a queue. The call then returns to the client, and the client can continue. The client knows that the message has at least been sent to the server, although it has most likely not yet been delivered to all the other clients that have subscribed to the topic. The message can then be taken from the queue later on to be processed.

You maintain two maps, one of which contains the currently available topics, and the other contains the currently registered clients. The topics are mapped to their `TopicInfo` data objects (recall that you implemented `equals` and `hashCode` methods earlier; this is where they become useful), and the listeners are mapped to their `ListenerInfo`.

```
String greeting = "Welcome to the 'Mastering RMI' chatserver!";

LinkedList queueList = new LinkedList();

int port = 0;
```

You have a string that contains the standard greeting to be sent to clients that register with the chat server. You also have a linked list of message queues. This is used to send messages to clients later on. Basically, when a message is to be sent to a client, the message is inserted into its queue,

Worker Threads

Now that you have the message in a queue, how do you distribute it to all the clients that are registered to that topic? To do this, you add *worker threads*. A worker thread is a thread that performs some piece of work repeatedly. In this case, it looks at the queue and checks whether there is a message to deliver. If there is a message, it takes the message off the queue and tries to send it to the destination. Typically, you have a pool in the server containing a number of worker threads that can work concurrently.

So far so good. Now the question is, how many worker threads should you have and how should they deliver messages? One option is to have worker threads assigned to each topic. When a message is sent to the topic, a worker thread takes it and tries to send it to all listening clients, one at a time. However, this suffers from the same problem as the initial solution: If one of the listening clients is slow, then the delivery to that client is going to take a significant amount of time. This means that the other clients will perceive the server as being slow, but in reality, it is one of the clients that is holding back the process. One other problem is that if there are many topics and each of them have a couple of worker threads, you will run out of memory quite soon because threads are somewhat heavyweights when it comes to memory usage.

Another problem is *thrashing*. If there are a lot of topics and they all have a couple of worker threads trying to deliver messages to the listeners as fast as possible, there will be so many threads that the JVM will spend most of its time switching between these threads. Very little time will be spent on actually performing useful work. This phenomenon is known as thrashing and limits the scalability of the server. It is obviously something you want to avoid as much as possible.

So, assigning worker threads to each topic is not a good idea. What about assigning a worker thread to each client? Then a slow client would not stop messages from being delivered to other, faster clients. Well, this solution has the same thrashing problems as the previous solution, although it's even worse because there are typically quite a lot of clients connected to the server, whereas there are typically relatively few topics.

The last option is to let the worker threads operate on the server level. When a message is published to a topic by a client, the topic tells the server to distribute this message to all the clients subscribed to that topic, and the server then has a pool of worker threads that performs this for the topic. Because the server manages all of the worker threads, the pool can be kept at a reasonable size in order to avoid thrashing and to keep memory usage to a minimum. Also, the problem with slow clients are now minimized because the same message can be delivered to different clients simultaneously by several worker threads running in parallel. This is the solution used in this example, and is in fact, the way most messaging servers work.

and the queue is then placed on this linked list. The worker threads then repeatedly take queues off of the list and send the messages to the clients. There is also an attribute for which port to export this server to. The default value of zero denotes "choose any port."

```
public TopicServerImpl(int workers)
{
    System.out.println("Creating "+workers+" worker threads");
    for (int i = 0; i < workers; i++)
    {
        Thread worker = new Thread(new Worker(this));
        worker.setDaemon(true);
        worker.start();
    }
}
```

The constructor is responsible for creating the worker threads that perform the delivery of the messages. The number of workers to create is read from the system properties by the manager class, which is described in the section "The Main Class." If you want, you can add functionality that tries to change the number of workers dynamically, depending on the load on the server.

How many workers should you have? The intuitive answer is to have as many as possible because that is what you would do in real life to get as much done as possible (some of you may have a contrary opinion, however). The real answer is given later on in this chapter (in the section "The MessageQueue Class"), but for now, just keep in mind that all worker threads share the same CPU, so more is not always better because computing resources are finite.

```
public void setGreeting(String greeting)
{
    this.greeting = greeting;
}

public String getGreeting()
{
    return this.greeting;
}

public void setPort(int port)
{
    this.port = port;
}
```

```
public int getPort()
{
   return port;
}
```

In the preceding code, you have a couple of administrative attribute accessors that are used to configure the server. As you can see, this server is not tightly coupled to any particular configuration files. This is desirable because configuration files typically change. You may want to start with a simple properties file for configuration, and then change it later on to an XML file. By decoupling your service objects that perform the main functionality of your server from the management of it, you make it significantly easier to change your mind later on. Or, why not have several ways to configure it at the same time?

```
public synchronized Topic createTopic(TopicInfo info)
   throws IOException
{
   Topic newTopic = new TopicImpl(this, info);
   topics.put(info, newTopic);
   sendMessage(new Message(Message.SYSTEM,
                           Message.TOPIC_CREATED,
                           info));
   return newTopic;
}
```

This method is used to create new topics. It creates an instance of `TopicImpl`, which is a remote object that exports itself, and then registers itself in the map of topics. It then sends out a message to all clients, notifying them of the availability of the newly created topic.

Next comes the implementation of the remote interface TopicServer.

```
public synchronized Collection getTopicInfos()
{
   return new ArrayList(topics.keySet());
}
```

This method is used to return a collection of topic information objects. The only thing special about it is that it is `synchronized`. Why is this? Well, because the RMI system does not do anything to make sure that several clients do not call your remote object concurrently, you have to deal with this yourself. In this case, what could possibly go wrong if two clients accessed the server at the same time? Think about what would happen if you tried to get the list of topics at the same time that a topic was being created. It is possible that the copying of the topic list could be done at the same time a new topic was inserted into the data structure. Modifying a structure while it is being read by another thread can lead to undefined behavior and should be avoided. To make sure this does not happen, you use the `synchronized` keyword to only allow one thread at a time to use the server. Any other threads have to wait until the one using it completes.

```
public synchronized Topic subscribe(TopicInfo info,
                                    ListenerInfo clientInfo)
{
   TopicImpl topic = (TopicImpl)topics.get(info);
   topic.addListener((Listener)listeners.get(clientInfo));

   return topic;
}

public synchronized void unsubscribe(TopicInfo info,
                                     ListenerInfo clientInfo)
{
   TopicImpl topic = (TopicImpl)topics.get(info);
   topic.removeListener((Listener)listeners.get(clientInfo));
}
```

The preceding methods are used by clients to subscribe and unsubscribe from a particular topic. You use the mapping from topic information to actual topics to acquire the topic being subscribed to, and again you use the `synchronized` keyword to make sure that no inconsistencies in data structures can happen.

```
public synchronized void addListener(ListenerInfo info,
                                     MessageListener callBack)
{
   Listener listener = new Listener(info, callBack);
   MessageQueue queue = listener.getMessageQueue();

   // Add listener to map without interfering
   // with possible concurrent message dispatches
   Map newListeners = (Map)((HashMap)listeners).clone();
   newListeners.put(info, listener);
   listeners = newListeners;

   sendMessage(queue, new Message(Message.SYSTEM,
                                  Message.GREETING,
                                  greeting));
}
```

The `addListener` method is used to add new clients to the chat server. You first create a `Listener` object that encapsulates all information about the client, and then register this object in the map of clients.

TIP

How to deal with event listener queues is a common topic when dealing with graphical interfaces, such as AWT or Swing, but is also relevant here. The basic idea is to have a list of objects that are interested in a particular kind of event, which is modified by calling add and remove methods. Events are then distributed by simply enumerating the list and sending the event to each of the listeners.

However, what happens if a listener tries to add itself to the list while an event is being sent to the list? It is very likely that the message sending will fail because the list structure that it is currently using is changing due to either the addition or removal of a listener. One of the most common ways to deal with this is to make a copy of the list before an event is sent to each listener. This way there is no way that a modification to the list interferes with event sending. The problem with this is that for each event that is sent, a new copy of the list will be made, which is not good.

A better way to deal with this is to make a copy of the list when the list is modified, and then remove or add listeners to the new copy of the list. By doing this, a possible concurrent event dispatch will not be interfered with, and there is no unnecessary copying being done for each event.

In this example, the method clone is used to create a new copy, and then the listener is added or removed from this clone. The clone is then assigned to the map attribute so that the next time an event dispatch occurs this new list will be used.

```
public synchronized void removeListener(ListenerInfo info)
{
    // Remove listener
    Map newListeners = (Map)((HashMap)listeners).clone();
    Listener listener = (Listener)listeners.remove(info);
    listeners = newListeners;

    // Remove all topic subscriptions
    Iterator enum = topics.values().iterator();
    while (enum.hasNext())
    {
        ((TopicImpl)enum.next()).removeListener(listener);
    }

    // Remove all posted messages to this listener
    synchronized (queueList)
    {
        // remove returns true while queue found in queueList
        while(queueList.remove(listener.getMessageQueue()));
```

```
      }
   }
```

The `removeListener` operation uses the same principle with regard to how modifications to listener lists are handled. You also remove this listener from all topics in case it did not remove itself properly, as would be the case if the client crashed. In addition, all currently pending messages to the client are removed from the list of queues to handle.

The next set of methods deals with placing messages in queues and also makes sure that the queues are handed out to worker threads.

```
void sendMessage(Message message)
{
   sendMessage(listeners.values().iterator(), message);
}
```

This method is used to send out a message to all connected clients and is typically used by the server for general messages, such as to notify the clients about new topics. The method delegates to another method, which is as follows.

```
void sendMessage(Iterator queues, Message message)
{
   while (queues.hasNext())
   {
      MessageQueue queue = (MessageQueue)queues.next();
      sendMessage(queue, message);
   }
}
```

This method is used to send a particular message to a list of message queues. The list could either be that of all clients connected to a particular topic or all clients connected to this server. The method simply enumerates the list and sends the message to the individual queues by using the following method.

```
void sendMessage(MessageQueue queue, Message message)
{
   queue.add(message);

   synchronized (queueList)
   {
      if (!queueList.contains(queue))
      {
         queueList.addFirst(queue);
         queueList.notify();
      }
```

```
        }
    }
```

This method has two parts. First, the message is added to this particular queue. Second, you add this queue to the list of queues to be dealt with by worker threads, but only in case it is not already scheduled. If it is indeed placed on the list of queues, you call `notify`. What happens then? Well, the method that hands out queues to be used by worker threads uses the `wait` method on the list of message queues in case it is empty. Calling `notify` wakes it up so that it can continue to get a message queue and hand it out to a worker thread. This process is shown as follows.

```
MessageQueue getNextQueue()
{
    while(true)
    {
        MessageQueue queue;
        synchronized(queueList)
        {
            // Wait for message to arrive in queue
            while (queueList.isEmpty())
            {
                try
                {
                // Wait for sendMessage to call notify()
                    queueList.wait();
                } catch (InterruptedException e)
                {
                    // Ignore
                }
            }

            // Get queue
            try
            {
                queue = (MessageQueue)queueList.removeLast();
            } catch (NoSuchElementException e)
            {
                continue;
            }

            // More queues waiting?
            if (!queueList.isEmpty())
            {
                // Wake up another worker
                queueList.notify();
            }
```

```
         }

         return queue;
      }
   }
}
```

Worker threads that want a queue containing messages to deliver will call this method. It has two main parts: wait until there is a queue available, and then remove it and return it to the worker thread. Because many threads will be used concurrently in this method (all worker threads that want to get a queue), it is not sufficient to simply wait for the notification. You must also check whether another thread has been notified and has already removed a queue to work with. If that is the case, then you continue to wait. Similarly, if there are more queues available after you have taken one off the list, you notify other worker threads about this.

This concludes the main chat server class. Now let's take a look at the classes that implement queues and worker threads.

The MessageQueue Class

As explained earlier, queues are a must-have in any message based application that requires a high level of performance. The queue class used in this example follows. It basically wraps an instance of the `java.util.ArrayList` class. Messages that are added to the queue are inserted at the end of the list in order to preserve the order of the messages. This also happens to be a very cheap operation on `ArrayList`, so the performance of inserting a new message is negligible.

The source for the queue class is as follows.

```
class MessageQueue
{
   ArrayList messageQueue = new ArrayList();
   Listener listener;

   MessageQueue(Listener listener)
   {
      this.listener = listener;
   }
```

Notice that the class is declared as `package protected` because it will only be used by other classes in the server package. After that, you declare the internal queue to be used as well as an attribute to hold the listener that this queue is associated with. As explained earlier, each client has its own queue.

Next, let's look at the code for adding messages to the queue and sending them to the client.

```
synchronized void add(Message message)
{
    messageQueue.add(message);
}

synchronized int send()
    throws RemoteException
{
    int messageCount = messageQueue.size();

    // Check nr of messages to send
    if (messageCount == 1)
    {
        // Send the message
        listener.
                getListener().
                messagePublished((Message)messageQueue.get(0));
    } else
    {
        // Send all messages
        listener.
                getListener().
                messagePublished(messageQueue);
    }

    // Remove messages
    messageQueue.clear();

    return messageCount;
}
```

The two methods are `synchronized` to make sure that you are not adding and sending messages at the same time. Adding a message is fairly trivial and is simply a matter of delegating to the internal list of messages.

Sending a message is a bit more complicated. You must make a distinction between sending one message and several messages. If you are only sending one message, you use the remote message listener interface method that only takes a message as a parameter. If there is more than one message, you use the remote message listener interface method that takes a collection as a parameter. Because your internal list is an implementation of the `java.util.Collection` interface, you can send it as is without having to transfer the messages into an intermediate structure. When all messages have been sent, you clear the internal list and return the number of messages that was sent. The message count is used by the worker thread to keep track of the total throughput of the server. See the "Message Delivery Performance" sidebar for a full explanation.

```
synchronized Listener getListener()
    {
        return listener;
    }
}
```

The last method is simply used to get the `Listener` object that is associated with this queue. The worker thread uses it in case the message delivery failed. The listener is then considered dead and is removed from the chat system by the worker thread.

With a full understanding of the message queues, you can now turn your attention to the last piece of the chat server internals, the worker threads, before rounding off with the server manager class.

The Worker Class

The rationale for using worker threads was explained in the description of the `TopicServerImpl` class. The implementation of such a worker thread is illustrated in this section. Its mission in life is to get a queue from the server and tell it to deliver its messages. And that is basically it. This is done repeatedly, and if no queue is available, it waits until one becomes available. The chat server, as shown earlier, implements this waiting procedure.

To make this class a little more interesting, I have added some metrics functionality, which can be used to determine the performance of the chat server. It regularly determines the throughput of the server, that is, the number of messages handled per second as well as the largest amount of messages that was sent at once. The first should be as large as possible and the latter as small as possible. If there are too many messages sent at once, the client's message viewer will be very hard to read

Message Delivery Performance

Although the message delivery seems relatively uncomplicated, the delivery mechanism implementation forms the hub of the entire chat application. Therefore, it is important that this little piece of code be optimized to achieve the best performance possible. It is also this code that gives you an idea of how many worker threads to use.

Why is this part so important? Consider a simpler alternative. Suppose that instead of having the ability to send several messages at once you only had a remote method to send one message at a time. If you had 10 messages on the queue, you would have to call this method 10 times. However, the overhead of an RMI call is so significant that the average time for a call is about 3 milliseconds per call. So, no matter what you do in your code, you will never be able to do more than about 300 RMI calls per second. This is a limit of distributed computing that you, as an RMI programmer, have to learn to live and work with. By employing simple design patterns, you can gain optimal performance for your applications.

This overhead will be there regardless of how many messages you send. If, instead of sending one message you send two messages at the same time, the relative difference between these two options is relatively small because the time it takes to serialize and send a message is fairly small. Basically, you get two for the price of one. How nice!

What is the conclusion? *Try to do as much as possible in each call!* This is the main reason that a method that takes a collection was introduced in the remote interface.

So now you know that you should send as many messages as possible in each call, and your message queue and remote interfaces have been modified to take advantage of this. Is there anything else you can do? Yes, there is one more thing to consider: the amount of worker threads. Let's consider the extremes. If you have as many worker threads as clients connected to the server, a worker thread will always be dedicated to sending incoming messages to a particular client as soon as possible. So, the *latency* (i.e., the time between when the message arrives at the server and the time it is sent to the client) will be relatively small. However, because the workers are so quick to send messages, they rarely send more than one message at a time. Hence, the performance will be close to the 300 calls per second that is the inherent limitation you have to contend with. If you choose the other extreme and only have one thread, what happens then? This poor thread will be responsible for delivering messages to all clients, and hence, if there are lots of messages coming in, it will take quite some time for each client's queue to be handled. Thus, the latency will be quite poor. However, the *throughput* (i.e., the number of messages handled by the server per time unit) will be very high.

Why? Well, because the worker thread has so many queues to handle, it will take some time between each usage of a queue. Consequently, a lot of messages will stack up in each queue. But as noted previously, this is good because you can then send a lot of messages all at once. As an example, I have measured a throughput of over 15,000 messages per second during a test of this chat application if only one worker thread is used. That is quite a bit more than the standard 300 messages per second if messages are sent one by one.

The conclusion is that if you use batched message sending, as is done by this chat application, having a low number of worker threads will result in high throughput as well as high latency, whereas a high number of worker threads will yield the opposite. Because the users of the chat client will perceive the chat as being choppy if too many messages are sent at once, you will have to tune the number of worker threads to produce high throughput and low latency. Balance is best, as always. The preceding information should hopefully give you some idea of how to decide on the number of worker threads to use.

One last, somewhat strange, side effect of multiple message delivery is that the more clients you have connected to the server, the higher the throughput! Again, the reason is the same: The client queues will be dealt with infrequently, hence more messages will stack up, and the RMI call efficiency will, as a consequence, be higher.

because messages will be scrolling by at a very high pace, and the user will not be able to make much sense of them.

```
class Worker
    implements Runnable
{
    TopicServerImpl server;
```

The `Worker` class is, as was the `MessageQueue` class, `package protected` because it is only used from other classes in the same package. You also let it implement the `java.lang.Runnable`, which allows you to assign instances of this class to be executed by threads.

Next is the metric code. This code is not essential for the implementation of the worker threads, but it provides you with valuable data that will help you tune the server for optimal performance. If you modify the number of worker threads or change the way messages are sent from the message queues, you will be able to see the results by reading this output.

```
// Metrics for throughput
// Count how many messages are being sent and calculate
// throughput every 5 seconds.

// When the last check was performed
static long lastCheck;

// Nr of sent messages since last metric check
static int messageCount = 0;
static int maxMessageSend = 0;
```

These are the `static` attributes that you will use. The `lastCheck` attribute is used to keep track of when you made the last metric calculation. The `messageCount` attribute contains the accumulated number of messages since the last calculation, and the `maxMessageSend` attribute contains the maximum number of messages sent at once since the last calculation.

Next, you create a thread that periodically performs the metrics calculations.

```
// Create throughput metric output thread
static
{
   new Thread(new Runnable()
   {
      public void run()
      {
         // Initialize check tracker
         lastCheck = System.currentTimeMillis();

         while (true)
         {
            // Wait 5 seconds
            try
            {
               Thread.sleep(5000);
            } catch (InterruptedException e)
            {
               // Ignore
            }

            synchronized (Worker.class)
            {
               // Calculate and pring throughput
               long now = System.currentTimeMillis();
               long throughput = (messageCount*1000)/
                                 (now-lastCheck);
```

```
        System.out.println("Throughput"+
            "(messages/second):"+throughput +
            ", Max message batch send:"+maxMessageSend);

        // Reset counter and note current time
        messageCount = 0;
        maxMessageSend = 0;
        lastCheck = System.currentTimeMillis();
      }
    }
  }
}).start();
}
```

You create an anonymous implementation of the `Runnable` interface
that waits for five seconds, computes and shows the desired metrics,
resets the counters, and then starts all over again.

```
// Add nr of messages to counter
static void increaseMessageCount(int sentMessages)
{
    synchronized (Worker.class)
    {
        messageCount += sentMessages;

        // Keep track of how many messages was sent in
        // one single batch transfer
        // If this is too high the client will experience
        // the chat to be choppy
        // and we should increase the number of worker threads
        if (maxMessageSend < sentMessages)
        {
            maxMessageSend = sentMessages;
        }
    }
}
```

This last method is used by each worker thread to update the counters
used for the calculations. Note that because you synchronize on the
class, only one worker thread at a time can perform this, so the gather-
ing of information will have some, although almost negligible, impact on
performance.

Next comes the bulk of the actual worker thread implementation.

```
public Worker(TopicServerImpl server)
{
    this.server = server;
}
```

```
// Runnable implementation --------------------------------------
public void run()
{
    MessageQueue queue;
    while(true)
    {
        // Get queue from server
        queue = server.getNextQueue();

        // Send messages to listener
        try
        {
            int count = queue.send();

            // Increase message count
            increaseMessageCount(count);
        } catch (IOException e)
        {
            // Client failed - remove it
            server.removeListener(queue.getListener().getInfo());
        }
    }
}
```

Not very complicated, right? The perfect worker really: All it knows is how to get work and which button to push. The rest is more or less automatic. The worker begins by requesting a queue to work on. The call to getNextQueue will not return until there really is a queue available for the worker to use.

After a queue has been obtained, the worker calls the send method, which tells the queue to send all its messages to the client. Finally, you make a note of how many messages were sent, which is used by your metrics calculations to enable you to tune the server.

The try/catch block takes care of any client failure. If the send fails, the client is considered dead and is removed from the chat server.

WARNING

Note that if there are a low number of worker threads, let's say only one, and a client dies, the chat server will come to a complete halt while the worker waits for the message delivery to this client to time out. This is one of the risks of having a low number of worker threads: The chat server becomes very vulnerable to slow and faulting clients. When deciding on how many worker threads to use, you should keep this in mind.

The last piece of the server is the manager class Main, which is next in line.

The Main Class

As with all the other examples, the chat server has a manager class that takes care of how it is configured and run. The chat server runs a Web server and registry internally in order to make it self-contained. There are a couple of configuration options, such as the number of worker threads and which RMI port to use, which are defined through the system properties. Because you are loading the file `system.properties` into the system properties, these settings can be defined in that file.

```
public class Main
{
    TopicServerImpl server; // To prevent GC

    // Static -------------------------------------------------
    public static void main(String[] args)
        throws Exception
    {
        // Load system properties
        System.getProperties().load(
            Thread.currentThread().
            getContextClassLoader().
            getResourceAsStream("system.properties"));

        new Main();
    }
```

You begin by declaring an attribute to hold the singleton chat server instance. The comment "To prevent GC" means that if you decide to use some naming service other than the RMI registry, you must hold an explicit reference to the server, or it will become subject to garbage collection. Why? Remember the warning in Chapter 2: The RMI registry counts as a remote reference; hence, a remote object bound in the registry will not be garbage collected. If some other naming service that does not count as a remote reference is used, then this will not hold, and the server might become garbage collected. You do not want this to happen, so hold on to it.

```
public Main()
{
    // Start server
    try
```

```
    {
        startWebServer();

        startNamingServer();

        startTopicServer();

        System.out.println("Server has been started and registered");

    } catch (Exception e)
    {
        System.out.println("The server could not be started");
        e.printStackTrace(System.err);
    }
}

public void startWebServer()
    throws IOException
{
    // Start webserver for dynamic class loading
    DynaServer srv = new DynaServer();
    srv.addClassLoader(Thread.currentThread().
                        getContextClassLoader());
    srv.start();
}

public void startNamingServer()
    throws Exception
{
    // Create registry if not already running
    try
    {
        LocateRegistry.createRegistry(Registry.REGISTRY_PORT);
    } catch (java.rmi.server.ExportException ee)
    {
        // Registry already exists
    } catch (RemoteException e)
    {
        throw new ServerException("Could not create registry", e);
    }
}
```

The preceding methods are similar to those in earlier examples, so I will not go through the details again. Refer to the explanation of the managers in the previous example for details. Basically, the constructor makes sure that all the services are started in the proper order. The last thing to be started is the actual chat server; the code for which is shown as follows.

```
public void startTopicServer()
    throws Exception
{
    // Create remote object
    server = new TopicServerImpl(Integer.getInteger(
                                   "chat.server.threads",
                                   5).intValue());

    // Load configuration
    server.setPort(Integer.getInteger(
                      "chat.server.port",
                      0).intValue());

    // Export server
    UnicastRemoteObject.exportObject(server, server.getPort());

    // Create a few topics
    server.createTopic(new TopicInfo("Beginner RMI",
                         "Welcome to the RMI beginner forum"));
    server.createTopic(new TopicInfo("Advanced Java",
                         "Welcome to the RMI advanced forum"));
    server.createTopic(new TopicInfo("Cool tricks in RMI",
                         "Welcome to the forum for RMI tricks"));

    // Register server with naming service
    new InitialContext().bind("topics",server);
    }
}
```

You begin by creating a new instance of the chat server class and pass the desired number of worker threads to be created. This, and the following port value, is taken from the system properties by using the helper method `Integer.getInteger`. Next, you explicitly export the chat server on the chosen port, and then you create a couple of topics. If you want, you can extend this example to read the list of topics from some configuration file.

The server is then created and initialized properly, and you can make it available to clients by binding its stub in JNDI to the name "topics."

Now that you have covered the entire chat server, let's continue with the client implementation. I will show you some useful tricks on how to build user interfaces with Swing and also how to do proper error handling in the client.

The ChatClient Class

The client consists of two parts. The `ChatClient` class takes care of the communication with the server, and the `ChatGUI` class is used to provide a GUI for the chat.

Why is this separation a good thing? For example, you may want to do automated testing of the chat application, in which case, a GUI is not needed. You would then only need the client model, and use it to test the server.

Also, by separating the GUI from the core client functionality, you add the possibility of having several different GUIs. For example, some users may want a snazzy interface with lots of bells and whistles, whereas others may prefer a simpler interface with less functionality (which is faster to load too!). The separation of the view from the model allows you to have several views of the same model, hence making it easier to reuse the code.

Let's take a look at the code for the chat client.

```
public class ChatClient
    extends UnicastRemoteObject
    implements MessageListener
{
    static final String TOPIC_SERVER = "topics";

    TopicServer server;

    DefaultComboBoxModel topics;
    DefaultListModel users;

    Topic currentTopic;
    TopicInfo currentTopicInfo;
    ListenerInfo info;
    String title;

    MessageReceiver messageReceiver;
```

Notice that this class extends `java.rmi.server.UnicastRemoteObject`, and that it implements the remote interface `MessageListener`. This is to allow the client to be used as a callback by the chat server for the purpose of delivering messages to the client.

Next, you define an attribute to hold the stub of the RMI server. Then, there are two data models for the topics and users. The values for these models are retrieved once you have connected to the server and have subscribed to a topic. The topic model is filled upon server connection, and the user model is continuously updated to contain the users subscribed to the topic you are listening to.

TIP

The data model classes I have chosen are from the Swing user interface API, but they are not strictly GUI classes. Instead, they are data models that can be wrapped and viewed by Swing's GUI components. Even though it is desirable to separate the GUI as much as possible from the model, that is, this ChatClient class, it can be a good idea to use the Swing data models to store data because this makes it trivial to show the data in a GUI.

You then keep some information, such as the currently selected topic and its accompanying topic information object. These two will change every time a new topic subscription is made. The listener info object holds information about the user and is used to log on to the server as well as when subscribing to topics.

Finally, you hold a reference to an object that implements the `Mes-sageReceiver` interface, which is an interface that is defined further down in the source. This interface is simply used to forward incoming messages so that they can be shown in a user interface. The class `ChatGUI` implements this interface and also registers itself as the receiver of messages. Because you only have one reference to this type of object, there can be only one such receiver at a time, and the GUI is that particular receiver.

As noted initially, the division of the client into model and view makes it easy to do automatic testing, and this is just what is done by the `ChatClient` if it is run as a stand-alone application. The normal usage is to wrap it in the `ChatGUI` applet, but you also have a mode of operation for testing purposes. This code is as follows.

```
public static void main(String[] args)
    throws IOException
{
    // Performance tests
    // This will test the throughput of the chat system
    // Typically you should get about 0 ms/message
    // The reason for this is that since the message delivery is
    // batched there will be a number of messages for each RMI call

    // Set security policy and security manager
```

```
// Policy allows everything
System.setProperty("java.security.policy",
                   ChatClient.class.getResource(
                   "/client.policy").toString());
System.setSecurityManager(new SecurityManager());

// Get test parameters
int clientCount = new Integer(args[0]).intValue();
int messageCount = new Integer(args[1]).intValue();
int topicIndex = args.length == 3 ?
                   new Integer(args[2]).intValue()-1 : 0;

// Create test clients and subscribe them
// to the default topic
Collection clients = new ArrayList();
ChatClient client = null;
for (int i = 0; i < clientCount; i++)
{
   client = new ChatClient();
   client.login("Hello"+i);
   client.subscribe(((TopicInfo)client.getTopics().
                         getElementAt(topicIndex)));
   clients.add(client);
   System.out.println("Client "+i+" created");
}

System.out.println("Clients created");

// Use the last client to send messages
long start = System.currentTimeMillis();
for (int i = 0; i < messageCount; i++)
{
   Message message = new Message("Hello"+clientCount-1),
                                 "Text","Hello "+i+"!");
   client.publishMessage(message);
   if (i % 100 == 0)
      System.out.println(i+" messages sent");
}
long end = System.currentTimeMillis();
long time = end - start;
System.out.println("Test done");

// Log off test clients
Iterator enum = clients.iterator();
while (enum.hasNext())
{
   client = (ChatClient)enum.next();
   client.logout();
}
```

```
        System.out.println("Clients removed");

        // Show results
        System.out.println("Total time:"+time);
        System.out.println("Nr of clients:"+clientCount);
        System.out.println("Total nr of messages:"+
                       (messageCount*(clientCount+1)));
        System.out.println("Time/message:"+(time/messageCount));
        System.out.println("Time/(message*nr of test clients):"+
                       (time/(messageCount*clientCount)));
        System.out.println("Time/(message*(nr of test clients + 1)):"+
                       (time/(messageCount*(clientCount+1))));
    }
```

The test code is fairly straightforward. It begins by setting the security
manager and policy so that you can use dynamic classloading, and then
reads in the test parameters from the command line. The test clients are
then created and registered in the server. One of the clients is used to
continuously send messages to the server, which is a task that is timed.
You then deregister the clients from the server and perform some statis-
tics calculations.

Server Interaction

Now that you have the test code covered, let's take a look at the main
code of the chat client.

```
    public ChatClient()
       throws IOException
    {
       getTopicServer();
    }

    public void login(String name)
       throws RemoteException
    {
       info = new ListenerInfo(name);

       getTopicServer().addListener(info, this);
    }

    public void logout()
       throws RemoteException
    {
       if (currentTopic != null)
         unsubscribe();
```

```
      getTopicServer().removeListener(info);
      server = null;
   }
```

The constructor of the `ChatClient` class calls the method `getTopic-Server`. As you will see later in this section, this method is used to make sure that you have the chat server's reference. The `login` method is used to log on to the server by registering the users info object as well as itself as a callback. Once you have logged on to the server, you will start receiving general messages, for example, if a new topic has been created. The `logout` method is used when you want to terminate your connection to the server. It begins by unsubscribing from a topic, if necessary, and then removes itself from the listener list by calling `removeListener` on the server. Finally, you set the reference to the server to null, indicating that you are not currently connected to the server.

```
   public void subscribe(TopicInfo topicInfo)
      throws RemoteException
   {
      if (currentTopic != null)
         unsubscribe();

      currentTopic = server.subscribe(topicInfo, info);
      currentTopicInfo = topicInfo;

      // Force user list to be loaded
      getUsers();
   }

   public void unsubscribe()
      throws RemoteException
   {
      server.unsubscribe(currentTopicInfo, info);
      currentTopic = null;
      currentTopicInfo = null;
      users = null;
   }
```

These two methods are used to handle subscription to a particular topic. The `subscribe` method first unsubscribes from any current topic to prevent it from listening to two topics at the same time. It then subscribes to the chosen topic and updates the user list model. The `unsubscribe` method first calls the server to notify it about the clients noninterest in the chosen topic. It then sets the internal structures related to topics to null.

Note that none of these methods handle any `RemoteExceptions` that are thrown by the server. Instead, these exceptions are simply delegated to the caller of these methods, which can decide how to deal with the exception. One option is to log off, but in some cases, it might be possible to recover from an exception.

```
public void publishMessage(Message message)
   throws RemoteException
{
   currentTopic.publishMessage(message);
}
```

This method is used to send a message to the topic that the client is subscribed to. It simply delegates to the RMI stub, which delivers the message to the server. Note that there is no performance optimizations in this method as was the case with the message queue on the server. The reason for this is that the user is not likely to be able to send a lot of messages very quickly in succession because the messages will be typed into a text field. So, even if this optimization were added, the messages would be sent one by one anyway. If you intend to modify this example to be used in a situation where it is a computer that sends messages, it would be a good idea to add the multiple message delivery optimization to messages going from the client to the server.

```
public void addMessageReceiver(MessageReceiver mr)
{
   this.messageReceiver = mr;
}

public void removeMessageReceiver(MessageReceiver mr)
{
   if (this.messageReceiver == mr)
      this.messageReceiver = null;
}
```

These messages are used to set the message receiver callback, which is typically the client's GUI. All messages that the client receives are forwarded or at least those that are not handled internally by the client model itself. As a security precaution, when removing the receiver, first check whether the current receiver is the one that is being removed.

```
public TopicServer getTopicServer()
   throws RemoteException
{
   if (server == null)
   {
```

```
       try
       {
          Properties cfg = new Properties();
          cfg.load(getClass().
                  getResourceAsStream("/jndi.properties"));
          server = (TopicServer)new InitialContext(cfg).
                              lookup(TOPIC_SERVER);
       } catch (NamingException e)
       {
          throw new ServerException("Could not access"+
                                "topic server", e);
       } catch (IOException e)
       {
          throw new ServerException("Could not load"+
                                "jndi.properties", e);
       }

       // Get topic list from server
       topics = new DefaultComboBoxModel();
       Iterator enum = getTopicServer().getTopicInfos().iterator();
       while(enum.hasNext())
       {
          topics.addElement(enum.next());
       }
    }

    return server;
}
```

This method is used to access the main chat server stub. As you can see, it is retrieved using lazy loading, that is, you only get the server stub if it has not already been retrieved. As a side effect of getting the server, you also update the list of topics. You look up the server by using JNDI (the `InitialContext` class) and load your settings from `jndi.properties`. Normally, this would be done automatically by JNDI, but unfortunately this does not work if done in an applet, so I added code to read `jndi.properties` explicitly. Once you have made sure that the server has been obtained and that the topic list is up-to-date, you return the server stub.

```
public ComboBoxModel getTopics()
    throws RemoteException
{
    return topics;
}

public ListModel getUsers()
    throws RemoteException
```

```
{
    // Get list from server
    if (users == null)
    {
        users = new DefaultListModel();
        Iterator enum = currentTopic.getListenerInfos().iterator();
        while(enum.hasNext())
        {
            users.addElement(enum.next());
        }
    }

    return users;
}

public ListenerInfo getClientInfo()
{
    return info;
}
```

The list of topics is, as was previously shown, created and updated as a side effect of obtaining the server, so the accessor is very simple. Getting the user list is also done through lazy loading and occurs the first time the list of users is accessed. It is possible to force this list to be reloaded by setting the reference to the user list to null. This causes the list to be retrieved again on the next access.

Accessing the client information that is associated with this user is also simply a matter of returning the listener information object that was created when you logged in this client.

The MessageListener Implementation

Next up is the implementation of the `MessageListener` remote interface. The `messagePublished` methods are called by the server when it has messages to deliver, and it is then your task to make sure that they are handled properly.

```
public synchronized void messagePublished(Collection messages)
    throws RemoteException
{
    try
    {
        Iterator enum = messages.iterator();
        while (enum.hasNext())
        {
```

```
            messagePublished((Message)enum.next());
        }
    } catch (RuntimeException e)
    {
        e.printStackTrace();
        throw e;
    }
}
```

This is how you handle a collection of messages. You simply split it into individual messages and handle each message as if it was sent individually.

```
public synchronized void messagePublished(Message message)
    throws RemoteException
{
    if (server == null)
    {
        // Not connected - ignore
        return;
    }

    if (message.getSender().equals(Message.SYSTEM))
    {
        // System messages
        if (message.getType().equals(Message.TOPIC_CREATED))
        {
            ((DefaultComboBoxModel)getTopics()).addElement(message.get-
Content());
        } else if (message.getType().equals(Message.TOPIC_REMOVED))
        {
            ((DefaultComboBoxModel)getTopics()).
                removeElement(message.getContent());
        } else if (message.getType().equals(Message.USER_JOINED))
        {
            if (currentTopic == null)
                return; // Ignore

            ((DefaultListModel)getUsers()).
                addElement(message.getContent());
        } else if (message.getType().equals(Message.USER_LEFT))
        {
            if (currentTopic == null)
                return; // Ignore

            ((DefaultListModel)getUsers()).
                removeElement(message.getContent());
        } else
        {
            // Normal message
```

```
         addMessage(message);
      }
   } else
   {
      // Normal message
      addMessage(message);
   }
}
```

The preceding code is the main message handler code. You start by checking if you are connected to the server at all or if you are receiving some stray messages. You then handle the messages that are relevant for the chat client. These messages include topic creation and removal as well as users joining and leaving the current topic.

If this was another type of message, you would call `addMessage`, which would delegate to the registered `MessageReceiver`.

```
void addMessage(Message message)
{
   if (messageReceiver != null)
      messageReceiver.handleMessage(message);
}

void addMessage(Throwable error)
{
   error.printStackTrace();
   addMessage(new Message(Message.SYSTEM,
                          Message.TEXT,
                          error.toString()));
}
```

These methods are used when a message is sent to the registered `MessageReceiver`, which is the GUI. For example, all messages of type "text" are sent to the GUI so that they can be displayed. You also have a convenience method for displaying a `Throwable` as a message.

The MessageReceiver Interface

Next, you have the `MessageReceiver` interface, which is implemented by any class that is interested in receiving the messages that the chat client has received from the server.

```
public interface MessageReceiver
{
```

```
        public void handleMessage(Message message);
    }
}
```

This interface simply contains a method that allows the implementation to receive a message. Typically, this interface is implemented by the chat client's GUI, but you could also make a test receiver that simply prints the messages on system out or in a text file for logging purposes.

This concludes the chat client data and functionality model. Next up is the applet GUI that you attach to this model, so that a user can interact with the chat server.

The ChatGUI Class

The last class in this example is the chat client's GUI, which is implemented by the ChatGUI class. The majority of this class is related to GUI building, but because this is not a book about how to use Swing, I will not detail that piece of the code. There are plenty of other resources available if you want to get the lowdown on how to create pretty user interfaces.

For this reason, I will skip most of the code and only show you how the chat message handling is performed, which is the most relevant part in terms of RMI programming. The complete source code for this class is of course available on the accompanying CD.

Figure 7.3 and Figure 7.4 display some screenshots of the client chat application.

Figure 7.3 displays the screen that appears when you first start the applet or if you are disconnected from the server. You enter your name and press Enter. This causes the chat client to log on to the chat server and display the second part of the GUI, which is shown in Figure 7.4.

At the top of the main chat GUI is a list of topics that you can choose from. To the right is a list of users in the selected topic. In the middle is the text area where all messages from other users appear. At the bottom is an input field where you enter messages to be sent to the currently selected topic.

As you can see in this screenshot, a user in this topic has started typing a message. Because all the clients, including itself, is notified of this, the username is shown with a slightly darker background. This is a custom

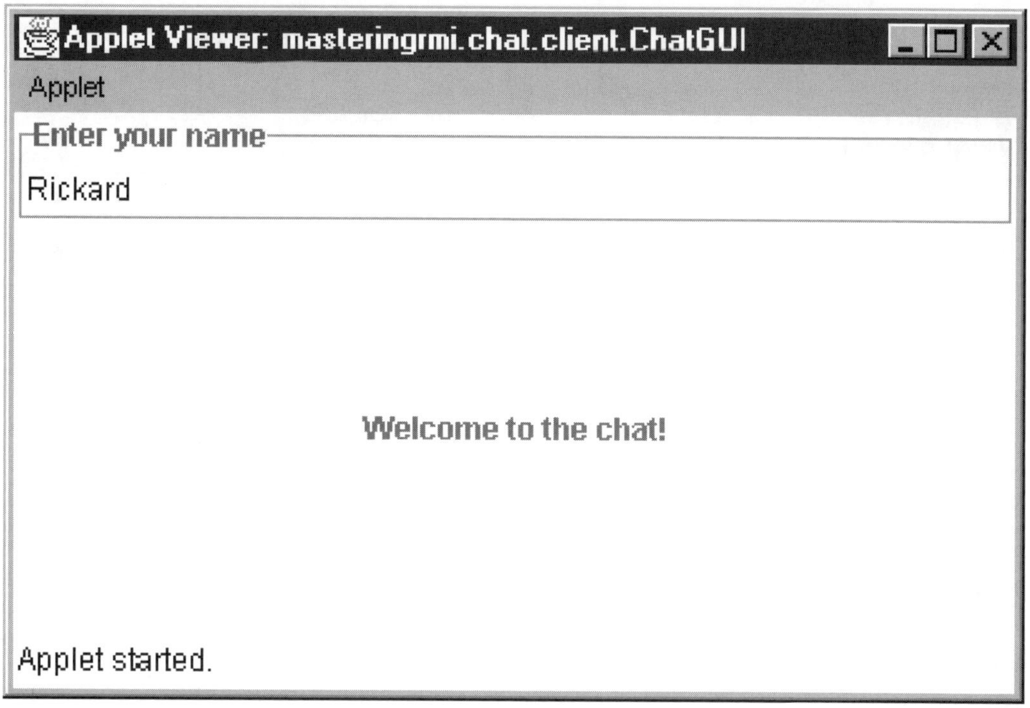

Figure 7.3   Chat login GUI.

extension to the generic message type system, and how this is done in practice is shown in the following code.

```
public void handleMessage(final Message message)
{
    SwingUtilities.invokeLater(new Runnable()
    {
        public void run()
        {
            if (message.getType().equals(Message.TEXT))
            {
                String msg;
                if (message.getSender().equals(Message.SYSTEM))
                {
                    msg = (String)message.getContent();
                    users.repaint();
                } else
                {
                    // Normal message
```

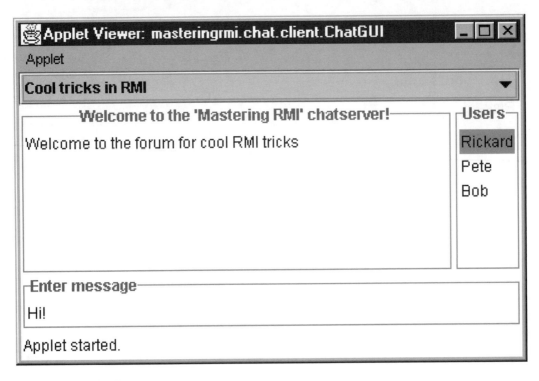

Figure 7.4 Main chat GUI.

```
            msg = message.getSender()+": "+message.getContent();

            // Reset typing
            isTyping.remove(message.getSender());
            users.repaint();
        }
        messages.append(msg+"\n");
        messages.setCaretPosition(messages.getText().length());
    } else if (message.getType().equals(Message.GREETING))
    {
        title.setTitle(message.getContent().toString());
        scroll.repaint();
    } else if (message.getType().equals(TYPING))
    {
        // Mark that this user is typing
        isTyping.put(message.getSender(), message.getSender());

        // Repaint user list
        users.repaint();
    }
```

```
      }
    });
  }
```

You first use the `SwingUtilities` class to allow this message to be handled asynchronously. Why do you do this? The reason is that because this method is called as a consequence of the server's delivery of messages, you would slow down the server if you handled the messages directly. So, instead you use the asynchronous functionality of Swing to allow the message to be handled after the method has returned. This is a very useful way to speed up Swing GUIs.

Once you have begun processing the message, it is quite straightforward. If this is a plain text message, you show it in the main text area of the client, and if it is a greeting message, you use this as a title for the text area. As you introduce more types of messages, you expand this portion of the code to handle them properly.

Next comes one of the custom extensions that this client has done. In the code that I have chosen not to show, there is code to send a special message once the user starts typing into the text field. This allows other clients to see that another user is active, and can then anticipate that a message is on its way. The benefits of this technique are that you can make the Message class extensible by adding the capability to have custom message types and content, and you only have to modify the client's GUI to introduce this functionality. The rest of the system remains unchanged. In addition, if another client does not have this functionality, it can still function; it simply discards the messages it does not understand.

And with this, you are finished with the first RMI application example. For details on how to run this example, please refer to the documentation on the CD.

Summary

In this chapter, you developed a complete, advanced, RMI chat application. The basic goal was to make a system that presented a GUI that someone could use to communicate in real time with other people. The real design goals were to make this as extensible as possible as well as to design for optimal performance.

In the implementation, you explored the notions of callbacks, which were used to allow the server to call the client. You were also introduced to the concepts of bulk operations, worker threads, and message queues, which are all design techniques that can be used in any RMI application to help achieve optimal performance.

For the contract between the client and server, you used data objects to encapsulate pieces of data to allow your system to function without having to change the interfaces between the client and server. For your `Message` class, you also looked at some performance optimizations to allow such objects to be serialized quickly. The optimizations included custom versioning and marshalling, so that the default serialization process did not perform these steps, which would have been slower. Any help that the system receives from the RMI programmer improves performance, but because it requires some effort, it is best to only add it when it is essential.

By delegating all configuration and setup code to a manager class, you learned how to make a singleton chat server that coordinates everything else, yet is not tightly coupled to the environment. The chat clients were added as listeners to the server, and for this you used a design pattern for managing listener lists, which ensured that there were no problems with concurrent access and that performance was good.

The core of this example was the worker threads and message queues. The queues were rather simple from an implementation point of view, but the design choice to allow multiple messages to be delivered in one RMI call substantially increased the throughput of the chat server. Had this not been done, the chat would have been limited in terms of performance because of the overhead involved with making a distributed RMI call.

You also examined how the number of worker threads impacted the throughput and latency of the chat system as a whole. Many worker threads reduced the throughput yet kept the latency of message delivery low, whereas a low number of worker threads increased the throughput, but increased the latency. At the same time, having a low number of worker threads made the server vulnerable to slow and faulting clients because a worker thread could be held up while waiting for a failed message delivery to time out. The increased latency also made the client perceive the server as choppy and slow. As always, balance is key, and knowing the characteristics of each of the extremes gives you a basis for choosing the proper setting. By adding some metric functionality to measure throughput, you can see how each setting impacts the server, which is often a useful thing to do when doing performance tuning.

You finished the code examination with the chat client. It was designed to contain two parts: the chat model and the chat view. By doing this, you made it easy to add automated testing and also to allow alternative GUIs to be added without having to change the main functionality of the chat client. When implementing the model, data models from Swing were used to make it easy to view the model in the GUI. Although it is desirable to keep the model and view apart as much as possible, using the Swing data models is often a good compromise between model purity and ease of coding.

Although you did not delve too deeply into the client code, you did look at the basic message handling and how to do it asynchronously so as not to keep the server waiting too long. In addition, the GUI introduced its own message types in order to add some custom functionality. Because of the careful design of the message, this was done without changing anything but the GUI of the chat client. Designing the system to allow for painless changes was apparently a good idea!

Now that you have finished your first complete RMI application, let's take a look at another example of how to use RMI to implement mobile agents.

CHAPTER 8

Developing a Mobile Agent Application

This chapter explores the design and implementation of a mobile agent system. The first question you will most likely ask is, "What is an agent?" or more specifically, "What is a software agent?"

A *software agent* is, more or less, some piece of software that performs some task on behalf of a user. It may do so by using some level of *intelligence* (this is the kind of agent that movies and science fiction literature likes). It may have some kind of *mobility* so that it can move physically between different hosts (hence a software virus is, ironically, an excellent example of a mobile agent). Finally, it *may interact with other agents* in order to perform its task. The key characteristic, however, is that it is somewhat *autonomous*: A user may tell it what to do, and the agent then goes and performs the task, returning only when it is finished. In this example, you are going to focus on the mobile aspect of agents-that is, you are going to make a system in which objects can move around between different servers.

What are the reasons for using mobile agents? There are a number of reasons involved, but one of the most significant is *processing locality*. Consider the following: A piece of software, A, needs to perform a task that involves an object B, and the two are relatively far away in terms of network distance. Because of the relative distance between the two, when A calls B it will have to wait fairly long for the reply from B. Now, if we were to move A to a position closer to B, then this interaction would be substantially faster. And this is what processing locality is all about. By moving the involved parties as close together as possible, the task that they are to accomplish together is completed much faster. If A is moved to the exact same location as B, then the possibility for network errors is also removed, which simplifies the process even further.

And the purpose of this example is to allow objects to be moved from a client to a server (i.e., moving A to B, instead of letting A talk to B over the network), in order to improve processing locality.

The application that you develop in this chapter is a mobile agent system, involving the agents themselves, a server to run them on, a client that you can use to create and deploy agents through, and a manager application that can work with agents running inside an agent server. Above all, you will explore how RMI's dynamic classloading allows you to have mobile objects whose code is not preinstalled on the servers they visit. After this chapter you should have a thorough understanding of dynamic classloading, and how to exploit it fully.

Overview of Agent Design

Creating a mobile agent system with RMI is quite straightforward and only requires a bit of imagination and ingenuity. Let's begin by introducing the players before looking closer at how this is intended to work.

- **Agent host.** Hosts are the equivalents of servers and are used to host mobile agents. You can add agents to a host, which is then made accessible as a remote object, so that you can talk to the agent later on. You should also be able to list the currently hosted agents and remove agents when they are done with their task. Preferably, there should be a way for hosted agents to access resources at the host; otherwise it would be of little purpose having them there.

- **Mobile agent.** You will implement mobile agents as simply being remote objects. Although the definition of mobile agents does not require the possibility to talk to them after their deployment, you will add this feature by making them remote objects. For this reason, an agent consists of at least two classes: the remote interface that can be used to talk to it and the implementation of the remote interface, that is, the agent itself. You can then instantiate and send these objects to an agent host, after which, they will be exported as regular remote objects. The remote objects can then access the resources of the agent host in order to perform their respective tasks.

- **Agent Client.** The client, in this scenario, is responsible for creating an agent and sending it to an agent host. The agent host accesses the implementation classes of the mobile agent through dynamic classloading. So for this purpose, you also let the client run a little Web server that provides the agent classes. It is, of course, possible to have only one Web server in the system to serve this purpose, but this way the clients are completely independent of each other.

- **Agent Manager.** Although you could run the system with just the pieces previously mentioned, I have decided to add another component, which is used to manage and interact the agents that are hosted at a particular server. It is able to ask the host for a list of agents and can then ask each agent for a management interface that it can use to talk to the agent. The manager, as was the case with the host, will not have any of the agent classes available when it starts, so they too will have to be accessed through dynamic classloading.

The different pieces that reside in the Java packages include `master-ingrmi.agent.server`, `masteringrmi.agent.agent`, `master-ingrmi.agent.client`, and `masteringrmi.agent.manager`, respectively. There is also a package called `masteringrmi.agent.interfaces`, which contains the contract classes that all of the involved parties need to have. An outline of the complete system is shown in Figure 8.1.

As you can see, there is an RMI registry that has been embedded in the server, which the agent host is bound into so that clients and managers can access it. Also, instead of only having a Web server in the server to allow the clients and any external registry to load the host's stub through dynamic classloading, you also have an additional Web server in the client. Because of this, when the agent is sent to the agent host, the host can get the classes from the client's Web server. So in this scenario, you are using dynamic classloading in two ways.

In addition, when the manager accesses the agent host and gets the list of agents, it requires the classes for the stubs. Although these classes are not available from the host, the manager is able to get these from the

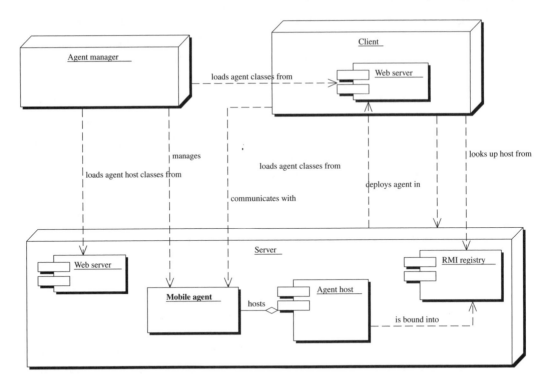

Figure 8.1   Mobile agent system overview.

client. How is this possible? Well, when the agent host receives the agent, it does not have the agent's implementation classes. It has to retrieve them from the client by creating a `java.url.URLClass-Loader` that points to the URL that was embedded in the remote call to the agent host. The `URLClassLoader` then loads the agent classes that have an association to that classloader. This means that if you call `get-ClassLoader` on the agent implementation classes, you will see that they were not loaded through the system classloader but instead by an RMI classloader. So, when the agent's stub (or any other agent class) is later sent to another client (such as the agent manager) through an RMI call, the codebase annotation rules defined in Chapter 2 come into play: Because the classes were loaded with a `java.url.URLClassLoader`, the URLs for that classloader are sent along with the call. The RMI implementation in the agent manager client then uses this information to access the classes from the client's Web server.

WARNING

It is unfortunately rather easy to make dynamic classloading of agent implementation classes fail! If the classes that are made to construct the agent are in the host's classpath, what will happen when the client sends the agent over to it? To answer this question, you need to understand the codebase annotation rule. Normally, you would have to use dynamic classloading, which implies letting RMI create a java.url.URLClassLoader to get the classes from the client's Web server.

However, if the class is loaded locally, then the classes are associated with the system classloader. So, when the agent's stub is sent to the manager, it is not able to get the stub because there is no codebase associated with the stub's classes; therefore, it does not know where to get them! Even worse, if the agent host is set up to provide dynamic classloading, the class is annotated with the server's codebase, which is completely wrong.

The solution is to be very careful with what part has access to what classes. If you have problems with dynamic classloading, this is one of the most likely causes.

How is the mobile object, which really is just a simple remote object, going to be transferred to the host? You are going to send it as a parameter of a remote method on the host! But all the other examples have shown you that if you send a remote object through RMI, it is going to be substituted with its remote stub. How come this does not happen here? The key is the remote object substitution semantics. If you remember what was said on this topic in Chapter 2, this is the time to apply that feature: Remote objects that are not exported will not be substituted with their stubs, but will be sent as-is through normal serialization. So, all you have to do is keep the remote object unexported, send it to the host and export it there, and then send it back. When you send it back, the remote object is exported, and the remote stub to the agent (which is now at the server) is returned. The client can then use this stub to communicate with the agent. This is the core principle that this example is based on.

One other important aspect of mobile agents is their ability to act as viruses or Trojan horses: What if the agent that is sent to the server decides to remove all the files for example? Well, that would not be very good. So, you need to pay attention to security in this case. What you would do is construct the security policy file so that only classes that you know are nice can do things such as read and write files. All other agents whose classes should not have access to such possibilities are restricted by not granting them these kinds of permissions in the policy file. Thus, you modify the security file to the following:

```
grant codebase "file:/-" {
        // Allow local classes everything
        // Remotely loaded agent classes can't do
        // any restricted actions
        permission java.security.AllPermission;
};
```

This allows all classes loaded from the local file system (this is denoted by the "file:/-" codebase) to do anything, but any class that is loaded through some other mechanism, for example HTTP, has no permissions at all. So if the agent, for example, tries to remove a file, it is not allowed to do so because it does not have that kind of permission-the wonders of the Java security framework at work!

These are the main design issues that have to be considered. Now let's look at the implementation of all of this. Let's begin by looking at the interfaces used in the application.

Agent Interface Classes

The contract classes of the mobile agent system contain two remote interfaces and one exception class. The first remote interface is the one that is used by the agent's hosts, and the second is a remote interface that contains methods that all agents must support. The exception is used by one of the host methods to indicate that the requested agent is not there.

The AgentHost Interface

The host's remote interface is as follows.

```
public interface AgentHost
   extends Remote
{
   public Agent addAgent(Agent agent)
      throws RemoteException;

   public Agent removeAgent(Agent agent)
      throws RemoteException, NoSuchAgentException;

   public Collection getAgents()
      throws RemoteException;
}
```

It is rather straightforward as you can see. It has one method to add an agent and one to remove an agent. For the addition method, the agent is serialized as the parameter, and the stub is returned. The removal method works the other way around by taking the agent's stub as a parameter and returning the agent through normal serialization. The remove method has an additional exception, `NoSuchAgentException`, which is thrown if the given agent is not registered at the host. For management purposes, it is also possible to get a collection of the stubs of the currently registered agents.

The NoSuchAgentException Exception

If a client tries to remove an agent that is not registered with the host, the following exception is thrown.

```
public class NoSuchAgentException
   extends Exception
{
   public NoSuchAgentException()
   {
   }
}
```

This exception simply extends `java.lang.Exception` and has a default constructor. There is no need to add any error message because the only reason that this exception is thrown is that the agent corresponding to the given agent stub is not registered in the host.

The Agent Interface

All agents have their own remote interfaces, but to ensure that they have a minimal set of methods that can be called, you let them all inherit the following remote interface.

```
public interface Agent
   extends Remote
{
   public java.awt.Component getComponent()
      throws RemoteException;

   public String getName()
      throws RemoteException;
}
```

Note that because this interface already extends `java.rmi.Remote`, there is no need for the subinterfaces to do this as well: All they have to do is extend this interface. The `getComponent` method is used to get a GUI component, which can be used to interact with the agent. The implementation of this can simply return some visual component that contains static information, but if it is going to be used to actually continually communicate with the agent, it needs some trickery. Especially, it needs to hold on to the stub of the agent so that it can call it. You will see an example of how to do this in the section "The HelloAgentImpl Class."

The last method is simply used to get a name for the agent that you can display. The manager uses this method to present a listing of agents by showing their respective names.

The only classes that are used for the contract between the different parts of this system are discussed in the following sections.

Agent Host Implementation

As usual, the server is divided in two parts: the implementation of the remote interface that provides the actual service to be provided and a manager class that sets it up along with the necessary environment.

The AgentHostImpl Class

Let's begin with the agent host. This is a remote object that implements the `AgentHost` remote interface. Its purpose is to hold a list of agents and provide them with services they can use to perform some task. For this purpose, I have chosen to use the *BeanContext API*. This is a standard API that is part of the JavaBeans API and can be used to order Java objects hierarchically and let them provide services to each other. The agents are added into such a tree, and any services can be added similarly to make them accessible to the agents. In this example, you do not have any such service, so if you intend to use this agent system for any practical purpose, you need to add a service yourself.

The following is the code for the agent host server implementation.

```
public class AgentHostImpl
    extends BeanContextServicesSupport
```

```
      implements AgentHost
{

   static AgentHostImpl host;

   public AgentHostImpl()
   {
      super();
      host = this;
   }
```

Notice that you do not extend any RMI base class, such as `java.rmi.server.UnicastRemoteObject`. This means that you must export this object yourself, and the manager class does this. You also have a `static` attribute that is used to hold a reference to the host, so that it does not get garbage collected. This `static` is then initialized in the constructor.

```
   public synchronized Agent addAgent(Agent agent)
      throws RemoteException
   {
      // Export agent
      UnicastRemoteObject.exportObject(agent);

      // Store agent in list
      add(agent);

      System.out.println("Added agent "+agent);

      // Return agent -- will be replaced with stub on clientside!
      // This allows the client to talk to it
      return agent;
   }
```

The method to add the agent receives the agent as a regular Java object because it has not been exported on the client. The first thing you do is to export it. After this point, if you ever try to send it as a parameter or a return value of an RMI call, it will, as usual, be replaced with the corresponding stub. Next, you add the new agent to the host. Because the host class extends `java.beans.beancontext.BeanContextServicesSupport`, which itself implements `java.util.Collection`, the `add` call is handled by the `BeanContextServicesSupport` superclass.

One important point is that if an object that is added to a `BeanContext` is of the type `java.beans.beancontext.BeanContextChild`, the method `setBeanContext` is called on the object, so that it knows what its `BeanContext` is (which in this case is the agent host). When you get to the agent, you will see how you can use this to implement some startup functionality.

When you return the agent, the client actually gets its stub because the agent is now exported. The client can then use this stub to call the agent remotely, just as with any other remote object.

```
public synchronized Agent removeAgent(Agent agentStub)
    throws NoSuchAgentException
{
    // Iterate through the list of agents and compare
    // their stubs with the given stub
    Iterator enum = iterator();
    while(enum.hasNext())
    {
        // Get the next agent
        Agent current = (Agent)enum.next();
        try
        {
            // Compare the agents stub with the given stub
            if (RemoteObject.toStub(current).equals(agentStub))
            {
                // Unexport the agent, forcibly
                UnicastRemoteObject.unexportObject(current, true);

                // Remove the agent from the list
                remove(current);
                System.out.println("Removed agent "+current);

                // Return the agent
                // Now that it is no longer exported,
                // it will be serialized
                return current;
            }
        } catch (Exception e) {}
    }

    // The agent was not found
    throw new NoSuchAgentException();
}
```

If a client wants to remove an agent for some reason, it can send the agent's stub to the `removeAgent` method. You iterate through the list of agents and use the `RemoteObject.toStub` method to get the stub of each agent, which you compare against the given one.

If the agent is found, you unexport it; thus making it yet again a normal Java object in terms of how RMI treats it. So, when you then return the agent, it is returned with all of its state. The client can then extract any state it wants from the agent by calling it locally.

Finally, in the case that the given agent is not registered at this host, you throw a NoSuchAgentException.

```
public synchronized Collection getAgents()
{
    return new ArrayList(this);
}
}
```

The last method is used by clients to get a list of registered agents. What happens during the creation of the `java.util.ArrayList` is that it copies the list of agents into itself. When the list of agents is returned, the agents are all replaced with their corresponding stubs. The client can then use these stubs to communicate with the agents. As you will see later on in the section "The AgentManager Class", the manager uses this method to acquire the GUI for each agent.

And that is all that is required of the agent host. Not very complicated, right? To summarize, you rely on the BeanContext API to provide you with all of the agent management functionality, and you use the RMI call semantics in order to be able to send the agents either as ordinary Java objects or their respective RMI stubs.

The Main Class

The manager class of the agent host is almost identical to the previous manager classes, so I will show the complete code directly and not explain the details.

```
public class Main
{
    public static void main(String[] args)
        throws Exception
    {
        // Load system properties
        System.getProperties().load(
            Thread.currentThread().
            getContextClassLoader().
            getResourceAsStream("system.properties"));

        // Set policy to use
        System.setProperty("java.security.policy",
                Main.class.getResource"/server.policy").toString());
```

```
        // Set a security manager
        System.setSecurityManager(new SecurityManager());

        new Main();
    }

    public Main()
    {
    // Start server
        try
        {
            startWebServer();

        startNamingServer();

        startAgentServer();

        System.out.println("Server has been started "+
                            "and registered");

    } catch (Exception e)
        {
            System.out.println("The server could not be started");
            e.printStackTrace(System.err);
        }
    }

    public void startWebServer()
        throws IOException
    {
        // Start webserver for dynamic class loading
        // The webserver can access any class
        // available from the default classloader
        // Start webserver for dynamic class loading
        DynaServer srv = new DynaServer();
        srv.addClassLoader(Thread.
                        currentThread().
                        getContextClassLoader());
        srv.start();
    }

    protected void startNamingServer()
        throws RemoteException
    {
        // Create registry if not already running
        try
        {
            java.rmi.registry.LocateRegistry.
                        createRegistry(Registry.REGISTRY_PORT);
```

```
        } catch (java.rmi.server.ExportException ee)
        {
          // Registry already exists
        } catch (RemoteException e)
        {
          throw new ServerException("Could not create registry", e);
        }
      }

      public void startAgentServer()
        throws Exception
      {
        // Create remote object
        AgentHostImpl server = new AgentHostImpl();
        UnicastRemoteObject.exportObject(server);

        // Register server with naming service
        new InitialContext().bind("agenthost",server);
      }
    }
```

The service startup code instantiates an agent host, exports it, and binds it into the naming service.

This completes the agent server. Next, you will look at an example agent and its implementation.

Mobile Agent Implementation

To begin with, what should your little agent do? There is of course a bunch of cool tricks it could perform for you, but let's settle for something reasonably silly. Basically, your agent will be an adaptation of the HelloWorld example: You will be able to say "hello" to it and get a greeting in response. In addition, the agent will keep track of how many times it has been greeted.

To show you how it can act without user intervention on the host, it will also start up a thread that continuously prints out the current date and time and keep track of how many times it has done that. You can of course replace this with some more interesting functionality, such as computing some function or having the agent query some database for information.

Another requirement for an agent is the ability to get a GUI from it with which you can interact. This can be a very basic GUI that simply shows the agent's name or something similar. I am going to make it a bit more advanced by actually making it possible to see the current status of the agent, have it update continuously, and also make it possible to get a greeting from the agent. To be able to do this, the GUI that is requested must contain a stub to the agent. In the section "The HelloAgentImpl Class" you will see how this is accomplished.

Let's take a look at the interface and the actual implementation of this agent.

The HelloAgent Interface

The `HelloAgent` interface contains methods to get a greeting from it and also accesses the internal counters.

```
public interface HelloAgent
    extends masteringrmi.agent.interfaces.Agent
{
    public String hello(String name)
        throws RemoteException;

    public int getQueryCounter()
        throws RemoteException;

    public int getRunCounter()
        throws RemoteException;
}
```

The interface is a regular remote interface with one difference: It extends the `Agent` interface instead. This means that the `HelloAgent` implementation not only has to provide the methods in the `HelloAgent` interface, but also those in the generic `Agent` interface.

The HelloAgentImpl Class

This is the class that actually implements the agent functionality. A great deal of the code is dedicated to supporting the remote interface, especially the GUI that can be used to manage it.

Let's take a closer look at the code.

```
public class HelloAgentImpl
    extends BeanContextChildSupport
    implements HelloAgent, Runnable
{
```

As you can see, this agent extends the `BeanContextChildSupport` class (which is part of the standard BeanContext API and is located in the `java.beans.beancontext` package). This allows the agent to be placed within a surrounding `BeanContext`, which it can use to access other agents and services. As stated earlier, you will not be exploring this capability, but it is a recommended task should you choose to expand this example on your own.

Next, it implements `HelloAgent`, which is the remote interface for this agent. It also extends the `java.lang.Runnable` interface. Why is this? As stated in the description of what the agent was supposed to do, it starts a thread that continuously prints the date. The agent itself provides the code to be executed in that thread, which means that you must implement the `Runnable` interface.

```
String localhost;
boolean running = true;
Thread runner;

int runCounter = 0;
int queryCounter = 0;
```

The attributes of the agent include the name of the local host, which is used in the greeting response. The running and runner attributes are used to manage the thread that prints the date, and the counters are used to keep track of the number of thread loops and sent greetings, respectively.

```
public synchronized String hello(String name)
{
   queryCounter++;
   return "Hello " + name + "! I'm an agent "+
          "running at "+localhost+".";
}
```

This is the first method of the `HelloAgent` implementation and can be used by the caller to get a greeting from the agent. You increase the counter and create a greeting that includes the name that was provided as well as the name of the local host. This greeting is then returned to the caller. As you can see, I have used the synchronized keyword on this method. Why is this? It is used to prevent two clients from calling this object at the same time, which could lead to the counter being improperly updated.

```
public java.awt.Component getComponent()
    throws RemoteException
{
    return new HelloViewer(this);
}

public String getName()
{
    return "Hello Agent";
}

public synchronized int getQueryCounter()
{
    return queryCounter;
}

public synchronized int getRunCounter()
{
    return runCounter;
}
```

The preceding methods are quite straightforward. The GUI component that is returned will be shown later on in this section. What is important is that you give it a reference to this agent. The GUI stores this internally and when it is serialized and sent to the client, the reference is replaced with the agent's stub (because it is an exported remote object). When the GUI is deserialized on the client, this stub is what it uses to communicate with the agent.

```
public void run()
{
    while (isRunning())
    {
        // Here we put the execution of the agent's task
        // In our case we simply print out the current date
        System.out.println("Date is now " + new java.util.Date());
        increaseRunCounter();

        // Wait for awhile
        try { Thread.sleep(5000); } catch (InterruptedException e) {}
    }

    // The agent was removed
    System.out.println("Ok, I'm done");
}
```

This method provides the implementation of the `Runnable` interface and is what is run in a loop once the agent starts the thread on the host.

It is basically a `while` loop that continues as long as the agent is on the host. It prints out the current date and updates the appropriate counter. It then waits five seconds and tries again. When the agent is removed, the method `isRunning` returns false, and the loop ends hence printing out the line "Ok, I'm done," signifying that the agent has completed its work. The thread that the agent used stops after the `run` method returns.

```
synchronized protected void initializeBeanContextResources()
{
    // Start the execution thread
    running = true;
    runner = new Thread(this);
    runner.start();

    // Get the name of this host
    try
    {
        localhost = InetAddress.getLocalHost().toString();
    } catch (Exception e)
    {
        localhost = "some nice agenthost";
    }
}

synchronized protected void releaseBeanContextResources()
{
    // Stop the execution thread
    running = false;
    runner.interrupt();// In order to not have to wait five seconds
    runner = null;
}
```

These two methods are overridden by the `BeanContextChildSupport` class. Remember that I said that `setBeanContext` is called on a `BeanContextChild` when it is added to a `BeanContext` (such as the agent host)? Well, the `BeanContextChildSupport` helper class is implemented so that if the `BeanContext` that is given as a parameter to the `setBeanContext` call is not null, it calls the `initializeBeanContextResources` method in which a subclass of `BeanContextChildSupport` can perform any initialization code. In this case, you start a new thread with the agent itself as the `Runnable` implementation. After that, you determine the agent hosts network name so that you can include it in the greeting. If the parameter to the `setBeanContext` call is null, it means that the object is being removed from its

BeanContext, and BeanContextChildSupport then calls the releaseBeanContextResources method, which subclasses can use to perform any cleanup code. In this case, you stop the thread.

```
synchronized protected boolean isRunning()
{
    return running;
}

synchronized void increaseRunCounter()
{
    runCounter++;
}
```

These are simply internal methods that you use to access the running flag and the thread loop counter. The reason they are synchronized is that there are issues with how threads share object state. Basically, if the reading and writing of object attributes is not done in a synchronized manner, the JVM sometimes caches these values so that different threads accessing the same attributes get different values. This is obviously not desired, so you add these synchronization procedures to ensure that this problem does not occur.

The following is the implementation of the GUI that the agent provides. I have made this as a static inner class. You could of course do this as a truly separate class if you want to, as long as you make sure that it, as the agent itself, is available for dynamic classloading by any agent client, such as the agent manager you will develop in the section "Agent Manager Implementation".

```
static class HelloViewer
    extends JPanel
    implements Runnable, ActionListener
{
    JLabel info = new JLabel("", JLabel.CENTER);
    JButton helloButton = new JButton("Say hello");

    HelloAgent agent;
    boolean running;

    HelloViewer(HelloAgent agent)
    {
        super(new BorderLayout());

        this.agent = agent;
```

```
        add("Center", info);
        add("South", helloButton);
    }
```

The GUI component extends `javax.swing.JPanel`, which is standard for any custom Swing component. It also implements `Runnable` as it creates a thread that checks the current state of the agent's counters. In addition, it implements `java.awt.event.ActionListener`, so that it can be notified when you press the `helloButton`.

Then you have a reference to the agent. As stated earlier, when the GUI is first created, it references the actual agent, but once the GUI has been transferred to the client, it is replaced with the agent's stub.

The constructor simply sets this reference and initializes the GUI.

```
public synchronized void addNotify()
{
    super.addNotify();

    // Start agent query thread
    running = true;
    new Thread(this).start();

    // Add action listener to button
    helloButton.addActionListener(this);
}
```

This method is called when this GUI is viewed in a client. You start up the thread that is used to update the GUI and also add the thread itself as a listener with the button.

```
public synchronized void removeNotify()
{
    super.removeNotify();

    // Stop agent query thread
    running = false;

    // Remove action listener from button
    helloButton.removeActionListener(this);
}
```

This code is called when a client no longer views the GUI. Setting the `running` flag to `false` stops the thread, and, as explained earlier, the method uses the `synchronized` keyword to ensure that the thread really sees this change. You then also remove the listener from the button.

```
public void run()
{
    while (isRunning())
    {
        // Get info from agent
        try
        {
            info.setText("Hello Agent. Run:"+
                            agent.getRunCounter()+
                            " Query:"+agent.getQueryCounter());
        } catch (RemoteException e)
        {
            e.printStackTrace();
            info.setText("ERROR: Could not access agent");
        }

        // Wait some time
        try
        {
            Thread.sleep(5000); // Sleep 5 seconds
        } catch (InterruptedException e)
        {
            // Ignore
        }
    }
}
```

This is the implementation of the `Runnable` interface. In it, you update the GUI with the current status of the two counters, and then let it sleep. For each loop, you check with the running flag to see if it is still necessary to perform this update.

```
public void actionPerformed(ActionEvent evt)
{
    String name = JOptionPane.
                    showInputDialog(SwingUtilities.
                        getRoot(HelloViewer.this),
                            "What is your name?");
    Component frame = SwingUtilities.getRoot(HelloViewer.this);
    try
    {
        String greeting = HelloViewer.this.agent.hello(name);
        JOptionPane.
            showMessageDialog(frame,
                        "HelloAgent says:\""+greeting+"\"",
                        "HelloAgent says",
                        JOptionPane.PLAIN_MESSAGE);
    } catch (RemoteException e)
    {
        e.printStackTrace();
```

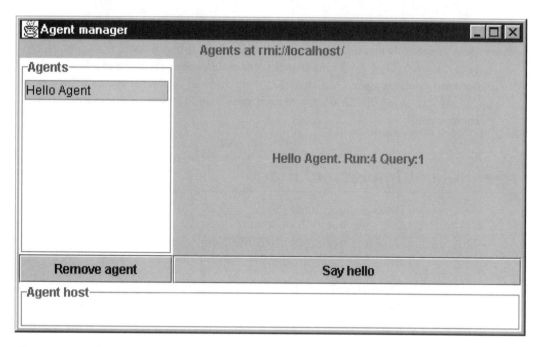

Figure 8.2 HelloAgent GUI.

```
JOptionPane.
    showMessageDialog(frame,
        "Could not contact agent:"+e.getMessage(),
        "HelloAgent error",
        JOptionPane.ERROR_MESSAGE);
        }
      }
    }
  }
```

This last piece of the code handles the button that is used to retrieve a greeting from the agent. You begin by showing a dialog prompting for the user's name. You then call the agent. This results in an RMI call to the agent at the remote host. You store the greeting and show it in yet another dialog. If something goes wrong, you show a dialog with an error message.

Figure 8.2 shows a screenshot of the agent's GUI as it appears when accessed through the agent manager.

And with this, you are finished with the agent implementation.

TIP

Most of the code was actually used to handle the GUI that talks to the agent. However, it is probably a good idea to make this code generic so that it can be reused between different agents, which makes it significantly easier for you to write your own agents. Using the JavaBeans API is a good way to create such reusable visual components.

Agent Client Implementation

The client in this scenario does two things: First of all, it creates a HelloAgent, which it registers with the agent host. Second, it allows the user to call the hello method on the agent.

Because the hosts use dynamic classloading to access the classes for the agent, the client also starts a Web server that is used to serve the agent's classes. For this reason, the client needs to be running until the agent is removed from the host, or any other clients wanting to get the GUI of the agent will not be able to access the necessary classes, that is, the agent's stub, the remote interface, and the viewer class. This is perhaps an unnecessary limitation that you can easily remove by simply running a Web server with the agent's classes separately.

The AgentClient Class

The client only consists of one class, namely AgentClient. The source code for this class is as follows.

```
public class AgentClient
{
   DynaServer srv;
   AgentHost host;
   HelloAgent agent;

   public static void main(String[] args)
      throws Exception
   {
      new AgentClient().talkToAgent();
   }

   public AgentClient()
      throws Exception
   {
      // Start webserver for dynamic class loading
```

```
    srv = new DynaServer();
    srv.setPort(8082);
    srv.addClassLoader(Thread.currentThread().
                    getContextClassLoader());
    srv.start();

    // Locate host
    host = findHost();

    // Create agent
    agent = new HelloAgentImpl();

    // Register agent
    agent = (HelloAgent)host.addAgent(agent);
}
```

The constructor takes care of all the interesting things. In it, you first create the Web server, which is used to serve up the classes for the agent. You then call `findHost` (this will be defined later in this section), which locates the host for you. Once you have a host, you create an agent and register it with the host. In return, you get the stub to the agent so that you can talk to it.

```
public void talkToAgent()
    throws IOException, NoSuchAgentException
{
    // Say hello
    BufferedReader in = new BufferedReader(
                        new InputStreamReader(System.in));
    String name;

    while (true)
    {
        System.out.print("Name:");
        System.out.flush();
        if ((name = in.readLine()).equals(""))
            break;
        System.out.println(agent.hello(name));
    }

    // Remove agent
    HelloAgentImpl result=(HelloAgentImpl)host.removeAgent(agent);
    System.out.println("The agent was run "+
                    result.getRunCounter()+
                    " times, and was queried "+
                    result.getQueryCounter() + " times");

    // Stop class-server
    srv.stop();
}
```

The purpose of this method is to read names from the system input, which is used to greet the agent whose response is printed to the console. When the user is finished, you remove the agent, print out the values of the counters, and stop the Web server. Note that the result of the remove call is the agent itself, so the result variable is bound to the actual agent. Consequently, the counter queries are local calls, not RMI calls.

Similarly, if you make an agent that is supposed to go to a host, compute some value, and then be returned, you can extract the computed value from the agent. The benefits of this are that it is only during the addition and removal calls that any network errors can occur, and that the calls to the agent are local so that there is no network overhead.

```
public AgentHost findHost()
    throws NamingException
{
    return (AgentHost)new InitialContext().lookup("agenthost");
}
}
```

Finally, you have a helper method that is used to locate the agent host. Because it too is a remote object that you have bound into a naming system, all you have to do is use JNDI to look it up. The preceding code assumes that the physical location of the agent host has been defined in the `jndi.properties` file. If you want to be able to access hosts on other machines, you could, for example, use the lookup string `rmi://mycomputer.com/agenthost`, which tries to locate an agent host running at `mycomputer.com`.

Agent Manager Implementation

Because it would be nice to be able to ask a host what agents it is currently hosting and be able to talk to these agents, you introduce a manager client for just that purpose. The agent manager shows a GUI that lets you connect to a given agent host, list the agents, and then retrieve GUIs from the agents that can be used to interact with them. Most of the hard work is already done in the client and the agent itself, so all you have to do is put it together.

Once run, the manager provides a user interface that is shown in Figure 8.3.

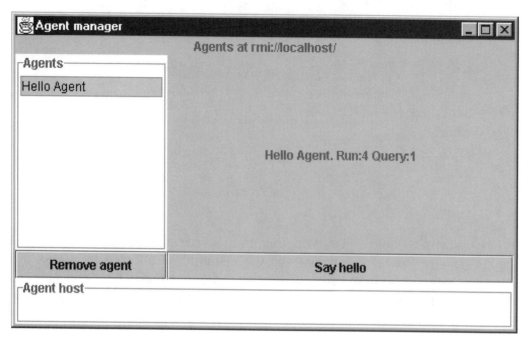

Figure 8.3 Agent manager GUI.

At the bottom of the figure is an input field for the location of the agent host. Once entered, the list to the left is populated with the agent's names. Then, when a name is selected, the agents GUI is presented in the middle. Below the list of agents is a button that allows the user to remove a selected agent from the server.

As mentioned earlier, the manager accesses the classes for the retrieved GUIs and agent stubs through dynamic classloading. So, the manager not only shows you how to let a server access a client's classes through dynamic classloading, but also how another client can access the same objects by using classes provided by the first client.

Sometimes the following question is asked, "Why can't the classes for the objects be retrieved as part of the RMI call? Setting up a separate Web server is too much extra work!" This example shows why: Sometimes the sender of the object, in this case the agent host, does not even have these classes! Remember that the agent host itself does not have the agent implementation available. So, because of this, there is no other option but to have a separate method for loading classes dynamically.

As with the agent host, you need to make sure that the GUIs of the agents do not do anything they are not supposed to do. Again, the solution is to construct the policy file properly. The following is the policy that is used by the manager.

```
grant codebase "file:/-" {
        // Allow local classes everything
        // Remotely loaded agent classes can't do
        // any restricted actions
        permission java.security.AllPermission;
};

grant {
        // Allow all classes to do network calls or the stubs will fail
        permission java.net.SocketPermission "*", "connect";
};
```

As with the agent host, you only grant all permissions to locally loaded classes. However, because the GUIs should be allowed to access the agents remotely in order to present a view of their state, you need to include permissions for all classes to make network connections. Because you do not know at this point which hosts you will be retrieving agents from, you denote the list of valid hosts with a star ("*").

The AgentManager Class

All of the code for the manager is contained in the class AgentManager. Most of the code is related to setting up and wiring together the GUI, but I will not describe this in any detail in the following code because you are primarily interested in the RMI aspects of the manager.

```
public class AgentManager
    extends JFrame
{
    AgentHost agentHost;

    JLabel agentLabel;
    JList agentList;
    JTextField agentHostField;
    JPanel agentPanel;
    JButton agentRemoveButton;

    Agent currentAgent;
    Component currentGUI;


    // Static ---------------------------------------------------
    public static void main(String[] args)
        throws Exception
```

```
    {
        // Set policy to use
        System.setProperty("java.security.policy",
                        AgentManager.class.
                            getResource("/client.policy").toString());

        // Set a security manager
        System.setSecurityManager(new SecurityManager());

        new AgentManager();
    }
```

The preceding code is the manager startup code. Because you are using dynamic classloading, you need to set a security manager and also make sure that the policy file you defined earlier is used. After that, you simply instantiate the manager.

Next comes the `AgentManager` constructor. This is a fairly large chunk of code, most of which is dedicated to setting up the GUI. Note that some of the inner classes defined call the agents, so examine how I deal with exceptions that may occur.

```
    public AgentManager()
        throws Exception
    {
        // Create GUI
        super("Agent manager");

        Container content = getContentPane();
        content.setLayout(new BorderLayout());

        agentLabel = new JLabel("Agent manager", JLabel.CENTER);
        agentList = new JList(new DefaultListModel());
        agentList.setBorder(BorderFactory.createTitledBorder("Agents"));
        agentList.setPreferredSize(new Dimension(150,150));
        agentList.setFixedCellWidth(150);
        agentHostField = new JTextField("rmi://localhost/");
        agentHostField.setBorder(BorderFactory.
                            createTitledBorder("Agent host"));
        currentGUI = new JLabel("Select agent host", JLabel.CENTER);

        agentHostField.addActionListener(new ActionListener()
        {
            public void actionPerformed(ActionEvent evt)
            {
                try
                {
                    // Get host
                    findHost(agentHostField.getText());
```

```
                    // Get list of agents
                    DefaultListModel list = (DefaultListModel)agentList.
                                                            getModel();

                    list.clear();
                    Collection agents = agentHost.getAgents();
                    Iterator enum = agents.iterator();
                    while (enum.hasNext())
                    {
                        list.addElement(enum.next());
                    }

                    setGUI(new JLabel("Select agent", JLabel.CENTER));

                    agentLabel.setText("Agents at "+
                                    agentHostField.getText());

                    // Clear host field
                    agentHostField.setText("");
                } catch (Exception e)
                {
                    e.printStackTrace();
                }
            }
        });

        agentList.addListSelectionListener(new ListSelectionListener()
        {
            public void valueChanged(ListSelectionEvent evt)
            {
                if (evt.getValueIsAdjusting())
                    return; // Wait until the selection has stabilized

                // Get the selected agent and show its GUI
                try
                {
                    currentAgent = (Agent)agentList.getSelectedValue();

                    setGUI(currentAgent.getComponent());
                } catch (Exception e)
                {
                    e.printStackTrace();
                }
            }
        });

        agentList.setCellRenderer(new DefaultListCellRenderer()
        {
            public Component getListCellRendererComponent(JList list,
                                                Object value,
                                                int index,
                                                boolean isSelected,
                                                boolean cellHasFocus)
```

```
                {
                    String name = "Error";
                    try
                    {
                        name = ((Agent)value).getName();
                    } catch (RemoteException e)
                    {
                        // Ignore - name will be "Error"
                    }

                    return super.getListCellRendererComponent(list,
                                                              name,
                                                              index,
                                                              isSelected,
                                                              cellHasFocus);
                }
            });

            agentRemoveButton = new JButton("Remove agent");
            agentRemoveButton.addActionListener(new ActionListener()
            {
                public void actionPerformed(ActionEvent evt)
                {
                    try
                    {
                        if (currentAgent == null)
                            return;

                        // Remove agent GUI
                        setGUI(new JLabel("Select agent", JLabel.CENTER));

                        // Remove agent from host
                        agentHost.removeAgent(currentAgent);

                        // Update list of agents
                        DefaultListModel list = (DefaultListModel)agentList.
                                            getModel();
                        list.clear();
                        Collection agents = agentHost.getAgents();
                        Iterator enum = agents.iterator();
                        while (enum.hasNext())
                        {
                            list.addElement(enum.next());
                        }


                        currentAgent = null;

                        Component frame=SwingUtilities.
                                    getRoot(AgentManager.this);
                        JOptionPane.showMessageDialog(frame,
```

```
                               "The agent has been successfully removed!",
                               "Agent removed",
                               JOptionPane.PLAIN_MESSAGE);
             } catch (Exception e)
             {
                e.printStackTrace();
             }
          }
       });

       agentPanel = new JPanel(new BorderLayout());
       agentPanel.add("Center", agentList);
       agentPanel.add("South", agentRemoveButton);

       content.add("North", agentLabel);
       content.add("West", agentPanel);
       content.add("Center", currentGUI);
       content.add("South", agentHostField);

       agentRemoveButton = new JButton("Remove");

       setSize(500,300);
       show();
    }
```

Phew! That was a pretty long constructor. It basically sets up the GUI and wires together the different visual components, so that they behave as described. Note the error handling that has to be done every time you want to interact with either the agent or the host. You may want to put all such error handling in a separate method that you can call from within the catch blocks. This allows you to easily unify how errors are handled. Currently, the exception handling is rather crude, and you may want to modify this to show the user an error message dialog.

```
    void setGUI(Component gui)
    {
       if (currentGUI != null)
          getContentPane().remove(currentGUI);

       getContentPane().add("Center", gui);
       getContentPane().doLayout();
       getContentPane().repaint();

       currentGUI = gui;
    }
```

The setGUI method is used to set the main GUI. You first remove the current GUI, add the new one, and finally repaint the whole thing.

```
      void findHost(String host)
         throws NamingException
      {
         agentHost = (AgentHost)new InitialContext().
                                   lookup(host+"agenthost");
      }
   }
```

This helper method is used to access the agent host. In the host field, you enter names such as `rmi://localhost/` (which is the default by the way), and then try to look up the RMI object `rmi://localhost/agenthost`.

And with this, you are finished with the example on mobile agents.

Summary

In this chapter, you built an application that supports the notion of mobile agents. In this case, an agent was simply a remote object that you could send to some agent host, which then exported it to the RMI run-time, so that it could be called remotely from clients. The agent could then perform any kind of task (although we settled for a rather simple one in this example). You also looked briefly at the BeanContext API, which is a part of the standard JavaBeans API, as a way to support this.

One of the primary features of this example was the use of advanced dynamic classloading to not only load RMI stubs, but also regular object classes. You also looked at how the codebase class annotations propagated to all users of the agent including any additional clients, such as the agent manager.

The remote method parameter marshalling semantics allowed you to send agents to the host in a serialized state, but after they were exported, their stubs were returned to the client that installed the agent.

In order to manage the agents, you looked at how the agent could create a visual component containing the stub to the agent, which was then used in an agent manager application. Again, the dynamic classloading feature allowed you to do this without preinstalling the agent's GUI in the manager, allowing you to easily view any agent without any hassles.

For the agent, you had to consider some thread synchronization issues by adding the synchronized keyword at certain points where different threads would access shared state in the agent. Proper handling of thread synchronization is one of the more complex problems you will encounter when working with remote objects that can be concurrently accessed by several clients or, as was the case in this example, custom threads in the server.

This was the last complete example of an RMI application. Hopefully, most of the common problems that you will encounter have been covered, and I hope I have provided you with some ideas on how to tackle them. Remote programming is not easy, but at least RMI takes care of some of the problems for you.

The next part of the book covers some of the related technologies, such as Enterprise JavaBeans (EJB) and Jini. These are both built upon the RMI API and provide additional features that are useful when building distributed applications.

PART FOUR

Advanced Applications

In the earlier parts of this book, you explored the fundamentals of RMI, looked in-depth at some of the key features of RMI, and learned how to construct entire applications in RMI.

As you may have noticed, RMI gives you a good set of fundamental features to help you build distributed systems. However, although you can get very far with just the fundamentals, as with all such technologies, there is a limit to how complex an application you can make without running into serious design troubles. Although you could solve all of these issues on your own, some of them are so common that specifications have already been created that describe in detail how to deal with them. In this part, you will look at some of the other technologies that have been created on top of RMI to help you to create even more advanced applications.

Chapter 9 introduces you to *Jini*. The basic goal of Jini is to help you create systems, or communities, of distributed services that are loosely coupled and that have a high tolerance for failures. The loose coupling allows you to plug in new services as they become available and make them available to other services to use. The high level of fault tolerance allows you to detect when services become unavailable and handle this in a well-behaved manner. You will look at which features of Jini allow this to happen. To show off this impressive technology, you will also create a sample Jini service and a client that uses it-high *wow* factor is guaranteed.

Chapter 10 describes the *Enterprise JavaBeans* (EJB) specification. Many people use RMI to create distributed systems that allow them to access relational databases, but with just the basic features of RMI, that can prove to be a very complex task. In particular, such systems must typically provide security, transactions, and persistent objects. In addition, because these classes of applications typically have a very large number of users, there are strict requirements on the system's ability to scale and handle failures. You will look at how the Enterprise JavaBeans specification provides a standardized way to create application components that can be plugged into EJB servers, which provide support for these types of features. The HelloWorld example will be adapted to EJB to show you how things work in practice.

Numerous tomes have been written on both of these topics, so I will, of course, not be able to cover them in as great detail. Instead, the goal is to give you some idea of what these two technologies can do and how they do it. Hopefully, you will then have such a good idea about what they provide that you will be able to determine if they are of use in your development and also be able to choose other literature that explains these two technologies in more detail.

After this part, you should have a pretty clear picture of where to go when you need more functionality than RMI can provide on its own.

CHAPTER 9

RMI and Jini

During your exploration of RMI technology, you will have seen at various points some drawbacks in how things are done. For example, all of your code examples would have failed if the system parts were not started in precise order. (And if any of the components fail, recovery is nontrivial.) Another drawback is the tight coupling between the different components. A client has to know the exact physical location and the JNDI name of the server it wants to access. If you had started several servers to serve the clients, the clients would have to be reconfigured in order to make use of them.

When building large systems of distributed services that together perform some task, these are issues that you want to handle in a slightly more intelligent way. And Jini provides just that kind of intelligence.

Jini was originally intended to be used by small devices that communicate on a network: printers, cameras, scanners, and so on. This kind of networked environment must be able to handle frequent failures of the various services. For example, if a printer is turned off or installed, this should automatically be recognized by the other members of the system. Jini is specifically designed to allow detection of these situations, and it also allows all members of the network to handle them in an intelligent way.

As it turns out, Jini technology is useful for pretty much any distributed service. Thus, it can be used for the small-scale services it was originally intended for as well as for large-scale systems implementing enterprise class applications. So, when you think about Jini, remember that its applicability is very broad.

Overview

So, what does Jini provide? Jini consists of a set of classes, which provides an API that allows servers and clients to work together in a flexible way. The Jini API is tightly bound to RMI as it contains predefined remote interfaces and remote objects, and a definition of how they should work together. As with RMI, and all of the other Java standard specifications, the API is fixed, but with a number of possible implementations. Sun provides a standard implementation of the Jini interfaces that you can download and use. Because you will always develop against the standardized Jini API, you will not be tightly bound to its particular implementation.

The functionality in the Jini API can be divided into five categories: Discovery, Lookup, Leasing, Remote Events, and Transactions, which are explained in the following sections.

Discovery

When dealing with normal RMI, you would typically run an RMI registry somewhere, and then let the server register itself with it. After that, the clients can look up the server's stub from it. This is a very simple approach, but it has one important drawback: both the client and server need to know where to find this registry. If it moves, everything will break because their common point of communication is lost.

Jini solves this by using a feature called *discovery*. Instead of the registry, there is a lookup service, which itself is a remote object. This is where the services register their availability for clients to find. However, instead of having the services and clients know the exact location of the lookup service, it uses multicast announcements to make itself available.

What does this mean? Basically, when a client needs a service, it sends a request to the network with the message, "Hey, I want to talk to a lookup service!" The lookup service, or services, "hear" this and send a response to the client saying, "Here I am. What can I do for you?" The client can then continue with a lookup of the Jini service it wants.

Because of discovery, you no longer have to configure your clients and servers to know exactly where the lookup service is located. Simply starting the service on the network makes it automatically available for anyone to use.

WARNING
There is a minor restriction to this method. When I say "network" as in the previous paragraph, I am not referring to the entire Internet. Instead, it refers to the physical subnet where the client, server, or lookup service is located, because multicast network packets cannot pass through network routers. This typically means a rather restricted set of network nodes, such as the local department within a company.

If these services are to communicate between several such subnets, a bridge that forwards a packet from one subnet to the others must then connect them. There is such a bridge available in the Jini implementation from Sun.

Lookup

Again, if you refer to the normal way of doing things in RMI, once you have found a registry where you can bind servers or let clients look them up, how should this be done? With the RMI registry, you are limited to using a simple string, such as "HelloServer." Unfortunately, this is not very flexible. For example, if there are two such services available, they will either overwrite each other's bindings into the registry (because they have the same name), or you will have to use two registries or two different names. However, it is then nontrivial for the client to decide where to find the best server. Which registry should it access, and what name should it use? The basic problem is that both the client and server have to be very explicit in their use of the registry.

Jini solves this by using an implicit declarative approach called *lookup*. Instead of binding a server to a name in the lookup service, it provides a set of *attributes* that describe it. The attributes can be the interface that the lookup implements, where the lookup is physically located, and if the lookup is some sort of hardware, what type it is (e.g., a printer interface may be implemented by lots of different types of printers, and thus, it is useful to know what printer a Jini service represents).

The client then also uses a declarative approach to finding a service by using a *template*. A template contains the minimal set of attributes that the service should have. The lookup service then compares this template with the registered services attributes and returns those that match the requirements. For example, the client can make a template with no attributes at all, which returns all available services during a lookup. Or it can just specify which interface the service should provide (which returns all services of a particular kind). Or it could specify which interface, type, and geographic attributes the service should have. The less specific the template is, the more available services become as possible options, and the more flexible the setup of the system becomes.

The lookup feature, along with discovery, allows Jini services and clients to be very loosely coupled.

Leasing

Let's again review an aspect of the earlier examples that can become a problem. When the client in the HelloWorld example acquired a stub to the server, what assurance did we have that the server was still available? The answer is none. For example, it might have crashed for some reason. The only way for you to detect the server is to invoke a method on the stub and see if an exception is thrown. This is not a very good thing, and it would be better if you could detect this situation before a call is made.

Jini solves this problem by using a concept called *leasing*. Basically, each service that can be used by clients has an associated lease (one for each client) that expires at a given time. The stub to the service is only valid if the lease has not expired. If the client wants to use the service for an extended period of time, he must *renew* the lease before it expires. If the client fails to renew the lease, the renewal fails because the service is not available. Or if the lease timeout expires, the lease is considered invalid. Also, if the client no longer wants to use the service, it can cancel the lease explicitly.

This serves two purposes: by successfully renewing a lease, the client knows that the service is still available, and the service knows that the client is still alive and using it. By actively keeping track of each other in this way, you make sure that there are no stale references to services. For example, if a client obtains a service, and after a while the renewal fails, it can try to obtain another similar service to use. If the client did not use the service between the time it failed and a new one was acquired, it will not have to deal with any network exceptions due to crashed services.

This approach makes it much easier to keep the system as a whole alive because each service and client must continually prove its aliveness in an active way.

For example, when a service registers itself in the lookup service, it becomes a client of the lookup service. Because of this, it gets a lease that is associated with the service registration. When the lease is cancelled or if the service crashes without explicitly canceling the lease, the service registration is removed from the lookup service. As a result, a client using the lookup service will not find the service during a lookup.

Compare this with the standard RMI registry, where the bound services are not removed if they crash. Clients are still able to get the stubs from the registry and do not find out that the service actually is unavailable until they try to invoke a method.

Remote Events

One very useful way of connecting components in applications is to use the concept of events: A component whose state changes can allow other components to register their interest in such changes by adding listeners to the component. When a change occurs, it sends an event object to all the listeners who may then act on this change somehow.

Jini has *remote events* that allow this to happen between distributed services. Basically, just as with the chat server you developed, clients can register a listener callback with a distributed service. When an event is created in the service, the service sends the event to all registered remote event listener callbacks.

However, the registration of clients is perceived as if they used the service. So, as described under leasing, clients must continuously renew the lease that is associated with the event listener registration. As with any other lease, if clients fail to renew it, the service considers the client as nonexistent and removes the listener from its list.

Although it is possible to let remote events be sent to a proprietary call-back interface, such as the `MessageListener` interface in the chat, Jini has a well-defined interface that should be used as well as a well-defined event object class to go with it (the equivalent of the chat's `Message` class). The reason for this is to make it possible to create generic event handlers that can sit in-between the distributed service and the actual client. For example, if a client is not always available, the client can register a generic event handler that stores the messages while the client is unavailable. When the client comes online, it can retrieve all the messages that have been produced and stored by the generic handler. This is only possible because of the generic interfaces that all remote events utilize. By chaining such generic event handlers together, you can gain more control over how events should be handled. It also becomes easier to reuse code that handles events in a certain way. This is shown in Figure 9.1.

In this scenario, the real listener registers a generic delegate, A, with the Jini service. Because A implements the generic remote event listener interface, it can handle any event sent from the Jini service. When it is finished with whatever it does, it sends the event to delegate B, which performs some action on the event. B finally delivers the event to the real, and final, listener.

Transactions

The last part of Jini deals with a common problem in distributed computing: *transactions*. The basic idea behind transactions is to allow several actions to appear as one; as if they were *atomic*. Consider this: A client talks to service A, which performs some state change. The client then talks to service B, which also performs some kind of state change. However, you want these two operations to be transactional, that is, as if they were one atomic operation.

What does this mean in practice? Consider this example: Service A contains an object Foo, and service B is initially empty. A client wants to remove the object Foo from A and move it to B. These are two operations: a removal and an insertion. So, you first remove the object Foo from A. Neither A nor B now contains any object; Foo is only available inside the client. Next, you insert Foo into B. If this succeeds, you then consider the operation, or transaction, to have succeeded as a whole.

However, what happens if the insertion fails? Then you have to reinsert Foo into A; otherwise it will be lost, which is not good. Instead of having moved Foo from A to B, it will have vanished.

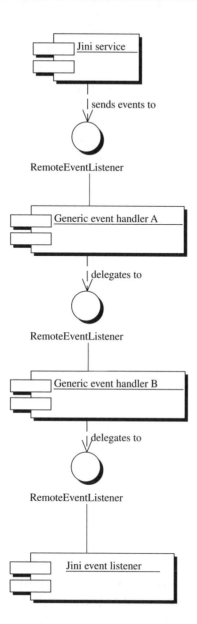

Figure 9.1   Jini event listener delegation.

To solve this problem, you use transactions. By using transactions, you make sure that the preceding scenario cannot happen. Because this is such a critical feature to have, Jini has a set of classes to support transactions.

Transaction Manager is simply a distributed service that can coordinate the transactions. When a client wants to make a series of operations within a transaction, it requests a new *Transaction* object from the Transaction Manager. This can then be sent to all *participants* of the transactions, such as A and B in the preceding example. These participants then register themselves with the transaction and perform their tasks. When the set of operations is complete, the client asks the transaction to *commit* the work that has been done. The Transaction Manager then tells the participants to finalize the work they have performed in the transaction. After this phase, the changes have either been made in all participants, or they will all have been undone, or *rolled back*, in the case that something went wrong along the way.

This completes the descriptions of the main five concepts that Jini uses. As a Jini programmer, you should be familiar with these five concepts. The descriptions I have provided are fairly brief, so be sure to pick up a book on Jini if you want more information about each of these concepts and how Jini handles them in practice.

Just to show you some of these concepts and the powerful paradigm they represent, let's adapt the HelloWorld example to Jini and see what benefits emerge.

Overview of the HelloJini Example

Let's begin with an overview of the pieces, and how this scenario differs from the previous ones. The system layout is shown in Figure 9.2.

The most obvious difference is that the RMI registry has been replaced with the Jini Lookup Service. Although they both implement the same basic concept, naming, the ways in which they accomplish this are radically different. With the registry, the client has to locate it first in order to perform a lookup. With the Lookup Service, this is performed by using multicast discovery, that is, the client shouts, "I want a lookup service!" and the Lookup Service responds to it. This reduces the amount of configuration that is needed on the client.

When the client has acquired an object that it can use to talk to the Lookup Service, the ensuing process is also radically different, as outlined in the "Lookup" section earlier. Instead of using a fixed string description of the service it wants, the client instead declares what the

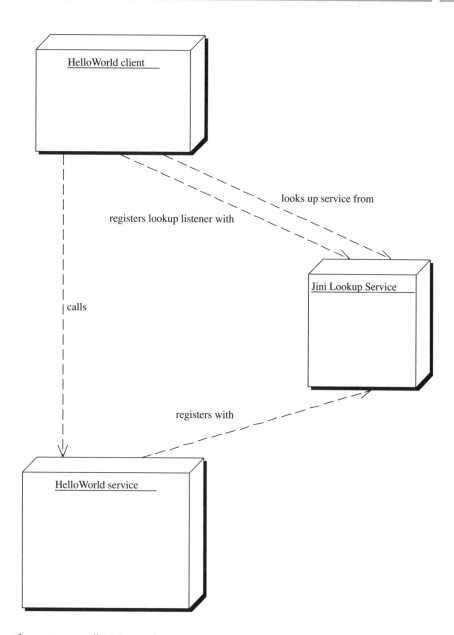

Figure 9.2   HelloJini overview.

service it wants should look like. This opens up the possibility of returning several registered services because there may be many services that
match the requirements.

But there is also another important difference between this scenario and the previous ones: The client has registered an event listener with the Lookup Service. What is the purpose of this? Well, consider the case when the Lookup Service is started, but not the HelloWorld service. What happens if you then start the client? It would find the Lookup Service, but it would not find any services to use. In the case of the RMI registry, that would be it; you would have to continually check the registry to see whether the service had been started and bound.

In this case, you can use the remote event listener feature: The client registers itself as interested in any changes to the Lookup Service. This means that whenever a service becomes available in the Lookup Service, the client will be notified. This makes it much easier to write your client, and it also makes it much more efficient because you do not have to poll the Lookup Service all the time.

So, in this scenario, you are using discovery, lookup, and remote events. What about leasing? Is that used in this scenario? Actually, yes it is. When the HelloWorld service binds itself into the Lookup Service, it can be seen as a client who uses its resources. Because of this, the Lookup Service wants to make sure that the information it holds about the HelloWorld service is valid, and thus requires the HelloWorld to renew a lease that is associated with the Lookup Service registration. In addition, the same applies for the client's event listener. Because the Lookup Service does not want to send events to services or clients that are no longer available, it associates a lease to each registered event listener.

This example does not make use of transactions, but it is useful enough to give you an idea of what Jini can do for you.

Although most of the Jini framework was introduced with Jini 1.0, there was a lot of manual administration that had to be done by the clients and services. This led to a rather large amount of similar code being written for each new service created. Jini 1.1 introduced a set of helper classes that can be used to perform these tasks for you. This example uses them, and you may find that the code, as a consequence, is rather simple, even verging on being simplistic. Do not be fooled though, as there is a lot of magic going on inside the helper classes. I will describe what each of these helper classes do, but for more details, you may want to read the source for these as well because it is available from the Jini home page.

The HelloJini Service

Let's start with the distributed service. This consists, as usual, of two classes: `HelloWorldImpl` and `Main`. The `HelloWorldImpl` is the remote object implementation, which implements the remote interface `HelloWorld` and performs the functionality of the service. The `Main` class is used to manage the `HelloWorlImpl` service and especially to make it available as a Jini service.

The code for `HelloWorldImpl` is as follows.

```
public class HelloWorldImpl
   implements HelloWorld
{

   private int counter = 0; // Invocation counter

   public String HelloWorld(String name)
   {
      System.out.println("Hello called");
      return "Hello " + name +"! You are caller nr "+(++counter);
   }
}
```

This may seem strange at first because this is just a regular remote object with no references to Jini at all. The trick here is that, as with the other examples, all the management functions of the service have been separated to the manager class `Main`. So, if you follow this pattern when you construct your own services, you will be able to convert them into Jini services without having to change the actual service class.

Without further ado, let's dive straight into the manager class `Main`, which is where the first reference to Jini appears.

```
public final class Main
{
   private DynaServer webserver;
   private JoinManager joinManager;

   private HelloWorldImpl server;

   public static void main(String[] args)
      throws Exception
   {
      // Load system properties from resource file
```

```
// This file is located in /lib/resources, and
// is included in classpath
// through the manifest in server.jar
System.getProperties().load(
    Thread.currentThread().
    getContextClassLoader().
    getResourceAsStream("system.properties"));

// Set policy to use
System.setProperty("java.security.policy",
    Main.class.getResource("/server.policy").toString());

// Set a security manager
System.setSecurityManager(new SecurityManager());

// Create server
Main main = new Main();

main.start();

System.out.println("Server has been started");
System.out.println("Press return to shutdown");

// Wait for return to be hit
BufferedReader in = new BufferedReader(
                        new InputStreamReader(System.in));
in.readLine();

// Shutdown gracefully
main.stop();

// Exit
System.exit(0);
}
```

So far there is not much new. One new attribute is the `JoinManager`. Later on in this section, you will see what this is used for. The most significant difference is that this class tries much harder to perform graceful shutdowns. As noted during the description of Jini leasing, a lease expires automatically if the client crashes. However, it takes some time before the lease grantor notices this, and by explicitly canceling the lease, as you will do in the shutdown procedure, your service will be much more well behaved. This will help your client immensely as you will see later on in the section "The HelloJini Client".

I have chosen to let the server wait for the user to press return in the console window. You can of course use some other mechanism for shutting down the server.

Next come the start and stop procedures.

```
public void start()
   throws IOException
{
   // Start all services in the right order
   startWebserver();
   startService();
   startJini();
}

public void stop()
{
   // Stop  all services in the reverse order
   stopJini();
   stopService();
   stopWebserver();
}
```

As you can see, there are three functions to perform, and you do them in reverse order in start and stop. You first start an internal Web server to be used for dynamic classloading. After that, you start the actual service, and lastly, you run the Jini associated code.

If you had started the Web server last, for example, the Jini code might fail because it could try to register the service with the Lookup Service. Because the Lookup Service needs the stub class of your service, this would have failed because the Web server that makes the classes available had not yet been started. This is the reason for this particular order.

```
protected void startWebserver()
   throws IOException
{
   // Create webserver for dynamic class downloading
   webserver = new DynaServer();

   // Add the classloader for this application
   // This will allow any client to download classes/resources that
   // are in the classpath for this application
   webserver.addClassLoader(Thread.
                              currentThread().
                              getContextClassLoader());

   // Start the webserver
   webserver.start();
}

protected void startService()
   throws RemoteException
```

```
{
    // Create remote object
    server = new HelloWorldImpl();

    // Export object
    UnicastRemoteObject.exportObject(server);
}

protected void startJini()
    throws IOException
{
    // Create attributes
    Entry[] attributes = new Entry[]
    {
        new Name("My HelloWorld service")
    };

    // Create a JoinManager
    // This will register our service with Jini lookup services
    joinManager = new JoinManager(server,
                                  attributes,
                                  (ServiceIDListener)null,
                                  null,
                                  null);
}
```

The first two start procedures are similar those you have seen before. You start a Web server and make the classes of your service available for download. You then instantiate and export your service as an RMI object.

And that's the Jini related code. As you can see, it is not much. You begin by creating the set of attributes that describe your service. There are a number of standard `Entry` types available, and `Name` is one of them. To keep things simple, I have only created one attribute for this service.

Next, you create a `JoinManager`. This is a Jini 1.1 helper class that takes care of the registration of your service with Jini Lookup Services. It uses the discovery mechanism to locate them, so there is no need to supply a URL or hostname to the Lookup Service. In the constructor, I have opted to not supply a couple of parameters.

The first null parameter is a `ServiceIdListener`. The first time a service is registered, it is given a unique ID that the service should try to reuse when making additional registrations. This makes it possible to determine whether two services from two different Lookup Services are actually the same service. The `ServiceIdListener` is notified when such an ID has been determined. The implementation of this interface typically stores the ID somewhere, so that it can be used if the service is restarted later on.

The second null parameter signifies a DiscoveryManagement object. The JoinManager does not perform the discovery mechanism itself, but instead delegates this to a DiscoveryManagement object. If you provide this object yourself, then you have the option of adding listeners to the discovery process (i.e., if you want to know when a Lookup Service was found). By supplying null, you tell the JoinManager that you are not interested in that kind of control, and the JoinManager then creates a DiscoveryManagement object internally. You can access this object from the JoinManager if you change your mind later on in the code.

The last null parameter is a LeaseRenewalManager object. Once the JoinManager has found a Lookup Service and has registered your service with it, the JoinManager then has to renew the lease that is associated with the registration. This task is delegated to a Lease RenewalManager object, which you may supply. As with the DiscoveryManagement object, this object lets you register your own listeners with the LeaseRenewalManager to receive leasing events. For this example, let's simply provide null, which allows the JoinManager to create a new LeaseRenewalManager. The relationships between the different objects are shown in Figure 9.3.

The startJini method is the only Jini related code you need to have in the server. Next, let's look at the shutdown code, which removes your service gracefully from the Jini community.

```
protected void stopWebserver()
{
   // Stop the internal webserver
   webserver.stop();
}

protected void stopService()
{
   // Unexport the Jini service
   try
   {
      UnicastRemoteObject.unexportObject(server, false);
   } catch (NoSuchObjectException e)
   {
      // Ignore
```

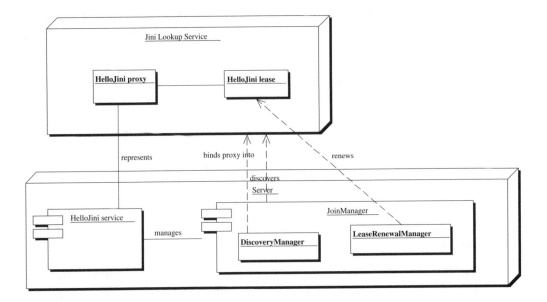

Figure 9.3 JoinManager services.

```
            e.printStackTrace();
        }
    }

    protected void stopJini()
    {
        // Stop the JoinManager
        // This will terminate any leases it has to Jini lookup services
        joinManager.terminate();
    }
}
```

Stopping the Web server and unexporting the remote object are tasks you are already familiar with. The last method also terminates the Jini JoinManager. Because the JoinManager runs a thread internally, which listens for Lookup Services, you need to explicitly shut it down. Also, the LeaseRenewalManager cancels the Jini leases that it has obtained from any Lookup Service. By doing this, all clients that are listening for changes in the Lookup Service are notified about the removal of the HelloJini service.

WARNING

▬▬▬ If you do not terminate the leases explicitly, they will expire only when the lease timeout expires, which means that clients will be able to retrieve the service from the Lookup Service although it is not really available. This in turn means that your clients need to be more fault tolerant because a normal shutdown means that the client receives connection exceptions when it calls the service.

The HelloJini Client

Because the remote interface is the same as the one used in all the other HelloWorld examples, let's skip directly to the client. In this example, you have to make the client an application instead of an applet. Why? Well, the client is going to be registering a callback with the Lookup Service so that it can be notified about newly registered services, and because you do not want to preinstall the stub class to this callback in the Lookup Service, you will use dynamic classloading. I have chosen to do this by embedding a Web server in the client from which the Lookup Service can access the callback stub class. Because this involves creating `java.net.ServerSocket` objects to listen for incoming HTTP requests, you cannot use applets because they are not allowed. If you want to change this so that the client is an applet, you have to provide a separate Web server that can be used for dynamic classloading.

The client presents the GUI shown in Figure 9.4.

There are three parts in this GUI. The top is used to show whether or not the client has found a service to use. The button at the bottom is used to

Figure 9.4 HelloJini client GUI before service startup.

Figure 9.5 HelloJini client GUI after service startup.

invoke the service once it has been found. As you can see, it is initially gray because no service has been found at this point. The empty space in the middle will be used to display a message from the HelloJini service.

When you start a HelloJini service, it is registered in the Lookup Service, and the client is notified of this. The GUI then changes to the screen shown in Figure 9.5.

The button is now enabled, and the label shows the text "Service is available." If you click on the button, the client invokes the HelloJini service through the stub that it has retrieved from the Lookup Service. The GUI then displays the response in the middle, as shown in Figure 9.6.

That was neat, was it not? So, what does the client code look like? The code is as follows.

```
public class HelloClient
extends Frame
{
    LookupCache serviceCache;
```

Figure 9.6 HelloJini client GUI after service usage.

```
Label serviceAvailability;

Label response;

Button helloButton;
```

You begin by declaring the variables you need. The first variable is related to Jini. Further down in the code, you create a Jini 1.1 helper object that helps you locate the HelloJini service. When the helper object finds a service that matches the client's needs, the service is put into a list of available services called the `LookupCache`. By not holding on to the service yourself, the reference to it becomes much easier to manage.

```
public static void main(String[] args)
    throws IOException
{
    new HelloClient();
}

public HelloClient()
    throws IOException
{
    super("HelloJini client");

    // Init security
    System.setProperty("java.security.policy",
        getClass().getResource("/client.policy").toString());
    System.setSecurityManager(new SecurityManager());

    // Start client
    startWebserver();
    startGui();
    startJini();
}
```

During the initialization of the client, you start the internal Web server for dynamic classloading, create the GUI components, and start the Jini client services.

```
protected void startWebserver()
    throws IOException
{
    // Create webserver for dynamic class downloading
    DynaServer srv = new DynaServer();

    // Add the classloader for this application
    // This will allow any client to download classes/resources that
```

```
        // are in the classpath for this application
        srv.addClassLoader(Thread.currentThread().
                              getContextClassLoader());

        // Start the webserver
        srv.start();
    }

protected void startGui()
{
        // Create GUI
        serviceAvailability = new Label("Service is not available");
        response = new Label()
        {
            public java.awt.Dimension getPreferredSize()
            {
                return new java.awt.Dimension(200,20);
            }
        };
        helloButton = new Button("Say hello!");
        helloButton.setEnabled(false);

        // Add listeners
        helloButton.addActionListener(new ActionListener()
        {
            public void actionPerformed(ActionEvent evt)
            {
                    // Call server again and show response
                    sayHello();
            }

        });

        addWindowListener(new WindowAdapter()
        {
            public void windowClosing(WindowEvent evt)
            {
                serviceCache.terminate();
                    System.exit(0);
            }
        });

        // Layout GUI
        add("North",serviceAvailability);
        add("Center",response);
        add("South",helloButton);

        pack();
        show();
    }
```

The creation of the internal Web server is identical to how it was done before.

When you create the GUI, the button is initially set to disabled. You will see later on in this section how to connect the state of the button with the Jini service lookup cache. When the button is pressed (which is only possible if there is a HelloJini service available), you call the method `sayHello`, which performs the actual call to your remote Jini service. As a last interesting point, you add a listener to the frame-closing event, which terminates the Jini service lookup properly. If this is not done, the lease that is associated with the callback, which you will be registering in the Lookup Service to listen for new services, will not be cancelled explicitly. This means that the Lookup Service will have an invalid call-back, which is unnecessary.

Next, let's look at the Jini related code in the client.

```
protected void startJini()
   throws IOException
{
   // Create Jini service discovery manager
   ServiceDiscoveryManager sdm;
   sdm = new ServiceDiscoveryManager(null, null);

   // Create service template
   Class[] types = new Class[] { HelloWorld.class };
   ServiceTemplate template;
   template = new ServiceTemplate(null, types, null);

   // Initialize service lookup
   serviceCache = sdm.createLookupCache(template,
                              null,
                    new ServiceDiscoveryListenerHelper());
}
```

In the client code, a little magic is performed. Just as the service created a `JoinManager` to help it communicate with the Lookup Service, the client creates a `ServiceDiscoveryManager` that helps it keep track of the available HelloJini services. As with the `JoinManager`, there are a few optional parameters, which I have chosen not to use. The first null parameter to the `ServiceDiscoveryManager` constructor is a `DiscoveryManagement` object. Just as the `JoinManager`, the `ServiceDiscoveryManager` needs to keep track of which Lookup Services it has found (as there can be many), and it uses a `DiscoveryManagement` object to do this. The second null is a

`LeaseRenewalManager`, which is used to renew the lease associated with the service availability listener callback that is registered in all found Lookup Services.

Once you have created a `ServiceDiscoveryManager`, it starts finding registered Jini services for you. Because you are only interested in the ones that implement the HelloWorld interface at this time, you initialize a lookup cache in which you want to contain the services filtered out by the given `ServiceTemplate`. You also register your own `ServiceDiscoveryListener` object, which is defined later on in this section, that updates the GUI according to the contents of the lookup cache.

Next comes the code that uses the lookup cache and invokes the Hello-Jini service.

```
protected void sayHello()
{
    ServiceItem si = serviceCache.lookup(null);
    HelloWorld service = (HelloWorld)si.service;
    try
    {
        String greeting = service.helloWorld("World");
        response.setText(greeting);
    } catch (RemoteException e)
    {
        serviceCache.discard(service);
    }
}
```

You first use the lookup cache to retrieve a reference to a HelloJini service. Because you do not want to filter the contents of the cache (any instance is ok), you simply provide null as a filter. Next, you extract the actual service object from the retrieved `ServiceItem`. How do you know that something was returned from the lookup? Can it not be null? In theory, yes, but because this method is only invoked as a result of a button click and the button is only enabled when there is something in the cache, this cannot happen. If you do not have these kinds of rules, then you must be prepared for the possibility of a null return value.

Next, you simply invoke the method and show the result in the GUI. If something goes wrong, remove this service from the lookup cache, so that you do not try to use it again. Note that because you have made the HelloJini service well-behaved in the sense that it deregisters itself from the Lookup Service, and because your client listens for such service removals through the `ServiceDiscoveryManager`, most of the time the cache will only contain valid service proxies, which enormously reduces the risk of getting a `RemoteException`. Although minimized, the risk is still present, so you need to do something with it. If the faulty service proxy was the only one in the cache, the button would be disabled until another HelloJini service became available.

Next, you define the helper class that updates the GUI to reflect whether or not the lookup cache is empty.

```
class ServiceDiscoveryListenerHelper
   implements ServiceDiscoveryListener
{
   public void serviceAdded(ServiceDiscoveryEvent event)
   {
      System.out.println("Service added");

      // Service is now available
      helloButton.setEnabled(true);
      serviceAvailability.setText("Service is available");
   }

   public void serviceRemoved(ServiceDiscoveryEvent event)
   {
      System.out.println("Service removed");

      if (serviceCache.lookup(null) == null)
      {
         // Service is now not available
         helloButton.setEnabled(false);
         serviceAvailability.setText("Service is not available");
      }
   }

   public void serviceChanged(ServiceDiscoveryEvent event)
   {
      // Ignore
      System.out.println("Service changed");
   }
}
}
```

This class is fairly straightforward. For all changes in the content of the Lookup Service, you check whether the lookup cache is empty or not. If it is not empty, you enable the button and show the string "Service is available" in the GUI. If the lookup cache is empty, you disable the button and show the string "Service is not available" in the GUI.

That is all you have to do in your client. The code that was coupled to Jini was quite simple. However, as you will see when you try this application, it is now much more robust as it properly handles server failures. Notice that you never had to specify where your server was located. This is a very interesting feature of Jini because it minimizes the need for client administration. You can move your server to any location you want as long as you can register it in a Lookup Service that the client can access.

Running the HelloJini Example

Now that you have finished all the code, let's look at how to run it. To make it interesting, execute the components in the following order:

1. Start the client.
2. Start the Jini Lookup Service.
3. Start the HelloJini service.
4. Start another HelloJini service.
5. Stop the first HelloJini service.
6. Stop the second HelloJini service.

The reason for the two HelloJini services is to see how your client reacts. Let's begin with the client. This can be started by executing the client.jar file in /bin with the following command:

```
java -jar client.jar
```

This command starts the client with its internal Web server, and the client starts looking for Jini Lookup Services. See Figure 9.4 to what it looks like.

You then start a Jini Lookup Service. How this is done is explained in the Jini package that you can download from Sun. The client discovers this Lookup Service, but the GUI remains unchanged because the Lookup Service does not yet contain a registration of the HelloJini service. The client, however, registers itself with the Lookup Service, so that it is notified when services become available.

You then start the HelloJini service by executing the following in the /bin directory of the HelloWorld example:

```
java -jar server.jar
```

The manager of the service first registers itself with the Lookup Service that you started; at which point, the client is notified of the availability of the new service. The client's GUI then changes to look like Figure 9.5. You can then invoke the service by clicking on the button, hence making the GUI look like Figure 9.6.

What happens when you start yet another HelloJini service? Well, it registers itself in the Lookup Service, and just as before, the client is notified about this. As a consequence, because this service matches the client's requirements (i.e., it implements the HelloWorld interface), the lookup cache that you created now contains two proxies. Does this matter to your client? Not really, but when the client looks up the service from the lookup cache in order to invoke it, it will get either of the services in a random fashion, so both are used if you click the button repeatedly. Thus, you get a basic form of load balancing.

You then stop the first HelloJini service. What happens? First of all, it is removed from the Lookup Service. This change is sent to the remote listener that the client's `ServiceDiscoveryManager` has registered in the Lookup Service, and the lookup cache is updated to only contain the service that is still available. What happens to your client? Nothing, because there is still one service in the lookup cache that you can use. If you click the button to invoke the service, the service that is still available is used.

Now, if you shutdown the last HelloJini service, the same happens as with the first one, but this time around the lookup cache is empty as a result. The button is hence grayed out, and the GUI shows the text "Service not available." You cannot call the service anymore.

What would have happened if the last HelloJini service had crashed instead of doing a proper shutdown? The Lookup Service would not have noticed this until the lease expired, so as a side effect, the client's lookup cache would continue to contain the service. If you then pressed the button before the lease timed out, the call would have produced a `RemoteException` because the connection had been closed. You have to catch this and handle it properly. In this example, I simply removed the defective service proxy from the cache (resulting in the button being grayed out), but you could also consider showing an error message.

So, what have you learned from all of this? That Jini provides a rather straightforward way to make your RMI applications quite a bit more flexible and robust. The declarative way of finding services makes your client and service much more loosely coupled, and the basic principle to anticipate problems removes many of the hassles that come with using RMI alone.

Summary

In this chapter, you took a look at Jini. Although an in-depth study of all of Jini's features was not provided, the basic principles were outlined: discovery, lookup, leasing, remote events, and transactions. You looked at how each of these affected RMI programming and how they helped you.

Discovery made it easy to find lookup services by using multicast. Lookup made it easy to find registered services by using a template-based approach. Leasing made it possible to detect failures of clients and services. Remote events made it possible to receive asynchronous notifications about changes in a service. And, transactions helped you keep systems consistent by grouping several changes into atomic actions.

To highlight these concepts, you adapted the HelloWorld example to use Jini. As you saw in the actual service, the remote interface did not have to change because of this new usage. You made a slight change to the service manager in order to use the new Jini Lookup Service as a naming system. You also modified the client to use the Lookup Service to find the service. The client became significantly more sophisticated as it could keep track of several instances of the service to use, and it also handled failures in a more robust manner.

Jini was initially marketed as a technology to get hardware devices to talk to each other, a kind of Java-based plug and play. Although Jini works great for that purpose, there is really nothing in Jini that prevents you from using it for pretty much whatever you want. If you think that the features of Jini make sense in your RMI project, you should definitely use it.

This completes your brief journey into the wonders of Jini. The next chapter will deal with the Enterprise JavaBeans technology and how it relates to RMI programming.

CHAPTER 10

RMI and Enterprise JavaBeans

One of the most common reasons to have distributed systems is to allow a set of clients to access a database with information and to perform tasks with that information. These types of systems often involve building servers with such functionality as database connection pools, logging facilities, and configuration tools. However, after doing a few of these systems, it becomes apparent that some of these features are highly reusable and not limited solely to the original application. For example, logging messages to files and communicating with databases are tasks that are common to many kinds of applications.

For this reason, developers often talk about three types of code: *system logic*, *business logic*, and *application logic*. System logic is the kind of infrastructure code described in the previous paragraph; it can be reused in a wide variety of applications. Business logic is code that is related to problems of a specific domain, such as order processing. Application logic is the part of your code that binds together various business logic parts to present a unified application to be used by clients. Typically, business logic is not tied to a particular application, but can be reused in many applications by using different kinds of application logic.

The question is: If system logic is so common, why should you have to bother writing system code for these things yourself? (It is like writing your own operating system, just to be able to create a word processor to run on it.) Not surprisingly, the answer is that you should not have to deal with these things. Instead, you should be able to write your business and application logic code and be able to plug it into a framework that provides the system logic for you, just as desktop applications use an operating system to provide things such as virtual memory management and file systems. But then you would have to have some API and guidelines for how to interact with the framework. And this is the precise purpose of the Enterprise JavaBeans (EJB) specification: It provides you with a standardized specification of how application and business components can be plugged into any system logic implementation provider (or EJB container in EJB lingo) and have them be executed by the framework in a well-defined way.

The EJB specification declares what you, as a component creator (or bean provider in EJB lingo), must do in order to be able to plug your component (or deploy it in EJB lingo) into an EJB container and what the EJB container must do with it. It defines an API that the bean provider can use to interact with the container and an API that the container can use to interact with your components. Hence, both sides of the interaction are covered by the same specification. Because it is preferable to allow many kinds of implementations of the system logic, most of the specification is declarative in the sense that you can declare "what" you want to happen, but not exactly "how" it should happen.

For example, your component can declare that it wants access to a particular database, that it wants transactions to be handled in a particular way, or that only a specified set of users can call it. Exactly how the container decides to implement these requests should not be important. The important thing is that it is done. This allows EJB components to be fairly loosely coupled to a particular container, and as a consequence, they can be used with various containers without any code changes.

So what does RMI have to do with all of this? Well, once you have deployed your beans in an EJB container, you need to access them somehow, and this is accomplished by using RMI. So, you will be using remote interfaces, stubs, remote exceptions, and all of those things that you know from programming regular RMI.

Also, all of the design guidelines that apply to RMI are valid in an EJB context as well. There is still a certain amount of overhead to network calls, security is something that should be considered, and serialization may be tricky to get right. Being the RMI wiz that you are by now, you should be able to tackle these issues with confidence.

We will begin this chapter by looking at the various things that EJB containers provide. Then, we will take a look at how EJB containers work to get a feel for what such a framework must do. Next, we examine the different kinds of components that you can create in EJB. Finally, we create an example that walks you through the different parts of an EJB component and discuss how they relate to each other.

Overview

What kinds of functionality does EJB containers make available to components? The EJB specification states that compliant containers should provide the following:

- **Transactions.** If certain actions in your component involve several steps, and especially if a database is used, then you often require them to be done in transactions, that is, atomic operations that either completely succeed or completely fail. EJB allows the bean provider to declare what transactional requirements the components have. The EJB container then implements these requirements by coordinating database interactions accordingly. EJB containers use the Java Transaction API (JTA) and Java Transaction Service (JTS) to do this.

- **Security.** EJB allows the bean provider to declare who is allowed to call the operations of the components. The EJB container then authenticates the clients and makes sure that they are only able to invoke methods that they are allowed to access. EJB may use the Java Authentication and Authorization Service (JAAS) to perform this. JAAS is an API that allows clients to declare their identity and servers to access this information for authorization purposes (or other similar purposes).

- **Environment properties.** The component may have certain features that should be configurable. Because of this, EJB allows the bean provider to declare environment properties and their respective values. The components can then look up the values of these properties at runtime. This makes it possible to configure components without having to hardcode values or provide custom configuration files.

- **Distribution.** Because EJB is a framework for distributed components, there has to be a way for clients to invoke the components through a network. EJB makes the components available through the JNDI naming system and allows clients to access them through RMI. EJB containers may use the RMI over Internet Inter-Orb Protocol (IIOP) technology to allow Common Object Request Broker Architecture (CORBA) clients to access EJB components (IIOP is the network protocol used by CORBA).

- **Database connectivity.** Because components typically access databases, EJB containers must be able to provide this functionality. Components can declare their database needs, and the EJB container then uses the Java Database Connectivity (JDBC) API to make databases available to the components.

- **Component relationships.** Quite often, components will want to make use of other components. For example, application logic components typically access business logic components in order to perform some complex task. EJB allows the bean provider to declare which other components a specific component wants to access, and the EJB container then makes those components easily available to it.

As you can see, EJB uses many other standard specifications (such as JTA, JDBC, RMI/IIOP, etc.) to perform its magic. The relationships between all of these technologies are described in the *Java 2 Enterprise Edition (J2EE)* specification. By using the J2EE specification, you can easily switch between different implementations of the J2EE technologies. Your application and the components that it consists of are thus portable between implementations of J2EE.

Many of the preceding features are declared by letting the bean provider write a special XML file with descriptions of the component and its needs and requirements. You will see in the section, "The HelloEJB Deployment Descriptor," what this file looks like and how to construct it.

EJB Containers

How do EJB containers work? What is it that they do to provide all of this functionality? And how do they make the components available to the client? There is quite a bit of magic involved, and I will not delve into all the details. However, the basic principles are shown in Figure 10.1.

EJB versus Jini?

If you look at the feature set provided by Jini, you might notice that many of the features are similar to those of EJB. They both provide transactions, distributed services, and lookup services. Many EJB containers also provide fault tolerance and scalability features, as do Jini's to some degree. So, the following question may seem logical at first: Should I use EJB or Jini?

However, this question has a serious flaw. The problem is that the functional overlap is only superficial because these two specifications serve different purposes: Jini is (primarily) used to create system logic code, and EJB is used to create application and business logic code. Hence, the system logic code that is used to implement an EJB container can use Jini to provide its services to the EJB components that have been deployed in it. For example, the JNDI implementation of the EJB container can use the Jini Lookup Service under the covers, i.e. as the basis for its implementation, and the failover features of the container can take advantage of Jini mechanisms to handle service failures.

For this reason, the question really should be: Should I use EJB and Jini? And the answer can very well be yes because they complement each other quite well. It is also quite possible to expose EJB components through the Jini Lookup Service, that is, use the Jini Lookup Service to wrap the JNDI implementation of the EJB container. This allows Jini clients to access EJB components as though they were regular Jini services.

For each component that you want the server to handle for you, it creates an EJB container that hosts your component and makes it available to callers. Especially, it creates one object called an *EJBHome* that clients can use to create, remove, and find instances of your component. When you tell the EJBHome object to create a component for you, it returns another object that is called an *EJBObject*. This object represents your component and allows you to make calls to your component. Both the EJBHome and EJBObjects are RMI objects, so they implement an interface that extends `java.rmi.Remote`. You will learn how to construct these interfaces later on in the section "The HelloEJB Component."

And this is the interesting part: When you make a call on the EJBObject, the call is handled by the EJB container, which may perform any tasks that it wishes (such as security checking or transaction management)

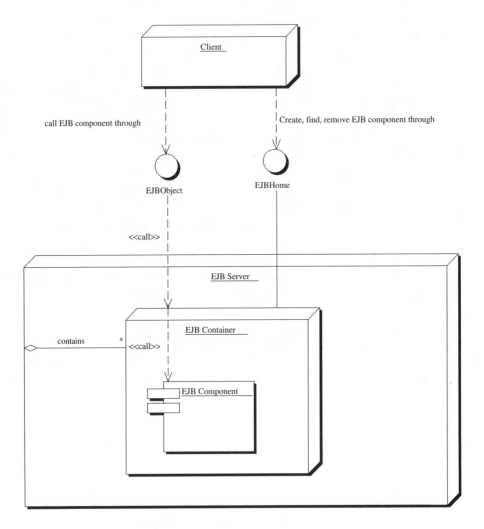

Figure 10.1 EJB container principles.

before forwarding the call to your component. By inserting itself in the middle, it can add quite a lot of services to your component, and the component itself does not have to be changed to allow this to happen. In fact, the component is not an RMI object; it is not exported to the RMI system. The EJB container is responsible for providing the remoteness by providing such RMI objects for you. How this is done depends on the actual EJB container implementation.

There are several options available to the EJB container implementor. For example, it can create just one remote object that is used to represent all of your component instances, or it can create one per instance. The important thing is that this really should not matter to the component provider. As long as the EJB container performs the tasks that you have told it to, and in accordance with the EJB specification, you should be happy.

EJB Components

So, just what are these components (or *beans* in EJB lingo) made of? Are there different kinds of components? There are, as of EJB 2.0, four kinds of components: *stateless session beans, stateful session beans, entity beans,* and *message-driven beans.* Session beans are coupled to specific clients, whereas entity beans are shared between clients. Message-driven beans are used to process asynchronous messages, such as Java Messaging Service (JMS) messages.

An EJB component is composed of four items:

- **EJBHome remote interface.** This is the remote interface that is implemented by the EJBHome object, and it must extend the `javax.ejb.EJBHome` interface. It mainly contains methods to create and remove EJBObjects. If the component is of the type entity bean, it also contains finder methods that allow clients to look up specific components with a particular identity. The implementation for this interface is entirely created by the EJB container provider. This part of the EJB component can be thought of as a factory in design pattern lingo. Message-driven beans do not have any EJBHome objects because clients cannot access them. The only way to talk to a message-driven bean is to send a message to the JMS topic or queue that the bean is listening to.

- **EJBObject remote interface.** This remote interface contains the methods that you want to be able to call in your component, and it must extend the standard remote interface javax.ejb.EJBObject. As with EJBHome, the EJB container provider is responsible for creating the implementation for this interface, and message-driven beans do not have any EJBObjects because they are not callable from clients.

- **Enterprise bean implementation.** This is the class that is the equivalent of the remote object implementation, with one difference; it does not explicitly implement the remote interface. Instead, it has the business methods of your EJBObject remote interface, and it also implements javax.ejb.SessionBean, javax.ejb.EntityBean, or javax.ejb.MessageDrivenBean (depending on which type of component it is), which lets the container interact with your component. So even though you need to make sure that the methods in your EJBObject remote interface and the bean implementation are the same, the bean does not implement the EJBObject interface. The reason is that it should not have to provide the methods of the javax.ejb.EJBObject interface, which are instead implemented by the EJB container provider. So, when you call a method on the EJBObject, there are two situations that can occur. If you define the method, then the method is forwarded by the container to your bean implementation, whereas if it is a method in the javax.ejb.EJBObject interface, the container can handle it without having to use the actual bean implementation. As previously noted, these EJBObject method considerations only apply to session beans and entity beans, not message-driven beans.

- **Deployment descriptor.** As stated before, much of the EJB magic comes from the fact that you can declaratively specify how certain tasks, such as transaction management and security, should work. For this purpose, EJB allows you to write a deployment descriptor, which is an XML file that contains a description of your component including how the EJB container should handle it. If you have several components that should be treated as a unit, you can write one descriptor that encompasses information about all of them.

Once you have created these four parts, you bundle them together into a JAR file, which you then can hand over to an EJB container for deployment.

The EJB container examines the descriptor and creates the EJBObject and EJBHome implementations for you, and then sets up the execution environment that runs the component. After that, your clients can look up the EJBHome object from JNDI and start creating and calling the component. Later on in this chapter you will create a sample component and client, which will allow you to see how all of this works in practice.

Let's take a closer look at each of these component types and see what their respective characteristics are.

Stateless Session Beans

The main purposes of stateless session beans are to model use-cases or workflow. They do not have any persistent data. Stateless session beans are stateless in the sense that instances of components of this type do not have any state that is tied to the clients that use them. What does this mean? It means that if the EJB container, for example, creates 10 instances of a stateless session bean, it can use any of those instances to serve a business method from a call. Why? Because each instance is not related to any one client. Why create 10 instances then? Why not just use one? Well, that would be perfectly okay, but the EJB specification states that only one thread at a time may execute any bean instance. So, if two clients want to call the same stateless session bean at the same time, there either has to be two separate instances or one of the clients has to wait for the other to finish. Basically, this makes stateless session beans components that simply contain a set of related methods that clients can call.

WARNING
The stateless part of stateless session beans is often misinterpreted as "their instances are not allowed to have any attributes at all." This is incorrect. They may have attributes that are not bound to the client that is using it, such as a JDBC connection or any other similar resource. Another possible use is to load configuration data from a database and store it in an attribute of the bean implementation.

Stateful Session Beans

If stateless session beans are completely client independent, stateful session beans are quite the opposite. When you create a stateful session bean through its home, an instance is actually created in the EJB container, which is dedicated to the client that created it. This instance may contain any state it wants, which may or may not be client related. For example, when the client creates a stateful session bean through the EJBHome, it may pass some data about the client that the session bean should keep during its lifetime. Each time the client calls it, the instance can then use the client specific information.

A common use for stateful session beans is to model business processes that involve a set of steps that acquire information from the client, such as a wizard style form or a shopping cart in a Web store. The information is accumulated during the separate steps and is then used in the last step to perform some action in the system.

Because stateful session beans contain client specific state, it may happen that there are so many instances around that the EJB container runs out of memory. The container may then swap an instance to disk, which is a process called *passivation*. The client does not notice this because the EJBObject that it uses to communicate with the session is not affected. If the client wants to make a call to the session, it is read back from disk, that is, it is *activated*. Because of this mechanism, the container can support a large number of clients without running out of memory.

Entity Beans

Entity beans are used to represent persistent objects or domain model objects. An entity bean has a primary key that is used to identify the individual instances, and their state is typically stored in a database.

They are not client specific. One client can create an entity bean with a particular primary key value, but a completely different client may later use a finder method on the EJBHome to find and use that entity bean, and a third client may remove it at some later point. Because they are not client specific, it is likely that several clients may try to use the same entity bean instance at the same time. The EJB container may then either serialize the different clients' access to it or create more instances that correspond to the same primary key and have the same state-all to preserve the rule that only one thread at a time may access an EJB instance.

If several instances are created, there is the possibility that conflicting changes are made to the different instances. There will be different versions for a short period of time. The solution to these conflicts is to use the database transaction facilities, which basically allow the EJB container to throw away the instance that was changed last. Does this seem senseless? Well, it is a trade-off, and the reasoning is that most of the usage will probably be read-only, so that conflicting versions will rarely occur.

Because entity beans typically contain quite a lot of state, there is a limit to how many can be kept in memory at any one time. For this reason, they are also subject to the activation/passivation mechanism that was outlined in the description of stateful session beans.

There are two ways to handle the state in entity beans: Either the container itself takes care of it, or you can put all the database interaction code in your own bean. The first option is called Container Manager Persistence (CMP), and the latter is called Bean Managed Persistence (BMP). If possible, you should try to use CMP because it makes your beans more portable. However, if you have a complex mapping between your database and the bean, which the container cannot handle, then you will have to use BMP. It is also possible to mix the two, so that the container handles what it can, and your bean handles the rest. You should also consider the fact that BMP requires you to write all the database interaction code, which can be quite complex.

Overview of the HelloEJB Example

Now that you have a fairly good understanding of what EJB is and how it works, let's put it to use by adapting the HelloWorld example to EJB and see how it turns out. Because it does not have any state, you can model it as a simple stateless session bean. When you start building your own EJB applications, you will find that this is the most frequently used type of EJB component.

Let's walk through the four different parts of the HelloEJB component and round off with a client that uses it.

The HelloEJB Component

Unlike the other RMI examples, there is no manager in this example because the EJB container implements the manager functionality for you (i.e., by taking care of the lifecycle of your object, placing references to it in the naming service, etc.). Instead, you can solely focus on the actual behavior of your component, and ignore the administrative issues. As you can see already, this is a great benefit of EJB. By taking care of the routine tasks, the business logic developer can focus more time on writing the business logic code instead of the system level code of the component.

Let's begin with the interfaces, the home and remote ones, followed by the bean implementation and see how they are all tied together in the deployment descriptor.

The HelloEJB Home Interface

Let's begin with the remote interface of the EJBHome object.

```
public interface HelloHome
    extends javax.ejb.EJBHome
{
    public HelloWorld create()
        throws javax.ejb.CreateException, RemoteException;
}
```

The primary difference compared to an ordinary remote interface is that it extends `javax.ejb.EJBHome` instead of `java.rmi.Remote`. Why is this? Have the rules changed for some reason? Fear not, the EJBHome interface contains methods that are common to all EJBHome objects (such as removal of EJBObjects and acquiring metadata for the component), and in fact, extends `java.rmi.Remote` itself. So all you have to do is to make sure that your EJBHome always contains a couple of methods that are always be available to clients.

The method that has been declared is used to create EJBObjects to talk to the stateless session bean. This EJBObject implements your own remote interface `HelloWorld`, which you will look at next. The create method also throws the EJB specific `javax.ejb.CreateException`, which is thrown by the container if the creation fails. As usual, because this is a remote method, it also throws `java.rmi.RemoteException`.

As noted before, the EJB container provides the implementation of this object and makes it available through JNDI.

The HelloEJB Remote Interface

The following code contains the remote interface of the HelloEJB interface. This is the interface that you will use to communicate with the component once you have created it through the EJBHome object.

JBoss

As noted in the description of EJB, you can choose any implementation of the specification and be able to deploy your component to it. However, because I happen to be the architect of one of these critters, it is time to put on my JBoss hat.

JBoss is an EJB server that has a couple of interesting features with regard to RMI. Instead of making each component a remote object, you have one object that all calls go to. This means that there is only one remote stub that has to be generated, and that is done when the EJB container itself is compiled, so it is nothing that you as a user have to worry about.

So, how can you access your components without having to make remote objects for the EJBObject and EJBHome objects? The trick is that the single remote object contains the following remote method:

```
public java.rmi.MarshalledObject invoke(java.rmi.Marshalled
Object mo)
```

So, what do these marshalled objects contain? They contain information about which component the call is meant for, which specific component instance should get it (in case of Stateful SessionBeans and EntityBeans where instances have identities), and the method and parameters for the actual call. With this information, the container can forward the call to the right instance for invocation.

But the client should see the remote interface, right? It should not have to call this "invoke" method! The trick I have used is to create a proxy on top of the remote object (by using the Dynamic Proxy API) that implements the remote interface of the EJB component. Thus, when a client requests a component from the EJBHome object (which also uses this trick), it gets a dynamically generated proxy that holds a reference to the remote object, which is the container. When the client then invokes this object, the proxy bundles the call information into a MarshalledObject and sends it to the container through the remote "invoke" method. When the container has forwarded the call to the component and has received a result, that result is put into a MarshalledObject and returned to the proxy, which unpacks the result and returns it to the client.

This trick gives you (mainly) three advantages: First of all, you need only generate one stub class (for the container). Second, it allows you to easily add custom information to the remote call (e.g., you can easily add information to the call about the client's identity). Third, it allows you to put custom logic into the remote proxy (e.g., failover and load-balancing code).

The JBoss server is OpenSource, so you can download the entire source and see how this has been implemented. See www.jboss.org for more information.

```
public interface HelloWorld
    extends javax.ejb.EJBObject
{
    public String helloWorld(String name)
        throws RemoteException;
}
```

As with EJBHome, this remote interface does not extend `java.rmi.Remote` directly, but instead extends the `javax.ejb.EJBObject` interface. And just as with EJBHome, the EJBObject interface contains methods that should be available regardless of what the component does.

Other than extending the `javax.ejb.EJBObject` interface, the EJBObject interface looks just like a regular remote interface: The method parameters and return values are serializable, and the *throws* clause must include `java.rmi.RemoteException`.

The HelloEJB Bean Implementation

The component implementation is fairly straightforward. The biggest difference compared to regular RMI is that any EJB component must implement the proper subinterface of `javax.ejb.EnterpriseBean`. In this case, a session bean is being developed, so you implement the `javax.ejb.SessionBean` interface. This contains various callbacks that the container uses during the lifecycle of the component instance. For example, once it has instantiated the `HelloBean` class, it calls `setSessionContext` in order to give the component an object that can be used to access the container.

```
public class HelloBean
    implements SessionBean
{
    String myName; // We can have state,
                   // but no client-specific state!

    public String helloWorld(String name)
    {
        return "Hello "+name+"! My name is "+myName;
    }
}
```

As you can see, the component implements the `javax.ejb.Session-Bean` interface, as was discussed earlier. It also has an attribute, `myName`, that you set to the name of this component. To make things interesting, you read this name from the configuration of the component. More about this later.

The component does not implement the `HelloWorld` remote interface. Why is this? As explained in the description of how EJB containers work, the container creates an EJBObject that is a remote object, which implements the remote interface. This is what clients will be calling methods on, and these method invocations will then be forwarded through the container to the component. Because of this, you do not have to implement the remote interface.

TIP

Because EJB components do not have to implement the remote interface, it is easy to get them to mismatch, for example, if you change the remote interface without making the same change in the component. This will not lead to compile time errors, but will cause the deployment in the container to fail.

To get around this, you can split your remote interface into two parts: one regular interface with all the methods and another that extends the first interface and javax.ejb.EJBObject. Then you can let your component implementation implement the interface with all the methods to provide you with compile time checking, which indicates that the interface and component implementation are equal.

Now let's take a look at the implementation of the EJB calls corresponding to the home interface.

```
    public void ejbCreate()
       throws CreateException
    {
       try
       {
          // Retrieve our name from the environment settings
          myName = (String)new
  InitialContext().lookup("java:comp/env/myName");
       } catch (NamingException e)
       {
          throw new CreateException("Could not get name for component");
       }
    }
```

Although the EJBHome interface does not contain a method called `ejbCreate`, it does contain a `create` method. When the client calls `create`, the container may create an instance and call `ejbCreate` on this new instance. The instance may then be used to execute calls to the

EJBObject. However, because the instance is not bound to the client (remember, it was stateless), the container may use this instance to handle calls from other clients as well. This mechanism is called *instance pooling*. Because of this, when another client calls `create` on the EJB-Home object, the container may find that it already has a created component instance and will not create another one.

This behavior only occurs with stateless session beans. If you create stateful session beans or entity beans, the container has to call `ejbCreate` on the component instance as a consequence of the `create` call on the EJBHome object. The reason is that the component instance must be tied to that particular client in the case of a stateful session bean or to a particular identity in the case of entity beans.

In this `ejbCreate` method, you access a configuration entry. This is defined in the deployment descriptor and is accessed through the component specific `java:comp/env` JNDI namespace. By component specific, I mean that each component has its own version of that namespace so lookups of the same name from different components may yield different results. In this case, you look up a string that signifies the name of the component. The name is used when the greeting is constructed in the `helloWorld` method.

The only thing left to do is implement the `javax.ejb.SessionBean` interface.

```
public void setSessionContext(SessionContext ctx)
{
   // Don't need the context so we don't store it
}

public void ejbActivate()
{
   // Only applies to stateful sessions
}

public void ejbPassivate()
{
   // Only applies to stateful sessions
}

public void ejbRemove()
{
   // Nothing to do here in our case
}
}
```

The `setSessionContext` method is called by the container directly after instantiation of the instance and allows the instance to get a context object that it can use to call certain operations on the container. The `ejbActivate` and `ejbPassivate` methods are not used because this is a stateless session bean. If this was a stateful session bean, you would, in `ejbPassivate`, drop any resources that are unsuitable for persistent storage (such as socket connections) and reestablish them in `ejbActivate`. The `ejbRemove` method is called when the container decides that it does not need this instance any longer.

TIP

Most of the time, you will not want to do anything in the session bean and entity bean EJB interface implementations, so you could make empty implementations of these interfaces, and then let your component extend these through inheritance. This allows you to define, in the component implementation, only the methods that actually do something interesting.

And with this, the HelloEJB component code is finished. Next you will look at the XML descriptor for this component.

The HelloEJB Deployment Descriptor

As mentioned earlier, an EJB component is not just composed of Java code. It also contains a descriptor that tells the EJB container how to deploy and execute the component.

The descriptor for this example only contains information about one component, HelloEJB, but if you have several components that should be deployed as a unit, or application, they should be described in the same descriptor.

```
<ejb-jar>
   <description>HelloEJB example for the book Mastering RMI
   </description>
   <display-name>HelloEJB example</display-name>
   <enterprise-beans>
      <session>
         <display-name>Hello EJB</display-name>
         <ejb-name>HelloEJB</ejb-name>
         <home>masteringrmi.helloejb.interfaces.HelloHome</home>
         <remote>masteringrmi.hclloejb.interfaces.HelloWorld</remote>
         <ejb-class>masteringrmi.helloejb.ejb.HelloBean</ejb-class>
         <session-type>Stateless</session-type>
         <transaction-type>Container</transaction-type>
```

```
    <env-entry>
        <env-entry-name>myName</env-entry-name>
        <env-entry-type>java.lang.String</env-entry-type>
        <env-entry-value>HelloEJB</env-entry-value>
    </env-entry>
  </session>
</enterprise-beans>
```

This first part of the descriptor is created by the bean developer. It contains a description of every component that is included: its name, the classes of the component, any environment entries, and so on. The bean accesses the environment entry `myName` in the `ejbCreate` method, and you can see how it is declared. The name, type, and value are given, and in this case, the string "HelloEJB" is bound to the JNDI entry `java:comp/env/myName`.

Next, you will look at the part of the deployment descriptor that has to do with how the container should execute this component.

```
<assembly-descriptor>
    <security-role>
<role-name>Guest</role-name>
    </security-role>
    <method-permission>
<description>Guest access</description>
    <role-name>Guest</role-name>
<method>
  <ejb-name>HelloEJB</ejb-name>
      <method-name>*</method-name>
    </method>
    </method-permission>
    <container-transaction>
<description>HelloEJB transaction</description>
    <method>
  <ejb-name>HelloEJB</ejb-name>
      <method-name>*</method-name>
    </method>
<trans-attribute>Supports</trans-attribute>
    </container-transaction>
  </assembly-descriptor>
</ejb-jar>
```

In this code snippet, you define all the security roles for your application. In this case, you simply define a role "Guest." You then use this role when you declare method permissions. The method permissions signify who is allowed to call what methods. When a client makes a call to a method in a particular component, the EJB container checks the component's method permissions to determine whether or not to allow the call to go through. You now have security constraints on your component without having had to write any code!

You then declare how transactions are handled. Because you do not work with any databases in this example, this is somewhat irrelevant, but set it to Supports anyway. This means that if the caller of the HelloEJB component has started a transaction, you will use it, but if a transaction has not been started, then that is okay as well. It does not really make a difference for this example.

In any case, you now have transaction management without having had to write any code! This means that you can change both the security and transaction requirements for the component without having to change any source code or recompile, which is a huge win. This is the wonders of declarative computing at work.

And with this, you are finished with the HelloEJB component. All that is left to do is to package the parts into a JAR file, which can then be deployed in an EJB container. This JAR file contains the classes and dependant classes of the EJB component(s) described in the deployment descriptor. The deployment descriptor must also be placed into the JAR file inside a file named `ejb-jar.xml`. The deployment descriptor must be placed into the `META-INF` subdirectory of the JAR file.

The HelloEJB Client

Let's take a look at the client for this component. As you will see, there are many resemblances to how it used to work with plain RMI: You use JNDI to look it up, and the calling of it is the same. What is different is that you first have to create an EJBObject from the EJBHome object. The code is as follows.

```
public class HelloClient
{
    public static void main(String[] args)
        throws Exception
    {
        new HelloClient();
    }

    public HelloClient()
        throws Exception
```

```
{
   // Find home for HelloEJB
   HelloHome home;
   try
   {
      Context ctx = new InitialContext();
      home = (HelloHome) PortableRemoteObject.narrow(
                        ctx.lookup("HelloEJB"),
                        HelloHome.class); // Use IIOP casting
      ctx.close();
   } catch (NamingException e)
   {
      System.out.println("Could not lookup HelloEJB home");
      throw e;
   }
```

You begin by looking up the EJBHome object from the JNDI namespace. You cast it to `HelloHome` and close the context. Note that the portable way to do casting is to use the `PortableRemoteObject.narrow` call. This is necessary because the EJB container may be CORBA-based, in which case, an externalized reference is stored in JNDI instead of a real object. The `PortableRemoteObject.narrow` call then replaces the externalized reference (or *IOR* in CORBA lingo) with a real object implementing the given home interface.

How did the EJBHome object get into the JNDI namespace? And who is responsible for starting this namespace? The answer to both these questions is the EJB server. When you start the EJB server, it also starts a naming service that clients can use to access the components. When the component is deployed, the server binds the created EJBHome object in the JNDI namespace.

```
   // Create HelloEJB
   HelloWorld helloEJB;
   try
   {
      helloEJB = home.create();
   } catch (CreateException e)
   {
      System.out.println("Could not create HelloEJB");
      throw e;
   }

   // Get greeting
   String greeting;
   try
```

```
    {
        greeting = helloEJB.helloWorld("World");
    } catch (RemoteException e)
    {
        System.out.println("Could not get greeting from HelloEJB");
        throw e;
    } finally
    {
        helloEJB.remove();
    }

    // Print greeting
    System.out.println(greeting);
    }
}
```

Next, you create an EJBObject that implements the component's remote interface, `HelloWorld`, and invoke the `helloWorld` method on it. The call, as previously described, is forwarded by the container's EJBObject to your component, which creates a greeting and returns it. You then remove the component, and print this greeting to the system output.

This may not seem very strange, but there is actually quite a bit of magic going on behind the scenes. To give you an idea of how the calls flow on create, invocation, and removal, let's take a look at a sequence diagram for those calls. Note that because the EJB specification allows flexibility in how these methods are implemented inside an EJB container, there can be variations in the sequence of events. Figure 10.2 illustrates one of the most likely ways that this scenario can be implemented.

At the beginning of this diagram, the component has been deployed, so the EJB container has created its EJBHome and has bound it into JNDI. No other client has used this component, so the container has not had any reason to create any `HelloBean` instances yet. The client then looks up the EJBHome and is ready to use it.

The first thing to do is to get an EJBObject that the client can use to call the component. This is done by calling `create` on the EJBHome. The EJBHome object forwards the call to the container, which instantiates a new EJBObject that implements the remote interface.

Next, the client invokes the `helloWorld` method on the EJBObject. This call is forwarded to the EJB container, which begins by doing the transaction and security checks, at least. It may also log the call or do

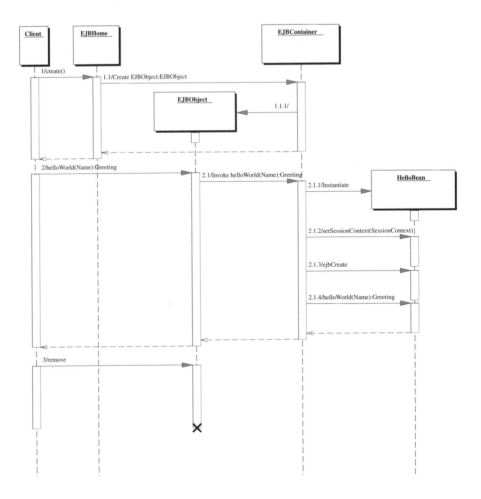

Figure 10.2 Creation, invocation, and removal of component.

some other useful task. Because it has not yet created any instances of the `HelloBean` class, it must do so now.

The HelloBean class is instantiated, and the container then casts it to `javax.ejb.SessionBean` and invokes `setSessionContext` on it to allow the instance to get a callback to the container. The container then calls `ejbCreate` on the instance; after which, it is ready to be used to serve client calls.

The container calls the `helloWorld` method on the instance, and returns the result to the client. Because the `HelloBean` instance may be reused for other client calls, it is stored in a pool of ready instances. The next time a client calls the component, it can use this pooled instance instead of creating a new one.

The last thing that the client does is to remove the component. This is done by calling `remove` on the EJBObject. Because there is no strong coupling between the `HelloBean` instance that the container created and the client that used it, the only thing that happens is that the EJBObject is destroyed. The instance in the container is still usable by other clients.

As you can see, EJB is very much about encapsulation of details. The container deals with all the complicated issues, such as threading and lifecycle management, by inserting itself between the client and the component. Although this can be a bit confusing to the EJB beginner, you will soon learn to appreciate not having to deal with these things yourself.

Summary

This chapter introduced you to the Enterprise JavaBeans technology. By acknowledging the difference in purpose of code in an application, you can draw the conclusion that system logic can typically be reused, whereas application and business logic changes quite a lot depending on the actual application. Enterprise JavaBeans introduces an API and semantics for that API, which allow system logic to be written so that application and business logic components can be easily plugged into it. This allows the component developer to focus on the problem domain of the application and use the features provided by an EJB implementation provider to supply the system logic parts.

The component host, or *EJB container*, provides features, such as transactions, security, persistence, and so on. It does so by using other APIs that are part of the *Java2 Enterprise Edition(J2EE)* specification. The components, or *Enterprise Beans*, come in four flavors (*stateless session beans, stateful session beans, entity beans*, and *message-driven beans*) and are comprised of four parts (*remote interface, home interface, bean implementation*, and *deployment descriptor*).

You looked at how the EJB container provides remote access to deployed EJB components by generating EJBHome and EJBObject classes that implement the remote and home interfaces. These can then be accessed remotely through JNDI and invoking them forwards the calls to the actual bean implementation through the EJB container. By inserting itself between the EJBObject and bean implementation, the EJB container can perform certain functions, such as managing transactions and security checks. What these functions should do is declaratively described by the developer in the deployment descriptor of the component.

You then converted the HelloWorld example to EJB. The component implementation was modeled as a stateless session bean, and the remote interface was converted to a valid remote interface for an EJB. You then added the EJBHome interface that allowed you to create and remove EJBObjects. Lastly, you created a deployment descriptor that contained all the information about your component.

To get a better feel for how EJB works, you followed the creation, invocation, and removal calls. You saw how stateless session beans allowed a rather decoupled relationship between the EJBObjects and the component instances. Because of this, the EJB container could pool instances of the bean implementation to be reused for other clients.

You should now have a reasonably good picture of what EJB is and what it can do for you. You should also be able to see how it relates to RMI: RMI is used as the interface through which you invoke EJB components.

You are now finished with this part of the book, which has shown you how RMI relates to other significant technologies that can help you when developing distributed applications in Java.

This part also concludes the book. During your journey in RMI land, you have examined the workings of the technology and its features, you have looked into the details of creating RMI applications, and finally you have looked at some technologies that can help you take applications to the next level.

The future is networked, and making sure that you are on top of it all is a good idea. And now you are.

Further Reading

M any of the topics covered in this book can be explored in more depth. Some recommendations for further reading related to the topics in this book follow. The order of this list mirrors the order of the book, so recommended reading related to topics covered early in the book are presented first.

Most of these references are to Web pages, which should be long-lived, but if you find that any of the references are no longer valid, please contact me by using the companion Web site at www.wiley.com/compbooks/oberg, and I will update the errata page.

Request For Comment (RFC) documents contain the definitions of all Internet protocols (including UDP, TCP/IP, and SMTP) and can be found through the home page of the Internet Engineering Task Force (IETF) at www.ietf.org.

All popular Web standards (such as HTTP and HTML) are created by the World Wide Web Consortium (W3C). You can find more information about them at www.w3.org.

All standard documents related to CORBA and IIOP can be reached through the Object Management Group (OMG) home page at www.omg.org.

For more information about RMI in general, you should take a look at the RMI home page at http://java.sun.com/products/jdk/rmi. Of special interest is the RMI specification at http://java.sun.com/j2se/1.3/docs/guide/rmi/spec/rmiTOC.html and the RMI FAQ at http://java.sun.com/j2se/1.3/docs/guide/rmi/faq.html.

Sun Microsystems runs a mailing list for RMI where you can get help and feedback from other RMI users. List archives and subscription information are available at http://archives.java.sun.com/archives/rmi-users.html. The archives for this list are full of solutions to common problems, and there are also extensive discussions on all complex RMI topics, such as threading, dynamic classloading, and socket factories.

The paper "A Note on Distributed Computing" is a must-read for anyone who is serious about creating distributed systems. This paper (by Jim Waldo et al.) discusses the differences between local and remote programming, why they differ, and why it might be a good idea to ignore or hide the fact that they are different. The paper can be found at Sun Labs' home page at www.sun.com/research/techrep/1994/abstract-29.html.

A related issue is that of whether java.rmi.RemoteException should be a subclass of java.lang.Exception or java.lang.RuntimeException. An article on exception design in general by Jim Waldo can be found at www.unixreview.com/archives/articles/1997/june/9706jabi.shtml. Combine this article with the preceding paper and you have very compelling reasons for the current design of java.rmi.RemoteException.

For more information on the security architecture, see the Security API home page at http://java.sun.com/security. Of special interest is the Java Security Architecture document, which defines how permissions work. As you have seen in this book, permissions are what you use to restrict classes loaded by dynamic classloading from performing undesirable functions or tasks. This document can be found at http://java.sun.com/products/jdk/1.3/docs/guide/security/spec/security-spec.doc.html.

The JNDI API was used quite extensively to hide the naming service implementation. For more information about this API, see its home page at http://java.sun.com/products/jndi. This Web site also offers you a list of other JNDI implementations that you can use.

In Chapter 4, you used the Java Plug-in to allow your client to be loaded as an applet. The best way to allow applets to run in Web browsers is to use the Java Plug-in. For information about this product go to http://java.sun.com/products/plugin.

Two articles by Frank Sommers have been published at JavaWorld regarding RMI Activation and Jini. They explain how the two can be used together and provide a nice example for how to use them in practice. Read these articles at www.javaworld.com/javaworld/jw-09-2000/jw-0915-jinirmi.html and www.javaworld.com/javaworld/jw-10-2000/jw-1027-jinirmi.html.

There are a number of good books available on GUI development in Java. Basic GUI development is described in most entry level Java books, such as Core Java by Cay S. Horstmann and Gary Cornell. There are also more advanced GUI books available, such as Core Swing by Kim Topley.

Regarding GUI development, you should also take a look at The Swing Connection, which is a forum hosted by Sun that provides quite a lot of resources about Swing programming. You can find it at http://java.sun.com/products/jfc/tsc/index.html.

The event notification optimization in Chapter 7 was inspired by the article "Speed Up Listener Notification" by Robert Hastings, which was published in JavaWorld February 2000. You can read it online at www.javaworld.com/javaworld/jw-02-2000/jw-02-fast.html. The article describes AWT event listener management, but the general pattern can be applied to any event listener implementation.

With regard to agents, I would like to refer to my own master's thesis titled "Software Agent Framework Technology," or SAFT. The thesis report covers the design and implementation of a mobile agent framework on top of J2EE. The report also discusses what an agent is and what it should be able to do. In addition, the report has an excellent set of references to relevant articles and papers on the subject, which are recommended reading for anyone interested in agent technology. The thesis report was coauthored with Karl-Fredrik Blixt. You can download the paper at www-und.ida.liu.se/~karbl058/saft.

For more information about the BeanContext API, please see the document "The JavaBeans Runtime Containment and Services Protocol Specification" at http://java.sun.com/products/javabeans/glasgow/beancontext.pdf. You can also read the BeanContext tutorial by Scott A. Hommel at http://java.sun.com/docs/books/tutorial/javabeans/beancontext/index.html.

The most comprehensive book on Jini is probably Core Jini by Keith Edwards. It covers all the tools and has quite a few good examples on how to use Jini. The book also introduces a set of utility classes that you can use in your own projects to simplify the coding. For other resources on Jini, please see the resource list at Bill Venners site at http://artima.com/jini/index.html.

The Jini tools and libraries can be downloaded from www.sun.com/jini. You can also find instructions on how to use these tools on this Web site.

As with RMI, there is a mailing list for Jini hosted by Sun. You can read the archives and subscription information at http://archives.java.sun.com/archives/jini-users.html.

The primary source for EJB information is the Sun Web site at http://java.sun.com/products/ejb. On this site, you can find the specification and links to other resources. If there is one EJB book that I would personally recommend it is Mastering RMI by Ed Roman, which has good coverage of the EJB specification and how to use EJB intelligently.

For more information about the EJB server I am working on (called jBoss), please see www.jboss.org. On this site, you can download it, read tutorials and documentation, and see what it is all about.

If you ever have any doubts or questions about EJB that are not answered elsewhere, there are two main EJB forums where you can find help. One forum is the EJB-INTEREST mailing list hosted by Sun. You can reach the archives and subscription information at http://archives.java.sun.com/archives/ejb-interest.html. The other forum is The Server Side community Web site located at http://theserverside.com.

For more information about J2EE and the various technologies that it comprises, please see the home page for J2EE at http://java.sun.com/j2ee. On this site, you can find links to information about JDBC, JTA, JNDI, and all the other enterprise Java technologies.

Finally, all of the examples in this book use the Ant make tool. This is a tool that helps you manage compilation and packaging of your applications and is an essential tool for any Java developer. For more information about Ant, see its home page at http://jakarta.apache.org/ant.

The CD contains all the examples from the book, plus a mini-version of the JBoss EJB server that can be used with the EJB example.

Some examples show the basics of RMI. Three examples showcase specific features of RMI. Two examples explore technologies that have been built on top of RMI, namely Enterprise JavaBeans and Jini. An additional bonus example (that is not explained in the book) shows how to use RMI without generating remote object stub classes statically.

What Is Freeware?

The examples are licensed as freeware. Freeware is software that is distributed for free by disk, through BBS systems, and through the Internet. There is no charge for using it, and it can be distributed freely as long as the use it is put to follows the license agreement included with it.

Hardware Requirements

To use this CD-ROM, your system must meet the following requirements:

Any platform and operating system supporting JDK 1.2.2 or higher

32 Mb RAM

30 Mb hard drive space

Installing the Software

To install the examples, the contents of the CD-ROM should be copied to a directory on your computer's hard drive. Then follow the general instructions in index.html and the example-specific instructions found in the document /src/docs/index.html of each example.

For the Jini example you must download and install Jini 1.1 (or higher) from the Jini homepage, which is located at www.sun.com/jini.

Using the Software

The examples must be compiled and built before they can be run. See the general instructions in index.html, which is located in the base directory of the CD-ROM. This basically involves executing the /src/build/ build.bat script of each respective example. After a particular example has been built, generally executable scripts are available in the directory /dist/bin of each respective example. Refer to the example accompanying each example for further instructions.

The JBoss server that is supplied to be used with the EJB example can be run by simply executing the script /bin/run.bat in Windows, and /bin/run.sh on UNIX platforms. Refer to the JBoss documentation on www.jboss.org for more information.

User Assistance and Information

If you need assistance with these examples or if you have any suggestions for improvement, you can contact me by email at rickard@dreambean.com.